Learning to Teach Mathematics in the Secondary School

A Companion to School Experience

Edited by Sue Johnston-Wilder, Peter Johnston-Wilder, David Pimm and John Westwell

RoutledgeFalmer
Taylor & Francis Group
LONDON AND NEW YORK

First published 1999
by Routledge
2 Park Square, Milton Park, Abingdon, Oxon OX14 4RN

Simultaneously published in the USA and Canada
by Routledge
270 Madison Avenue, New York, NY 10016

Reprinted 2001, 2002, 2003 (twice), 2004 (twice), by RoutledgeFalmer

RoutledgeFalmer is an imprint of the Taylor & Francis Group

Typeset in Bembo by
J&L Composition Ltd, Filey, North Yorkshire
Printed and bound in Great Britain by
T.J. International, Padstow, Cornwall

British Library of Cataloguing in Publication Data
A catalogue record for this book is available from the British Library.

Library of Congress Cataloging in Publication Data
Learning to teach mathematics in the secondary school: a companion to school experience/edited by Sue Johnston-Wilder . . . [*et al.*].
p. cm.
Includes bibliographical references and indexes.
1. Mathematics—Study and teaching (Secondary)—United States.
I. Johnston-Wilder, Sue
QA13.L4 1999
510′.71′2—dc21 98–31035
CIP

ISBN 0–415–16280–7

Learning to Teach Mathematics in the Secondary School

This book covers a wide range of issues in the teaching of mathematics and offers supporting tasks to students to enable them to translate theory into practice. Topics covered include the nature of mathematics as a subject; mathematics in the National Curriculum; pupil learning; different teaching approaches; using ICT; mathematics education for pupils with special needs in mathematics; communicating mathematically; assessment and public examinations; teaching mathematics post-16; and professional development.

Sue Johnston-Wilder is lecturer in mathematics education at the Open University; **Peter Johnston-Wilder** is lecturer in mathematics education at De Montfort University Bedford; **David Pimm** is Professor of Mathematics Education at Michigan State University, USA; and **John Westwell** is advisory teacher for secondary mathematics in the London Borough of Barking and Dagenham.

Learning to Teach Subjects in the Secondary School Series

Series Editors
Tony Turner, Institute of Education, University of London; Sue Capel, Canterbury Christ Church College; and Marilyn Leask, De Montfort University Bedford.

Designed for all students learning to teach in secondary schools, and particularly those on school-based, initial teacher training courses, the books in this series complement *Learning to teach in the secondary school* and its companion, *Starting to teach in the secondary school.* Each book in the series applies underpinning theory and addresses practical issues to support students in school and in the training institution in learning how to teach a particular subject.

Learning to Teach English in the Secondary School
Jon Davison and Jane Dowson

Learning to Teach Modern Foreign Languages in the Secondary School
Norbert Pachler and Kit Field

Learning to Teach History in the Secondary School
Terry Haydn, James Arthur and Martin Hunt

Learning to Teach Physical Education in the Secondary School
Susan Capel

Learning to Teach Science in the Secondary School
Tony Turner and Wendy DiMarco

This book is dedicated to our children, the maths students of the next generation:

Robin, Ruth, Jaclyn, Daniel, Alex, Alastair, Olivia, Hannah

and is offered in memory of Jill Bruce and Rita Nolder, inspirational teacher-researchers who died before their time.

Contents

Introduction to the Series

Learning to Teach Mathematics in the Secondary School is one of a series of books entitled Learning to Teach Subjects in the Secondary School covering most subjects in the secondary school curriculum. The books in this series support and complement *Learning to Teach in the Secondary School: A Companion to School Experience* (Capel, Leask and Turner, 1995), which addresses issues relevant to all secondary teachers. These books are designed for student teachers learning to teach on different types of initial teacher education courses and in different places. However, it is hoped that they will be equally useful to tutors and mentors in their work with student teachers. In 1997, a complementary book was published entitled *Starting to Teach in the Secondary School: A Companion for the Newly Qualified Teacher* (Capel, Leask and Turner, 1997). That second book was designed to support newly qualified teachers in their first post and covered aspects of teaching which are likely to be of concern in the first year of teaching.

The information in the subject books does not repeat that in *Learning to Teach*; rather, the content of that book is adapted and extended to address the needs of student teachers learning to teach a specific subject. In each of the subject books, therefore, reference is made to *Learning to Teach*, where appropriate. It is recommended that you have both books so that you can cross-reference when needed.

The positive feedback on *Learning to Teach*, particularly the way it has supported the learning of student teachers in their development into effective, reflective teachers, has encouraged us to retain the main features of that book in the subject series. Thus, the subject books are designed so that elements of appropriate theory introduce each behaviour or issue. Recent research into teaching and learning is incorporated into this. This material is interwoven with tasks designed to help you identify key features of the behaviour or issue and apply them to your own practice.

Although the basic content of each subject book is shared, each book is designed to address the unique nature of each subject. In this book, for example, some of the reasons for the special status often afforded to mathematics within the curriculum becomes clearer. Many different groups have an interest in mathematics education and so seek to have an influence on it. Among many other things, the book examines the consequences of this including some of the controversies that can sometimes develop. Mathematics education has also acted as a significant stimulus for the development of new theories of learning and new teaching approaches and so the book also explores many of these developments.

We, as series editors, have found this project to be exciting. We hope that, whatever the type of initial teacher education course you are following and wherever you may be following that course, you find that this book is useful and supportive of your development into an effective, reflective mathematics teacher.

Susan Capel, Marilyn Leask and Tony Turner
January 1997

Illustrations

FIGURES

TABLES

TASKS

Notes on Contributors

Maria Goulding originally taught secondary mathematics in Liverpool schools. She then taught at the Department of Education in the University of Liverpool before moving to the School of Education at the University of Durham. She teaches on primary and secondary mathematics education courses and is the Deputy Director of the secondary Postgraduate Certificate in Education (PGCE) course. Her recent book *Learning to Teach Mathematics* (David Fulton, 1997) draws on her research of the students' learning experiences on these courses.

Peter Johnston-Wilder works at De Montfort University Bedford, where he is a lecturer in mathematics education. Before coming to Bedford, he taught mathematics in a secondary school in Inner London. He is an examiner for A-level mathematics and joint editor of *Micromath*. He has particular interests in the assessment of coursework and group work in mathematics and statistics. His research interests are in the impact of new technology on the teaching and learning of mathematics and statistics, especially probability.

Sue Johnston-Wilder (formerly **Sue Burns**) is a lecturer in mathematics education at the Open University. Originally, she taught secondary mathematics in London. She then worked at King's College London on Graded Assessment in Mathematics and at the Institute of Education on Computer-Based Modelling Across the Curriculum. For four years, she was Deputy Director of Nuffield Advanced Mathematics and taught PGCE students at King's College London. The main focus of her work is encouraging the use of history of mathematics and of information and communications technology (ICT) in mathematics teaching. She is a joint editor of *Micromath*.

Keith Jones taught mathematics in a number of multi-ethnic, inner-city comprehensive schools for twelve years, rising to become head of department. Following a period as an advisory teacher for both primary and secondary mathematics, he became a lecturer in mathematics education at the Institute of Education, London. He now works at the University of Southampton, where he leads both the mathematics PGCE course and the Masters course in mathematics education. He is particularly interested in the development of mathematical reasoning and how teachers can promote this.

Ann Kitchen was a secondary mathematics teacher for nine years before she left to work with the Mechanics in Action Project at the University of Manchester. As a writer for some of the texts for SMP (School Mathematics Project) 16–19 Mathematics, she continues to be involved in syllabus design and assessment for SMP A level. She is at present (1999) Chair of the Association of Teachers of Mathematics (ATM). Her current work at the Centre for Mathematics Education at Manchester University involves research into learning post-16 and the mathematics interface between A level and Higher Education, as well as in-service training for A-level teachers.

Candia Morgan was a secondary mathematics teacher and advisory teacher in London schools for thirteen years. She currently works at the Institute of Education, London, where she co-ordinates the mathematics component of the secondary PGCE course. Her research interests include mathematical language and assessment issues.

David Pimm worked in mathematics education at the Open University from 1983 until 1997. He is currently Professor of Mathematics Education at Michigan State University in the USA. The main area of his work has been in exploring interactions between language and mathematics education, thinking specifically about the issues of spoken language and written notation in mathematics classrooms. He is the author of two books: *Speaking Mathematically: Communication in Mathematics Classrooms* (Routledge and Kegan Paul, 1987) and *Symbols and Meanings in School Mathematics* (Routledge, 1995).

Melissa Rodd was a secondary mathematics teacher in Oxfordshire and first became involved in initial teacher education as a school teacher mentor for the Oxfordshire Internship PGCE. From there, she went to the University College of St Martin, Lancaster, to teach mathematics and work in teacher education. She has recently (1998) completed a Ph.D. at the Open University and now works in the Centre for Science and Mathematics Education at the University of Leeds.

Christine Shiu has taught mathematics in secondary schools in London and Leicestershire and carried out research into mathematics classrooms mainly in Nottinghamshire. She joined the Open University in 1985, where she is now Director of the Centre for Mathematics Education, and has worked on distance-taught undergraduate courses in mathematics and mathematics education and on the production of professional development packs. Her research interests are in practitioner-research and the professional development of mathematics teachers.

John Westwell is advisory teacher for secondary mathematics in the London Borough of Barking and Dagenham, where his principal work is on the Axiom Project, a Key Stage 3 numeracy initiative. Formerly, he was head of mathematics at a school in Chelmsford, where he was also the mathematics tutor for the Mid-Essex School-Centred Initial Teacher Training (SCITT) consortium. He was one of the editors for the Charis mathematics project.

Foreword

There are likely to be few more important jobs at the beginning of the twenty-first century than that of a mathematics teacher. Knowledge in many of the key contemporary growth areas, and the ability to harness them for the benefit of humanity, requires a competence with the appropriate underlying mathematical ideas. These key areas include:

- the software and hardware associated with information and communication technology;
- finance and economics, including the control of risk;
- design in a variety of fields, from machinery to fabrics, and from graphics to architecture;
- all branches of science, from the biotechnology of genetic engineering and medicine to the physics of cosmology;
- the quantification of performance, and the statistics and modelling involved in research and development in all fields.

For children to be able to hold their own in the new century, it is thus critical that they have an appreciation of, a competence in manipulating, and a positive attitude towards, the big mathematical ideas that are central to the functioning of our global culture. This means understanding the development of these ideas by individuals and groups within particular social contexts, and enjoying the elegance and beauty of their patterns and symmetries for their own sake, as well as an ability to participate in the implementation and the shaping of future advances which rely on them.

Mathematics teachers therefore have a significant part to play in ensuring that the next generation is both excited and well-equipped. The job is uniquely challenging in requiring familiarity and engagement simultaneously with the unsullied abstraction of mathematics and the sometimes crude realities of classes of teenagers. However, many of us who have experienced great enjoyment in the role of mathematics teacher have found that the successful bringing together of these diverse worlds is at the same time uniquely rewarding and very worthwhile.

I am pleased and honoured to have been asked to contribute the Foreword for this book. It has been written by a group of people all of whom I respect as themselves excellent and knowledgeable teachers, both of secondary students and of intending and serving mathematics teachers. Indeed, I know most of the authors well as former PGCE students, MA students, colleagues on research and development teams, and fellow members of committees, working groups and conferences.

The various chapters introduce new teachers to the leading edge of theory and research, made meaningful through practical examples, often drawn from personal experiences. Because it will cause careful thinking about the what, the why and the how of teaching mathematics, it is a very important book. I believe it will help to continue, and to disseminate more widely, the tradition of excellence in mathematics teaching which both respects and seeks to build connections within and between mathematics and secondary school students.

Margaret Brown
Professor of Mathematics Education,
King's College London.
November, 1998

Acknowledgements

John Hibbs, HMI, for permission to use his report of Jill Bruce at work.
Helen Osborn, for reading, and for friendship.
Rachel Eyres, without whom this would not have been finished.
Douglas Butler, for permission to use screen-shots from the Oundle School maths site.
Yale Babylonian Collection, for permission to use the photograph of Babylonian tablet YBC 7289 in Figure 4.2.
The Open University, for permission to use the transcription of the same tablet, previously published in Fauvel and Gray, *The History of Mathematics: A Reader.*
Rosie Hunt for providing the handwriting in Figure 6.1.
The graph in Figure 11.1 is reproduced from NICCEA *Comparing Examination Boards and Syllabuses at A Level* (Executive Summary) © 1994 with the permission of the Northern Ireland Council for the Curriculum, Examinations and Assessment.
QCA for permission to reproduce Table A3.1, taken from page D7 of the *Mathematics National Curriculum Non-Statutory Guidance* (NCC, 1989).

Introduction

Learning to teach mathematics is not something you will do in just a year. This book might have been more appropriately titled *Beginning to Learn to Teach Mathematics in a Secondary School*. For how ever long you continue to teach mathematics, you will also continue to learn about this extremely complex and challenging profession. Having said that, the lessons you learn about teaching mathematics as a student teacher will have a significant impact on your future career. This book will guide you through the very important first stage of your formal development as a mathematics teacher.

Start to think of yourself as a mathematics teacher right from the beginning of your course. The work on which you are embarking is multi-faceted. Not only will you be developing as a teacher, but you will also be developing as an educational researcher, as a mathematician, as a writer, as a counsellor, as a team worker and as a reflective practitioner. You will find yourself stretched intellectually, physically and emotionally, and there may be times when you wonder why you ever decided to teach. However, along with the challenge, there will also be the rewards and satisfaction that come from working with young people and with your colleagues.

MAKING THE MOST OF YOUR SCHOOL EXPERIENCE

There have been some significant changes in the structure of teacher education courses in recent years. As well as there being more central government control over the aims and content of courses, there has also been a considerable increase in the time spent by students in schools. Many people see this as a positive development. They would argue that it is essential that new teachers learn 'on the job' in the school environment. However, there is a danger that you will not get the maximum benefit from your school experience unless you use it as an occasion for a full range of learning experiences.

It is important that your school experience is organised so that you have the opportunity to learn in a number of different ways. Some of the possibilities are outlined in what follows.

Reflective journal

It is widely accepted that reflecting on your experiences in a structured way is essential if you are to develop as a practitioner. You will be bombarded by experiences during your time in school, so it is essential that you do indeed make time to reflect. Perhaps the most effective way of supporting this process is through writing down your thoughts as a record that you can look back on. Indeed the practice of using a reflective journal as a tool for personal development goes back many centuries. If you establish the habit of keeping a reflective journal during your training, you will be well prepared to continue the practice throughout your career.

Classroom research

During your training, you will spend much of your time in classrooms. For a significant proportion of this time, you will not be primarily responsible for the teaching. Instead, although you may be supporting a teacher, you will have an excellent opportunity to observe and investigate aspects of classroom life in some detail. Whilst student teachers often complain that they have to spend too long just observing, many experienced teachers complain that they have too few chances to observe their colleagues, or their pupils. It is important that you use this special time effectively to undertake a variety of classroom research activities.

Investigating the school and department

Given how much time you spend in school, it is important that you are familiar with how both the school and its mathematics department are organised and operate. However, you should go further than just finding out enough to survive. You have the opportunity to develop an understanding of factors that lead to an effective school or department. Comparing your school and department with those of fellow students will also support this process. The teachers in your school will also benefit from the presence of a student who can ask perceptive questions and cause them to reflect on their policies and practices.

Researching the curriculum and resources

Even if you have gone straight from school to university to teacher training, you can still expect the mathematics curriculum to have changed in the intervening years. It is important to understand the structure and content of the curriculum for different phases of schooling and to be familiar with associated qualifications and/or assessment arrangements. There is an abundance of teaching resources available to maths teachers. Your period of training is an ideal time to investigate these resources and to evaluate them critically. You may find that your department will also appreciate hearing about the results of such research.

Studying mathematics

As you begin to teach, it is important that you continue to study mathematics. This can include both exploring new areas of mathematics and going deeper into areas you have previously studied. In particular, you are required to develop your subject knowledge in the areas of the mathematics curriculum in which you are less confident. However, even in topics with which you have no difficulty, you will also need to think more deeply about the ideas involved in order to teach them effectively. A further aspect to studying the subject is learning more about its diverse applications and history.

Interviewing staff and pupils

You will have plenty of opportunity to discuss education informally with both staff and pupils, but it is also valuable to explore issues more formally. At the end of lessons, teachers may well need to prepare for the following lesson or they may want a break. However, arranging to interview staff, even for a short time, will mean that both you and the teacher have a chance to reflect in more depth about their thinking and their practice. Meeting pupils on a one-to-one basis or perhaps in a pair outside the classroom environment allows you to listen to what pupils really think about their education.

Reading about education

With much of your time spent in schools during your course, it is important that you still try to make time to read widely about education. This will contribute towards the development of a personal theoretical base from which you can reflect more effectively on your school experience. It is worth planning to include reading time and visits to your education library.

Teaching

Many student teachers consider taking sole responsibility for teaching classes mathematics as the main point of their school experience. Obviously, you have to have enough opportunity to learn how to cope with the complex demands that teaching lessons on your own can bring. However, in order to develop your understanding and skills for teaching, you will need to have experiences in which you just focus on particular areas. You can do this by teaching just a small group, or pair or individual, or by taking responsibility for just part of a lesson, or by team teaching with a colleague. Whatever form the teaching takes, be sure that it also includes experience of planning, assessment and evaluation.

HOW TO USE THE BOOK

The book is divided into twelve chapters, each addressing an important theme. Each chapter has an introduction and objectives, which should help you to clarify the key ideas to be addressed in the chapter. There is also a summary of each chapter that highlights the main points made. You may find it helpful to read a chapter prior to addressing the theme in a tutorial (either at school or university). You may also find it helpful to dip in and out of the book when you want to read something to support your reflection on particular school experiences. You will obviously need to read more than just this book, so, in order to support your further reading, each chapter ends with some recommendations for relevant reading on the same theme. In addition, the chapters are fully referenced, thereby offering you alternative sources of further reading.

An important feature of the book is the tasks; these comprise a key element in each chapter, and provide you with many suggestions of how you can make the most of your school experience. There are tasks to support each of the types of learning experience addressed in the previous section. Your course will place various requirements upon you, but there will be opportunity to negotiate with your school tutor the details of how you use your time in school. You may wish to suggest some of the tasks from this book to your tutor as possible elements of your school experience programme. The tasks will be of more value if you can talk them through with your tutors and/or your fellow students.

At the end of the book, you will find a glossary of useful terms (Appendix 1) and a collection of useful addresses for resources and organisations (Appendix 2). You will find that you add to these as you progress through your career. The training will be hard work; at the end, you will emerge as a qualified teacher of mathematics, to inspire and encourage the next generation of young people. You are much needed; welcome to the challenge.

1 Mathematics Education – Who Decides?

John Westwell

INTRODUCTION

A recent publication from the Mathematical Association, one of the two professional organisations for mathematics teachers, begins with these thoughts.

> To teach Mathematics is a high calling. The truth of mathematics is real and fundamental, and we believe it is right for all pupils to study mathematics throughout all of their compulsory schooling. The questions we address in this booklet are:
>
> **Why** does mathematics deserve its place in the curriculum?
> **What** mathematics will it be appropriate to learn in the early 2000s?
> **How** can mathematics best be learnt by each individual pupil?
>
> (MA, 1995a, p. 1)

As you learn to teach mathematics, you will need to seek answers to these key questions. However, you will soon discover that there are no simple answers, and may also be surprised to find that there is often much disagreement about the issues raised and even whether these are the best questions to explore.

Indeed, some people go even further, beyond the issues raised by these questions, and argue that what really needs to be addressed is mathematics itself. The American mathematician Reuben Hersh claims that 'The issue, then, is not, What is the best way to teach? but, What is mathematics really all about? . . . Controversies about . . . teaching cannot be resolved without confronting problems about the nature of mathematics' (cited in Ernest, 1991, p. 296). Your time spent as a student teacher can provide opportunities to develop your understanding of the ideas that underlie these controversies. You will then be better prepared to make teaching decisions in the best interests of your pupils.

OBJECTIVES

By the end of this chapter, you should:

- understand how your experiences of mathematics have shaped your views about mathematics education;
- be able to articulate clearly your current rationale for mathematics education;
- be aware of how different groups have influenced the current shape of mathematics education in the UK;
- be able to respond more confidently to the different expectations that will be placed on you as a mathematics teacher.

MATHEMATICS AND YOU

You are about to begin learning how to teach mathematics. But in reality you are not a beginner. You already have a wealth of experience of mathematics education upon which to draw. Whether you have studied mathematics at degree level or not, you will have spent many hours of your life engaged in learning and using mathematics. 'The teacher's view of mathematics is shaped to a very large extent by his/her own mathematical experience as a student' (Dörfler and McLone, 1986, p. 87). Indeed, not only will these experiences inform your views on the nature of mathematics, they will also influence your personal philosophy about mathematics education. It is a valuable exercise then, at the beginning of your course, to look back and reflect on where you have come from. Task 1.1 leads you through this process.

Task 1.1
Mathematics – your story so far

In this task, consider your experience of mathematics and mathematics education. Read the following passage, 'Mathematical memories', which consists of a substantial number of questions and prompts. Give yourself some undisturbed time, at least 30 minutes, to reflect upon the thoughts stimulated by what you read. Note down ideas and memories as they occur to you in your reflective journal. Read the sections slowly and do not worry if your thoughts wander; be aware of this happening and record what you believe to be important.

Mathematical memories

- What is your earliest memory of learning mathematics? Call to mind where you are, what you are doing, how old you are. Is it a positive memory?
- When did you last *do* some mathematics? Think about why you were doing it and how you felt at the time.
- Have you ever called yourself 'a mathematician'? If you have, think about when this first happened and what it meant to you at the time. If you have not, think about why not, and who you think can use such a title. Do you expect to meet mathematicians during your school experience?
- How do you rate your ability in mathematics? Think how this view was formed and whether it has changed over time. Consider whether your ability was something you believe you were born with or whether it was a product of your education to date, or both, or neither. How does your ability compare with others? What basis are you using for your comparison?
- Can you remember a time when you have used mathematics for something important? Think about the type of mathematics that was involved and whether it was something you learnt at school. Would other people share your opinion about the importance of the activity?
- Can you remember a time when you have chosen to do mathematics for pleasure? Think about where you were, who you were with, if anyone, and how long you spent doing it. Do you think other people would derive pleasure from the same task? Why?
- Try and remember some times when being mathematical has been enjoyable and satisfying. Think about what brought about the enjoyment or satisfaction. Now try and remember other times when mathematics has been boring or frustrating. How do you account for your different responses?
- Who was your best mathematics teacher? Think what it was about this person that impressed you. Try to remember some particular moments that exemplify all that was good about his/her teaching. What aspect of this person's teaching would you like to emulate?
- Who was your worst mathematics teacher? Think what it was about this person that led you to such a judgement. Try to remember some specific occasions that exemplify what was poor about his/her teaching. Which aspects of this person's teaching would you wish to avoid?
- Think about all the qualifications that you have in mathematics. Consider all that you had to do in order to earn those qualifications. Do you think they offer a fair assessment of your mathematical abilities? Are there other ways in which you would have preferred to be judged?
- Try and remember some times when learning mathematics was difficult and times when it was easy. Why was there a difference? Consider other people with whom you have learnt mathematics. Did they find it easier or harder? Why do you think that was? Do you think you have a preferred way of learning mathematics?
- Why did you decide you wanted to be a mathematics teacher?

Having looked back over your encounters with mathematics, you are now in a better position to look forward. You will already have hopes for your life as a maths teacher, but you may also have doubts about your decision. To grow and develop as a maths teacher, you will need to go on reflecting about mathematics, about education and about your place in relation to both.

Task 1.2 Your personal vision for mathematics education

It is important to be clear about your opinions about mathematics and mathematics education, because they will influence your practice. In order to articulate your views clearly, it can be helpful to try writing them down in a concise form. Write a statement outlining your personal vision for mathematics education. This could be kept in your reflective journal and referred to at different times during your course. For instance, you might consider reviewing it prior to any job interview and also at the end of your course.

Limit yourself to a maximum of 250 words. Include answers to the following questions:

- Why is mathematics education important?
- What is mathematics?
- How is mathematics best taught and learnt?

Having finished your statement, you might like to ask other students on your course how it compares with their own views. How will the differences among you have an impact on the pupils you teach?

MATHEMATICS AND EDUCATION

While you are learning to teach mathematics, you may feel that you have more important priorities than considering the somewhat abstract issues of the nature of mathematics and the purpose of education. You may quite reasonably wish to focus instead on surviving in a classroom full of pupils. However, it is important to understand at this early stage the way in which these philosophical issues do impinge significantly on classroom practice.

The nature of mathematics

Is the nature of mathematics a controversial issue? Surely everyone has a fairly clear idea of what the subject is and consequently what should be taught in schools? If you have had a chance to talk to other students about the issues raised in either Task 1.1 or 1.2, you may already have encountered varying perspectives, if not conflicting views, on what is important about mathematics.

The two quotations that follow, written by professional mathematicians and published in the same year, illustrate that mathematics can mean different things to different people.

> It is security. Certainty. Truth. Beauty. Insight. Structure. Architecture. I see mathematics, the part of human knowledge that I call mathematics, as one thing – one great glorious thing.
>
> (Halmos, quoted in Albers, 1986, p. 127)

> Mathematics does have a subject matter, and its statements are meaningful. The meaning, however, is to be found in the shared understanding of human beings, not in an eternal non-human reality. In this respect, mathematics is similar to an ideology, a religion, or an art form; it deals with human meanings, and is intelligible only within the context of culture. In other words, mathematics is a humanistic study. It is one of the humanities.
>
> (Davis and Hersh, 1986, p. 410)

You might conclude that although the responses of these people are different, they are nonetheless still talking about the same thing. However, there is a significant difference between these two views, and it is rooted in different understandings of human knowledge. For Paul Halmos, mathematics seems a fixed, objective body of true ideas, independent of culture. For Philip Davis and Reuben Hersh, mathematics is a fallible, yet correctable, product of human thought rooted in human culture. Developing your standpoint on the nature of mathematics is important because it will influence the values about mathematics that you convey to your pupils.

The aims of education

Aims express intentions of individuals or groups; they are not just abstract ideas. It is important, then, in order to understand educational aims fully, to ask whose aims are being expressed. As with the nature of mathematics, there is no universal agreement or happy consensus. This is because different groups can and do have different sets of values which are in turn rooted in their different world views or belief systems.

There are, however, some broad categories that help to illuminate the area of educational aims. These are indicated in Table 1.1, which presents a simplified

Table 1.1 The aims for education – different types of development

Academic development

Education should help pupils to develop a thorough knowledge and understanding of the subject. At the same time, pupils are encouraged to form appropriate attitudes towards the subject. The desired outcome is sufficient people inducted into the academic community, including an adequate supply of good teachers at all levels. This is in order that the subject's place within our cultural heritage and its future development are guaranteed.

Vocational development

Education should provide pupils with the relevant knowledge and skills that they need in the world of work. The desired outcome is a suitably equipped work force ready to adapt to the needs of a growing economy.

Personal development

Education should provide opportunity for the all-round development of the individual. The desired outcome is fulfilled and autonomous people who have a well-developed self-awareness and who continue to grow and mature in adult life.

Social development

Education should provide the forum within which pupils can develop socially and find their roles within society. The desired outcome is individuals who will be confident in their interpersonal relationships and in their role as critical citizens.

categorisation of the possible purposes for education. Each of these areas of development has, at some time within the history of mathematics education, been the focus of concern for different groups. Considering your aims for education is a further important part of clarifying the values that will inform your mathematics teaching.

Further issues

Your perspectives on the nature of mathematics and on the aims of education come together to form your aims for mathematics education. However, having established the purpose of mathematics education – a sense of 'why?' – there remain the further questions, 'what?' and 'how?'. The way in which you answer these questions will be strongly connected to your aims. Table 1.2 lists questions that follow on from the more philosophical ones you have been considering. You will explore many of these areas in more detail in later chapters of this book. However, you might immediately begin to see how different aims might lead you to answer these questions differently. You are faced with the challenge of developing your own considered responses to these questions, consistent with your aims.

Table 1.2 Fundamental questions

Area of interest	*Questions raised*
Philosophy	Why should pupils learn mathematics?
Curriculum	What mathematics should be included in the school curriculum? Which pupils should learn which aspects of the subject?
Learning	How do pupils learn mathematics?
Teaching	What teaching methodologies will best support your aims?
Resources	What resources are most appropriate to the tasks and the learners?
Assessment	How should/could/might pupils' development in mathematics be measured?
Differentiation	What accounts for the diversity of pupil response to mathematics? How should/could/might you respond to this diversity?

Task 1.3 The aims of the mathematics department

During your school experience, you will find out much about how your mathematics department works. It is also useful to find out what aims or vision the department has for mathematics education and how this comes through in its policies. Ask to read the department handbook, and in particular consider:

- what views about the nature of mathematics and education underpin any statement of aims;
- how well policies and procedures relate to the department's aims;
- the extent to which the official aims are shared by all members of the department;
- whether classroom practice supports the achievement of the department's aims.

COMPETING INFLUENCES ON THE MATHS CURRICULUM

This section includes various aims for maths education and some discussion of the implications these could have on your work as a maths teacher in the classroom. Below are descriptions of the mathematical perspectives of four different social groups: the Mathematical Purists, the Industrial Pragmatists, the Progressive Educators and the Social Reformers. These groups are not real, organised associations of people, but instead represent a categorisation offering a framework for exploring the competing influences within mathematics education. No claim is made that all individuals fit neatly into any particular group; indeed, as you read the descriptions, you may find you have certain sympathies with some or even all of the groups. However, the origins of much current practice in maths education have their roots within the opinions attributed to one of these four groups. Many of the ideas expressed here are due to the work of Paul Ernest (for example, Ernest, 1991).

Mathematical Purists

This group is primarily concerned with the academic and some aspects of personal development of pupils. Its members strongly reject any utilitarian emphasis on work or the applications of mathematics for its justification as a school subject. They also assume that it is obvious that mathematics education has no role in the social development of young people.

Members of this group have a long tradition within mathematics which can be traced back to Greek philosophy, where mathematics was seen to be educationally valuable in the development of thought rather than for learning about any applications.

> Now that we have mentioned the study of arithmetic, it occurs to me what a subtle and widely used instrument it is for our purpose, if one studies it for the sake of knowledge and not for commercial ends . . . it draws the mind upwards.
>
> (Plato, trans. Lee, 1987, p. 332)

The tradition of emphasising the importance of mathematics as a subject for the improvement of the mind continues to be maintained by some today.

The Mathematical Purists consider mathematics to be an objective form of knowledge, a complex hierarchical structure of ideas linked together through proof and rational thought. They celebrate its significant contribution to our cultural heritage, identify it more as an art than a science, and believe it to have aesthetic qualities. The Cambridge mathematician G. H. Hardy wrote:

> The mathematician's patterns, like the painter's or the poet's, must be *beautiful*; the ideas, like the colours or the words, must fit together in a harmonious way. Beauty is the first test: there is no permanent place in the world for ugly mathematics.
>
> (Hardy, 1940, p. 25)

They see the role of the teacher as enabling the effective transmission of this body of knowledge and encouraging particular qualities in the pupils, such as concern for rigour, elegance and precision. This tends to involve a lecturing and explaining style that makes use of standard texts and traditional mathematical equipment, but makes little use of other resources. Teachers will have an enthusiasm for the subject that will be conveyed to the pupils.

This group supports major competitions for pupils such as Mathematical Olympiads, partly because these help identify the next generation of mathematicians. Assessment on the whole is not a major concern. However, it is important that qualifications such as A-level mathematics preserve their high standards, and so members of the group express concern if they think this is becoming less demanding. On the whole, there is little consideration given to what form of mathematics education is appropriate for pupils who will not be part of the new mathematical élite, and it is just to be accepted that some people are born with a talent for the subject.

Industrial Pragmatists

This group is primarily concerned with the vocational development of pupils through mathematics. There is some recognition of the need for social development, but only in as far as it prepares young people for the world of work. Academic development is acknowledged to be relevant for a few, but the dominant focus of maths education must be on the great mass of ordinary people. Everybody needs an adequate mathematical education, so that they can contribute to the development of a successful economy.

Members of this group are most likely to be found amongst employers in industry or leaders of technical and scientific professions. There is a tradition of this group trying to influence maths education from the last century. At that time, their argument was mainly with the Mathematical Purists. One strong advocate of this group's views was Professor John Perry, an engineer and former science teacher. At the 1901 meeting of the British Association for the Advancement of Science, he said:

> The study of Mathematics began because it was useful, continues because it is useful and is valuable to the world because of the usefulness of its results, while the mathematicians, who determine what the teacher shall do, hold that the subject should be studied for its own sake.
>
> (cited in Griffiths and Howson, 1974, p. 17)

This group has grown considerably in numbers and strength throughout the twentieth century and is arguably the most influential at the end of the century.

The Industrial Pragmatists see mathematics as an established collection of very useful techniques and skills that can be applied to a large range of technical and scientific contexts. They recognise that there is a body of knowledge to be learnt, but consider that it is only to be learnt in order to be applied. There is, however, sometimes a tension within this group as to which areas of mathematics are most important. Some advocate a strong emphasis on arithmetic and basic numeracy, whilst others require pupils to learn the mathematics most helpful for them to function in a rapidly changing technological society and so welcome an increased emphasis on the use of calculators and, especially, computers.

They see the role of the teacher as being to instruct the pupil in skills and to motivate them by the use of real work contexts. Learning requires thorough practice and pupils benefit from doing practical and possibly experimental work. At a higher level, pupils should learn the skills required for applied problem solving and modelling.

Assessment has a dual function for the Industrial Pragmatists. On one level, it acts as a simple aid to selection – what has been termed a 'critical filter'; for instance, unless pupils have a Grade C at GCSE level, they will not be considered for a particular job. However, there is also an emphasis on assessment ensuring that core skills have been developed and verified. Concern is expressed by this group if standards of numeracy are falling, and so the new vocational qualifications, which all include an element of 'the application of number', are welcomed.

Progressive Educators

This group is primarily concerned with the personal development of pupils, with the individual child as focus of attention. It rejects the adult-orientated nature of vocational development, and supports social and academic development only to the extent that these are supportive of personal development.

Members of this group have, like the Industrial Pragmatists, grown in prominence during the twentieth century, but there is a tradition rooted as far back as the work of Jean-Jacques Rousseau in the eighteenth century. His advice to potential teachers included:

> Your first duty is to be humane. Love childhood. Look with friendly eyes on its games, its pleasures, its amiable dispositions. Which of you does not sometimes look back regretfully on the age when laughter was ever on the lips and the heart free of care? Why steal from the little innocents the enjoyment of a time that passes all too quickly?
>
> (cited in Boyd, 1973, p. 33)

Here we find a concern to put the child, not the future adult, at the centre of the educational project.

Whilst accepting that mathematics is a body of knowledge, this group is not very concerned about the particular mathematics to be learnt. Instead, it is much more interested in the process of learning and rejects any attempt to impose mathematics on the pupils. It believes that pupils should be supported in exploring and discovering the subject for themselves. There is a concern for the child to remain motivated and to have positive feelings and attitudes towards the subject. Learning mathematics should build up children's self-esteem and help them to become confident and autonomous. They are encouraged to pursue their own open-ended investigations, to engage in projects related to personal interests, and to find their own ways of expressing and communicating their own mathematics.

They see the role of the teacher as coming alongside the pupil and acting as a guide in the pupil's journeys of discovery. This means that it is the responsibility of the teacher to create an appropriate learning environment, both in terms of stimulating resources and supportive social dynamics. Mathematical educators within this group have been influential in developing specialist maths equipment, such as Cuisenaire rods and Dienes structural apparatus. Computers and calculators are considered important for offering new environments within which mathematical exploration can happen. There is also an emphasis on developing caring, supportive relationships in the classroom, with children being shielded from significant social conflict.

Children are to be treated as individuals and allowed to learn at different rates. It is important to recognise and celebrate their success, so records of achievement and criteria-based assessment are to be welcomed. External examinations are not considered helpful, as they have the potential for bringing discouragement and disappointment to the child. They are also seen as skewing the curriculum towards short-term goals.

Social Reformers

This group is primarily concerned with the social development of pupils, in the sense that education should empower the individual to participate fully and critically in a democratic society. Consequently, aspects of personal development are considered important. Encouraging vocational and academic development is appropriate only through negotiation with the pupil.

Members of this group have only relatively recently begun to influence mathematics education, but the origins of this group within education (also called 'Public Educators') can be traced back to the nineteenth century. Then, the concern was for education for all. In more recent times, Social Reformers have had more influence in the emerging education structures of developing countries. For example, president Julius Nyerere expressed the aims of a Tanzanian education programme as being:

> to prepare people for their responsibilities as free workers and citizens in a free and democratic society, albeit a largely rural society. They have to be able to think for themselves, to make judgements on all the issues affecting them; they have to be able to interpret the decisions made through the democratic institutions of our society.
>
> (Ernest, 1991, p. 202)

The other stimulus to the work of the group of Social Reformers has been the need to work towards equality of opportunity for all within education. Within mathematics education, significant work has been done in the field of gender issues, multicultural and anti-racist mathematics.

The view of mathematics held by some in this group is also relatively new. Mathematics is seen to be 'a social construction: tentative, growing by means of human creation and decision-making, and connected with other realms of knowledge, culture and social life' (Ernest, 1991, pp. 207–208). This offers a much wider definition of mathematics than is the norm, and challenges the Mathematical

Purists' exclusive ownership of 'real mathematics'. Pupils should experience mathematics as relevant to their own lives; as important in addressing wider social issues; as a vehicle for social emancipation; and as enabling a critical stance towards society.

They see the role of the teacher as facilitating pupils in both posing and solving their own problems. This requires the teacher to set conditions in which pupils can participate in decisions about their learning and in which they feel able to question their mathematics course and its associated teaching methods. Resources need to be socially relevant and include authentic materials such as newspapers and sources of real data. Discussion is central to the learning process and conflicting ideas are welcome in promoting greater understanding.

Any form of assessment must be seen to be fair to all pupils and should not disadvantage any social grouping. This requires a greater variety of modes of assessment, and so project work and the on-going assessment of coursework is highly valued. The GCSE qualification initially had scope for a large percentage of assessment by coursework, and so was welcomed by the Social Reformers. Because of the status that certain mathematical qualifications have within UK society, helping pupils to pass external exams remains crucial, so teachers have to work within the existing assessment system.

AGENCIES FOR CHANGE

Given that there is a range of views about the aims of mathematics education, you may wonder how these competing influences actually bring about change in the school curriculum and teaching approaches. In this final section, you will see how the social groups discussed above have acted through different agencies to bring about the reforms that they seek. You will also consider the influence of people who express their expectations at ground level within your school context.

Mathematics teaching associations

The influence of different groups can be seen in the history of the two main maths teaching organisations. The Mathematical Association (MA) was established in 1871 as 'The Association for the Improvement of Geometrical Teaching', with an overt agenda for change. The initial focus was on reforming the teaching of Euclidean geometry. The Association of Teachers of Mathematics (ATM), which was set up in 1953 as 'The Association for Teaching Aids in Mathematics', was a splinter group from the MA. Articles in the early issues of the journal of the newer association (*Mathematics Teaching*) show clearly the dominance of the Progressive Educator group (Cooper, 1985, pp. 69–90). These two organisations are discussed further in Chapter 12.

Curriculum development projects

Mathematics education has had its fair share of curriculum projects. Some succeed and have a large impact in schools across the country; others do not extend much beyond the initial project schools and are soon forgotten. In either case, projects will normally have the strong support of one of the four social groups listed above, which recognise that courses and materials are a significant way of influencing the way in which teachers work. The School Mathematics Project (SMP), established in 1961, was perhaps particularly successful in establishing itself because it was the product of an alliance between members of both the Mathematical Purists and the Industrial Pragmatists (Cooper, 1985, pp. 235–266).

Official reports

Every so often, the climate within education reaches such a level of concern that an official inquiry is commissioned. The reports then produced can become key reference points against which all future proposals are tested. Consequently, many groups wish to influence the findings of these inquiries. Dr W. H. Cockcroft chaired the most influential inquiry into mathematics teaching in recent times. Its report was entitled *Mathematics Counts* (DES, 1982). Its terms of reference included considering the needs of employment, but perhaps its most famous paragraph (para. 243 – see Chapter 4) is about the need for a broad range of teaching methods. It can be interpreted as being supportive of the views of both Industrial Pragmatists and Progressive Educators (Ernest, 1991, pp. 220–222).

Curriculum and assessment policy

All four groups described above have long recognised that qualifications and their associated exams have a significant impact on teaching and learning. Some of their particular views on assessment were outlined above. In comparison, the most far-reaching government policy in this area, the National Curriculum (NC) for England and Wales, and the corresponding curricula for Scotland and Northern Ireland (see Chapter 2), is still relatively new. Plainly, the NC will remain a crucial battleground for competing groups, and indeed the present NC can be seen to embody ideological aspects of some of the groups. Certain of the key debates surrounding the various national mathematics curricula are explored in the next chapter.

Local expectations

Finally, it is important to recognise the influence of much more localised groups on your teaching. Parents, colleagues in the mathematics department, and the school's senior management will all have expectations of you as a maths teacher. These expectations may coincide with your own views or may be in conflict with them. You will need to learn to negotiate with different individuals and groups, if you are to remain in contact with your own values while working to meet the legitimate demands of others. In particular, pupils will certainly let you know their own expectations; this theme is addressed in Task 1.4.

Task 1.4 What do the pupils want from their mathematics education?

Pupils are arguably the group that will most regularly express to you their views about maths education – and much else besides. It can be valuable for you to understand what they are wanting from their mathematics education. There is scope for exploring this in every maths lesson, but there is not normally the time to consider the issue in depth with individuals.

Design an interview sheet that you could use with pupils to explore their views. The prompts in 'Mathematical memories' (Task 1.1) offer possible questions, but you may also want to add some of your own. If you ask questions about teachers, make sure the pupils understand that you do not want to know names; you just want to know what teaching styles work well for them. If it is possible within your school, ask to interview three Year 7 pupils, three Year 10 pupils and three A-level pupils, and arrange with your head of department to speak with them for about fifteen to twenty minutes. Also check with your head of department that your interview questions are acceptable to the staff.

Record the results of your interview and write some notes in your journal, indicating the extent to which you believe you could accommodate the pupils' perspectives within your teaching.

SUMMARY

The role of mathematics education in our society is complex. There is no simple consensus as to which mathematics is important or how it should be taught. Indeed, there is controversy about the nature of mathematics itself. Different social groups have influenced and will continue to influence the shape of mathematics education. Maths teachers experience the influence of such groups through their teaching associations, curriculum projects, recommendations of official reports and government policy on curriculum and assessment.

The chapter title posed the question 'Mathematics education – who decides?'. Now you must prepare to decide where you stand on the issues raised within it.

FURTHER READING

Cooper, B. (1994) 'Secondary mathematics education in England: recent changes and their historical context', in Selinger, M. (ed.), *Teaching Mathematics*, London: Routledge, pp. 5–26.

This introductory chapter from an Open University reader for PGCE mathematics students offers a helpful historical overview of the forces for change within English mathematics education. It also provides an extensive section of references.

DES (1982) *Mathematics Counts*, London: HMSO.

This volume, often referred to as the Cockcroft Report, remains a key text for mathematics education in Britain. It is much referred to, although often quite selectively, and so it is worth being familiar with its contents.

Ernest, P. (1991) *The Philosophy of Mathematics Education*, Basingstoke: Falmer Press.

This book is an ambitious work that seeks both to offer a new philosophy of mathematics and to examine its impact on mathematics education. The influence of different ideologies on mathematics education is explored in some detail.

MA (1995a) *Why, What, How? Some Basic Questions for Mathematics Teaching*, Leicester: The Mathematical Association.

This booklet provides a good example of an outcome from the recent attempt by one of the mathematics teaching associations to produce a coherent rationale for mathematics teaching. As well as offering answers to why, what and how in relation to mathematics teaching, it also includes a small number of classroom examples.

2 Mathematics in the National Curriculum

John Westwell

INTRODUCTION

In the introduction to his book on mathematics national curricula around the world, the English mathematics educator Geoffrey Howson writes:

> It is well known that teachers throughout the world do not slavishly (or even unslavishly) follow their national curriculum. What is 'intended' by those who draw up national curricula is never 'implemented' in all classrooms. . . . Moreover, what is learned by students may bear little relation to the implemented curriculum. Much that is taught is misunderstood, not understood or not retained. . . . Are national curricula, therefore, so important?
>
> (Howson, 1991, p. 1)

This chapter addresses Howson's question, examining just how influential national curricula can be in shaping pupils' learning experiences. As you embark on your teaching career, you will need to have a detailed knowledge and understanding of the structure and content of your own national curriculum, so that it can inform the processes of your planning, assessment and evaluation.

In order to interpret some of the intentions that lie behind a curriculum, you will have the opportunity to examine some of the debates that have surrounded the development of the English/Welsh Mathematics National Curriculum. Results of international surveys of pupils' mathematical achievement have received a much higher public profile in recent times, which has led to more focused attention on the mathematics curricula and teaching approaches used abroad. In consequence, this chapter makes reference to mathematics curricula and practices from overseas, particularly when they provide alternative models to those currently employed in Great Britain.

OBJECTIVES

By the end of this chapter, you should:

- understand the structure and be more familiar with the specific content of your Mathematics National Curriculum;
- be aware of some of the main issues and debates that surround the development of mathematics curricula;
- understand some key aspects of the mathematics programmes of study;
- be aware of alternative curricular models and possibilities for future development.

THE SCOPE, PRESCRIPTION AND PRESENTATION OF THE CURRICULUM

Mathematics curricula can have very different structures, can apply to different ranges of pupils and can be presented in a variety of forms. When examining any mathematics curriculum, the following questions are worth considering.

- Who is the curriculum for and to what ages of pupils does it apply?
- Is there a common curriculum for all pupils in all schools?
- Is the curriculum statutory, with legal requirement, or is it advisory, solely offering guidance?
- How much prescription is there in the curriculum and how much freedom is there for teachers?
- What forms of documentation are used to present the curriculum?
- In which ways are teachers expected to interpret the curriculum requirements?
- To what extent are textbooks used to dictate or elaborate the curriculum?

Scope and prescription

England and Wales share the same Mathematics National Curriculum. The current version (DfE, 1995) was published in January 1995 and began to be implemented from August of that year. It is the third version of the curriculum since the Mathematics NC was first introduced in 1989. Mathematics is one of the three core subjects in the NC, along with English and science. There are statutory requirements that apply to all pupils in state schools from the ages of 5 to 16. The NC is organised into four *Key Stages* (see Table 2.1), and so in secondary schools your main concern will be with KS3 and KS4.

Table 2.1 Key Stages in the National Curriculum

Key Stages	*Pupil ages*	*Year groups*
Key Stage 1 (KS1)	5–7	1–2
Key Stage 2 (KS2)	7–11	3–6
Key Stage 3 (KS3)	11–14	7–9
Key Stage 4 (KS4)	14–16	10–11

In Scotland, there are no statutory requirements for the curriculum. Instead, the Scottish Office Education Department has issued *National Guidelines* (SOED, 1991) on the curriculum and assessment. These mathematics guidelines, published in August 1991, relate to ages 5 to 14 and are commended to teachers as a basis for mathematics programmes in all Scottish state schools. These guidelines cover the primary years, P1 to P7, and the first two years of the secondary school, S1 and S2.

The move towards a more centralised and prescribed mathematics curriculum in England and Wales had been developing over a number of years (see Johnson and Millett, 1996, Chapter 1). Although there has been some movement towards more prescription in England and Wales, the degree of specification of and control over mathematics curricula in some countries can be much greater still. In Greece, for example, the primary school mathematics curriculum is specified in such detail to the extent of setting out the time to be spent on particular topics (see Howson, 1991). The balance between prescription and guidance will continue to be an issue in future revisions of your own National Curriculum.

Presentation

There are two types of documentation for the English/Welsh Mathematics NC. There is the official Order, made by the Secretaries of State for Education and Wales (DfE, 1995), which contains the legal requirements. However, as well as this, the various curriculum and assessment authorities established to oversee the National Curriculum have continued to produce documents offering guidance. These have sometimes been issued in conjunction with the curriculum Orders and sometimes separately.

The first *non-statutory guidance* (NCC, 1989) gave extensive support and is still a helpful and relevant document for teachers. The current curriculum body, the Qualifications and Curriculum Authority (QCA), has details of publications currently available (its address can be found in Appendix 2). In Scotland, because there is no statutory element, the recommendations and the supplementary guidance are all issued in a single document (SOED, 1991).

An alternative or supplementary way in which mathematics curricula are presented in some countries is through the use of official textbooks. In the United Kingdom, although publishers produce new textbooks that are claimed to meet the various National Curriculum requirements, these are not officially recommended

Task 2.1 Reading the curriculum

It is essential that you have a personal copy of your Mathematics National Curriculum and that you become increasingly familiar with its structure and contents. Begin by skimming the document to establish its structure and to gain a broad sense of its contents. Then, start to read for the details. You may initially wish to concentrate on the secondary curriculum, but do also read about the primary curriculum. Make notes in your journal, so that you can follow up your reading, and:

- seek clarification on any aspects of the document that you do not understand;
- discuss with others questions that the document raises for you;
- resolve any areas of ambiguity within the text;
- start to investigate any aspects of the mathematics that seem new or unfamiliar to you.

texts. By contrast, there are many countries where there is either a required textbook or a range of approved texts. For example, in Japan, there are various series of textbooks, but they all have to be approved by the Education Ministry.

In whichever way a national curriculum is presented, there will always remain the issue of how teachers interpret it. In the research study carried out for the School Curriculum and Assessment Authority (SCAA – a forerunner of the QCA) on the implementation of the Mathematics National Curriculum for England and Wales, the problem of interpretation was examined in relation to 'Using and applying mathematics' (Johnson and Millett, 1996, pp. 99–112). For some teachers, the title of this Attainment Target (see later) informed their view more than its actual contents. This led to a restricted view and little stimulus to change. Here is an example, then, of a possible gap that can form between the 'intended' and the 'implemented' curriculum that Howson described. You, too, may encounter this problem, both during and after your course. As you read the documents, form your own views on what you think is actually required by them. You need to continue refining your understanding through discussion with teachers and other students.

THE DEVELOPMENT AND REVISION OF THE CURRICULUM

The development of a mathematics curriculum is a complex process. The ways in which this is carried out will have a significant impact on the success of its implementation. When examining how curricula are developed or revised, it is worth considering:

- who is involved in the development or revision of the curriculum;
- how teachers are included in the process;
- the time-scale for development, revision and implementation.

In the case of England and Wales, a working group (established in July 1987) developed the first version of the Mathematics NC. Their final report (DES/WO, 1988) was produced in August 1988 and, following consultation, the first Mathematics NC was published in March 1989. The working group included people with sympathies towards the different standpoints on mathematics and its teaching addressed in Chapter 1. Not surprisingly, there was much debate within the group. Teachers were required to begin implementation in the autumn term of 1989, and many teachers felt that they were given inadequate time to prepare for implementation. The pace of change, coupled with the feeling of poor consultation, led to increasing unrest amongst teachers in the years that followed.

Two revisions of the curriculum followed, one as a result of the then Education Minister Kenneth Clarke's intervention (see Johnson and Millett, 1996, Chapter 1) and the second as a result of the Dearing Review (see Capel *et al.*, 1995, unit 7.3). By contrast, the time for the development and consultation on the guidelines in Scotland was extended further. Also, because the guidelines were not statutory there, teachers could respond in a more systematic way over a period of time.

At the time of writing, the process of revising the National Curriculum for England has begun. The stated intention of QCA is that the first draft of the new National Curriculum should be published one year ahead of its implementation in schools.

Task 2.2 The impact of the National Curriculum

The Mathematics NC (or National Guidelines) has had a significant impact on the work of secondary school mathematics departments. In this task, examine the extent of that impact on the mathematics department within which you work, by:

- reading the departmental handbook to see what reference is made to the mathematics NC;
- examining the department's schemes of work to see how the NC is used within the planning process;
- investigating what changes have been made to the department's resources following the introduction and/or later revision of the curriculum;
- discussing with teachers in the department what they believe has been the main impact of the NC on their practice;
- finding out how often and for what purpose teachers in the department refer to the NC documentation.

ATTAINMENT, DIFFERENTIATION AND ASSESSMENT WITHIN THE CURRICULUM

National curricula are partly introduced with the intention of raising standards of attainment in schools. It is an important element of developing a national curriculum to clarify the standards of attainment that will be expected of pupils. In order to do this, a range of issues needs to be addressed, including:

- how the standards of attainment are presented within the curriculum;
- whether fixed standards are defined for particular ages;
- whether there is a defined progression of attainment for the entire curriculum;
- whether there are different targets of attainment for different types of schools;
- how the different rates at which pupils learn are catered for;
- the purpose, form and timing of any assessment prescribed by the curriculum.

In England and Wales, different *Attainment Targets* (AT) set out the expected standards of pupil performance. An Attainment Target is actually a collection of different levels of attainment relating to a particular area of mathematics. For each target, there is a scale of eight level descriptions and a description of exceptional performance. These descriptions convey 'the types and range of performance that pupils working at a particular level should characteristically demonstrate' (DfE, 1995, p. 22). Attainment Target 3 (AT3), for instance, concerns Shape, Space and Measures, so, for example, pupils working at level 8 in AT3 should 'understand and use mathematical similarity. They use sine, cosine and tangent in right-angled triangles when solving problems in two dimensions. They distinguish between formulae for perimeter, area and volume, by considering dimensions' (DfE, 1995, p. 28).

The England and Wales curriculum does not have particular targets for pupils at certain ages. Instead, pupils are expected to progress along the eight-level scale. However, it is said that by the end of KS3 the great majority of pupils should be within the range level 3 to 7. Level 8 and the description of exceptional performance is provided for very able pupils. The scale of level descriptions does not apply at KS4, where GCSE (with grades A to G) becomes the principal way in which attainment is measured. There are no firm descriptions for the various GCSE grades.

There are four Attainment Targets for Mathematics (DfE, 1995, pp. 23–30). These are:

- Attainment Target 1 (AT1): Using and Applying Mathematics;
- Attainment Target 2 (AT2): Number and Algebra;
- Attainment Target 3 (AT3): Shape, Space and Measures;
- Attainment Target 4 (AT4): Handling Data.

The second Attainment Target has double weighting and brings together number and algebra. The main reason that number and algebra are grouped together is that at the lower levels there is very little algebra and at the higher levels there is very little number. Also, certain aspects of algebra can be understood as generalised arithmetic, and there are a number of topics on the boundary between number and algebra.

The Scottish curriculum is organised into broad *attainment outcomes*, within which there are a number of *strands* (see Table 2.2). For most of the strands, there are *attainment targets* at five levels of attainment (A to E). (Note: the term 'attainment target' is used in a different way from the English/Welsh National Curriculum.) For example, the level D attainment target for the 'interpret information' strand is that 'Pupils should be able to interpret from a range of displays and databases by retrieving information subject to one condition' (SOED, 1991, pp. 24–25).

Table 2.2 The structure of the Scottish attainment outcomes and targets

Attainment outcomes	*Strands*
Problem solving and enquiry:	• Starting a task • Doing a task • Reporting on a task
Information handling:	• Collect information • Organise information • Display information • Interpret information
Number, money and measurement: • number and number notation, including money • methods of calculating using number, including money • patterns sequences and relationships, including symbolic representation • measure	• Range and type of numbers • Money • Add and subtract • Multiply and divide • Round numbers • Fractions, percentage and ratio • Patterns and sequences • Functions and equations • Measure and estimate • Time • Perimeter, formulae and scale
Shape, position and movement: • properties of two- and three-dimensional shapes • properties of position and movement	• Range of shapes • Position and movement • Symmetry • Angle

Source: SOED, 1991, pp. 12–41.

The exception to this structure is the 'problem solving and enquiry' strand, for which a range of desirable process strategies is described, along with some indication of how pupils will improve. As in the English/Welsh curriculum, there are no age-related targets, but instead there are broad criteria as to when pupils should attain certain levels. For example, 'Level D should be attainable by some pupils in P5–P6 or even earlier, but certainly by most in P7' (SOED, 1991, p. 10).

The English/Welsh Mathematics NC working group adopted a ten-level model (since revised to eight) for describing attainment; this model was originally proposed by the Task Group on Assessment and Testing (TGAT) (see DES/WO, 1987 for further details). Members of the Task Group believed that, by having a single scale for ages 5 to 16, there would be a clear sense of progression for pupils throughout their schooling. Furthermore, it was thought that this approach would help improve the continuity of provision for pupils as they move between phases of schooling, such as at primary–secondary transfer. Members of the Group were concerned that having age-specific targets might lead to limitations on the most able or no reward for the least able (DES/WO, 1987).

Some of the most heated debates within the Mathematics NC working group occurred over the issue of how to set standards for attainment. Most members of the group were supportive of the TGAT proposal, but a few members favoured having fixed age-related targets, particularly for what they felt were core areas such as arithmetic (Johnson and Millett, 1996). The TGAT model was eventually adopted, but has continued to receive criticism from a number of quarters. Howson criticises it because:

> The TGAT model (as used within mathematics) makes a remarkable assumption: that curricula can be independent of the student's age and ability. Differentiation through depth of treatment or expected outcome is largely ignored. Students of all abilities are expected to follow the same path – the only accepted variable is the rate of progress.
>
> (Howson, 1991, p. 33)

He is concerned that all pupils should be able to take courses of mathematics that have a sense of unity and completeness and are relevant to the pupil's future study. There is a danger with the TGAT model that, by age 16, a pupil has just completed part of a whole course. However, if the continual scale model is not used, then alternative approaches are needed. Different models can be found abroad (see Howson, 1991).

Once a model for attainment and differentiation is established, there is also the need to assess the levels of attainment achieved at some stage. The English/Welsh approach of national tests at ages 7, 11, 14 and 16 has no parallels elsewhere. By contrast, in Scotland and in many other countries, there is no use of externally directed assessments until school-leaving age. However, assessment is still seen as a crucial aspect of a teacher's work, especially where it has an influence on whether pupils have to repeat a year or not. It is this assessment aspect of the English/Welsh NC that has possibly attracted the most criticism of all. For example, the mathematics educator Richard Noss believes that the curriculum is assessment driven:

> My thesis is that the content of the National Curriculum provides nothing more than a thin veneer for its essential form: that the National Curriculum is about testing and grading *per se*, and that what is tested is of less than secondary importance.
>
> (Noss, 1992, p. 62)

In addition to this, it was the problem of unmanageable assessment that acted as the main stimulus for the first revision of the Mathematics NC (see Johnson and Millett, 1996).

PROGRAMMES OF STUDY FOR THE CURRICULUM

Right at the heart of the debate about mathematics curricula is the question of what pupils should be taught. The final section of this chapter addresses a range of issues stimulated by this question, including:

- the breadth and balance of mathematical topics included in the curriculum;
- whether certain aspects of mathematics are considered foundational and therefore requiring special emphasis;
- how the applications of mathematics and the contexts in which maths is used are addressed;
- the place given to process skills of problem solving, enquiry and investigation;
- the value placed on promoting personal qualities and attitudes towards mathematics;
- the impact of calculators and computers on the content of the curriculum;
- how calculators and computers are expected to be used.

In England and Wales, the *programmes of study* specify what pupils should be taught in each Key Stage. The programmes of study for KS3 and KS4 are organised into five sections (see Table 2.3). There is also a section of further material for Key Stage 4 (DfE, 1995, pp. 20–21). In each of the five sections, there is a description of the opportunities that should be offered to pupils and a description of what pupils should be taught. Details of the latter are organised in sub-sections known as *strands*.

In the Scottish guidelines, the term 'programmes of study' refers to any plan of action for teaching mathematics, so this section in the guidelines addresses important principles and issues in the design of these plans (SOED, 1991, pp. 42–61). The section does not attempt to cover the structure of a pupil's experience, as this is addressed in the earlier sections on the attainment outcomes and the general rationale. Guidance is also given on programmes for pupils who reach level E before the end of S2 (SOED, 1991, pp. 63–75).

In devising programmes of study, there is a tension between wanting to offer all pupils a broad experience of mathematics and ensuring that they all develop mastery of core knowledge and skills. This tension was certainly evident within

Table 2.3 The structure of the programme of study for KS3 and KS4

Sections	*Strands*
Using and Applying Mathematics	• Making and monitoring decisions to solve problems • Communicating mathematically • Developing skills of mathematical reasoning
Number	• Understanding place value and extending the number system • Understanding and using relationships between numbers and developing methods of computation • Solving numerical problems
Algebra	• Understanding and using functional relationships • Understanding and using equations and formulae
Shape, Space and Measures	• Understanding and using properties of shape • Understanding and using properties of position, movement and transformation • Understanding and using measures
Handling Data	• Processing and interpreting data • Estimating and calculating the probabilities of events

Source: DfE, 1995, pp. 11–19.

the Mathematics NC working group and is partly rooted in different views about the nature of mathematics. Mathematics educator Zelda Isaacson finds a contradiction within the National Curriculum documents 'between mathematics as a necessary and utilitarian skill for the market place, and mathematics as an aesthetic subject within which creative effort plays a central role' (Isaacson, 1992, p. 26). Although these criticisms were made prior to the preparation of the third version of the NC, the issues she raises still merit consideration.

The way in which both programmes of study and Attainment Targets are presented could lead to a mathematical experience for pupils that is fragmented, yet at the same time has a rigid progression. However, guidance linked to the English/Welsh Mathematics NC warns against this. Planning should 'span the programmes of study and the five broad areas of mathematics they contain, cross-referencing ideas and leading to a coherent and holistic view of mathematics' (NCC, 1989, p. C2). This guidance also quotes the original TGAT report, cautioning against an over-simplified, hierarchical view of pupils' learning: 'It is not necessary to presume that the progression defined indicates some inescapable order in the way children learn, or some sequence of difficulty in the material to be learnt' (NCC, 1989, p. C2).

However, whilst bearing these warnings in mind when studying the mathematics curriculum, it can be helpful to consider the particular issues relevant to its different aspects. Using the structure of the English/Welsh programme of study, five areas of mathematics are examined in the sub-sections that follow.

Using and applying mathematics

The interpretation of this aspect of the Mathematics NC has presented a problem. Think about the following three dimensions to the use or application of mathematics. The first is the context within which mathematics is deployed, the second is the mathematical processes that are used and the third is the mathematical concepts, facts and techniques that are employed. Figure 2.1 illustrates the way in which these three dimensions can be integrated.

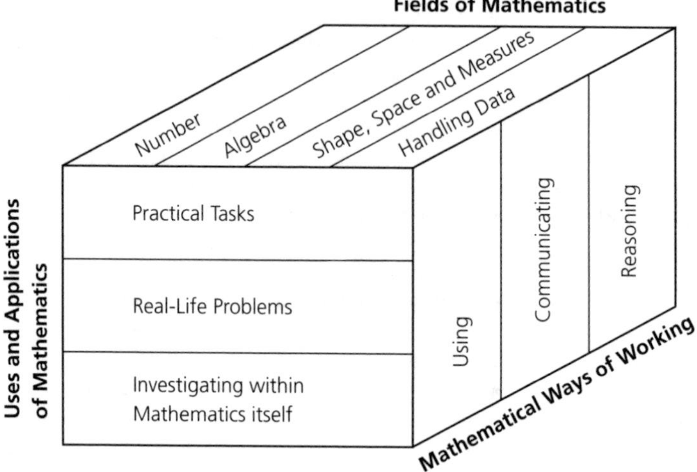

Figure 2.1 Three dimensions of applying mathematics
Source: adapted from ATM (1993b)

The English/Welsh programme of study suggests that pupils be given opportunities to use and apply mathematics:

- in practical tasks;
- in real-life problems;
- within mathematics itself.

The Scottish curriculum expands slightly on the range of contexts by including:

- real-life and everyday problems;
- imaginary or simulated contexts;
- problems and investigations where the structure of mathematics itself provides the setting.

The skills, processes and strategies that are employed when using mathematics are diverse and not easy to classify. The English/Welsh programme of study for using and applying mathematics has three quite different strands (Table 2.3) from the Scottish attainment outcomes for problem solving and enquiry (Table 2.2). However, if you look more closely at the detail of both curricula, you will find many of the same processes, just organised in a different way. The third dimension of mathematical concepts, facts and techniques, sometimes labelled 'mathematical content', can be found in the rest of the programmes of study (England/Wales) or attainment outcomes (Scotland).

Many members of the Mathematics NC working group had wanted significant emphasis placed on 'applications of mathematics'. They proposed three elements: using mathematics, communication skills and 'personal qualities' (DES/WO, 1988). However, they did not think it was possible or appropriate to fit these elements into the ten-level structure. Partly because of this difficulty, the 'personal qualities' element was taken out of the first Mathematics NC (DES/WO, 1989a) and only appeared in the *Non-Statutory Guidance* (NCC, 1989). In Scotland, this same problem of defining 'progression' was acknowledged but handled differently by indicating 'broad trends in improvement' (SOED, 1991, p. 9).

Even with the place of 'applications' somewhat less central than some of the working group had wanted, the emphasis on this aspect of mathematics is still considerably greater in the United Kingdom curricula than overseas. This is linked to the increased emphasis on problem solving and investigational work in mathematics teaching encouraged by the Cockcroft Report (DES, 1982, paras. 243, 249–250) and the reports and projects that followed it. Consequently, it is this area of the British mathematics curricula that is perhaps of most interest to mathematics educators abroad.

Task 2.3
Investigating number chains

In this task, you will apply your knowledge of mathematics 'within mathematics itself'. Begin by carrying out this mathematical task.

A number chain is generated by the following rule from any starting number:

- if the number is even, halve it to generate the next number in the chain;
- if the number is odd, multiply it by three and add one to generate the next number in the chain.

Investigate. Keep a record of your work and produce a written report when you have finished investigating.

When you have completed the task, read through either of the following as appropriate: the 'Using and Applying Mathematics' programme of study and Attainment Target (DfE, 1995, pp. 11–12 and 23–24) or the 'Problem-Solving and Enquiry' attainment outcome (SOED, 1991, pp. 12–17). As you do this, evaluate your performance on the activity in light of the curriculum requirements. Then return to the task and improve your work accordingly.

Number

The programme of study for number within the English/Welsh curriculum is also organised into three strands (Table 2.3), but it is mainly the second strand, with its emphasis on developing methods of computation, that attracts most interest. The curriculum encourages the use of mental methods, estimation and approximation, and the use of calculators, as well as pencil-and-paper methods. It is the balance within the curriculum among these different approaches to calculation that is the cause of many debates (see also Chapter 8). The section from the non-statutory guidelines on pupils doing calculations suggests:

> For most practical purposes, pupils will use mental methods or a calculator to tackle problems involving calculations. Thus the heavy emphasis placed on teaching standard written methods for calculations in the past needs to be re-examined. Mental methods have assumed a greater importance through the introduction of calculators, and use of mental methods as a first resort in tackling calculations should be encouraged.
>
> (NCC, 1989, p. E6)

The importance of mental methods is widely accepted, but there is now an increasing awareness that this consists of much more than knowledge of arithmetic facts. It is recognised that pupils need to be helped to develop mental strategies for handling calculations, an area that had, on the whole, been neglected. Instead, pupils would have been taught how to use a narrow range of standard algorithms. Many people, however, express concern that if pupils are allowed easy access to a calculator, they will become too dependent on it. This was part of the reasoning behind the then Minister of Education Kenneth Baker insisting in 1988 that some non-calculator long multiplication and division be included in the number curriculum. However, the teaching of any particular algorithm is not required. This is important, given that both studies of people at work and international school-based studies show that there are many different calculation algorithms as well as *ad hoc* personal methods.

Teaching pupils how to estimate or approximate answers has also been an undeveloped aspect of the mathematics curriculum. Pupils, who often place more value on finding exact solutions, tend to resist it. However, these skills become more significant in a calculator age, when the reasonableness of answers needs to be checked. The appropriate use of the calculator is much discussed. Some people would like to see it removed from primary and early secondary school. Others think it can be an invaluable tool for promoting understanding of number and so should be used as early as possible. International comparisons lean more towards the former view, especially at primary level (but see Kitchen, 1998); a few countries like Spain welcome the use of any calculating device. Japan offers a further contrast, where teachers are expected to introduce pupils to the use of the *soroban*, the Japanese abacus.

Task 2.4 Pupils' calculation methods

In this task, you will interview some of your pupils to investigate how they carry out calculations and their relative confidence with different methods. You will need to arrange to interview six pupils, either individually or in pairs. There are three stages to the interview. Tell the pupils that you are interested in how they do calculations. Explain that you will specify whether they should do the calculations mentally, with pen and paper, or by using their choice of calculator or pen and paper.

Stage 1

Ask pupils to do the first set of calculations mentally, without the use of pencil and paper. Tell them that you particularly want to know what they do in their heads and what their approach was.

(a) $23 + 48$ (b) $82 - 37$ (c) 15×7 (d) $96 \div 4$

Record details of their methods as they explain them to you. Also note down any problems they have, whether in doing the calculation or in explaining their approach. Read what you have written back to them and see if they agree.

Stage 2

For the second set of calculations, tell the pupils that they can use pen and paper if they wish to.

(a) $267 + 584$ (b) $645 - 178$ (c) 23×57 (d) $624 \div 12$

Ask them to talk through their methods, noting down and checking with them afterwards as you did in Stage 1.

Stage 3

For the final set of calculations, tell the pupils that they may use a calculator or pen and paper if they wish to.

(a) $247 + 345 + 692 + 701$ (b) $10{,}000 - 2{,}637$ (c) $16 \times 18 \times 20$
(d) $325 \div 17$

If they use the calculator, note which keys they press and in which order. Ask them to explain the reasons behind their choice of method and device.

Having carried out the interviews, analyse the results and consider what implications they have for the way you might teach pupils to calculate. Write a short report of your investigation in your journal.

Algebra

One of the impacts of the Mathematics NC was to encourage a much broader algebra curriculum than before, and consequently this resulted in a reduced emphasis on algebraic manipulation. For example, there is much more attention given to working on patterns and generalisations. Guidance from the National Curriculum Council states:

> Traditionally the curriculum has contained a great deal of routine imitative algebraic manipulation. Pupils were taught and rehearsed through a collection of standard rules and methods, often with little understanding or appreciation of the power of algebra in dealing with generality.
>
> (NCC, 1992, p. E1.1)

It is believed that early work on number patterns and the relationships between numbers lays the foundation for the subsequent development of algebra. Pupils are expected to learn more about the interpretation and use of formulae and equations and how to use graphical and trial and improvement methods for solving equations.

Some of this shift in the algebra curriculum had begun with the GCSE. Some teachers at both university and post-16 level soon raised concerns that their students no longer had adequate algebraic skills for higher courses. These criticisms have continued to be made, particularly from amongst the Mathematical Purists group (see Chapter 1). However, at the same time, the place of certain algebraic manipulation skills in the curriculum is being questioned as symbolic manipulator software becomes more widely available. Just as the easy availability of numerical calculators has stimulated much debate about the number curriculum, so the increasing presence of symbolic manipulators will fuel the debate about the algebra curriculum.

Shape, space and measures

This area of the curriculum brings together ideas of shape, location, movement and measure, and is a long way from a traditional geometry curriculum. The measures strand of the curriculum has been shifted around in the course of National Curriculum revisions. This is mainly due to it having close links with both number and shape/space; it therefore provides a good instance of a topic where the curriculum cannot be neatly divided into discrete chunks. Aspects of co-ordinate and transformation geometry had become well established since the 1960s and retained a significant place in the National Curriculum.

Most countries have also moved away from a more traditional Euclidean geometry curriculum. However, there are some countries, like France for example, where aspects of this sort of geometry have been retained. In France, this is principally because it is thought that the teaching of geometry contributes to the development of reasoning powers. There are also some British mathematics educators who consider that traditional approaches to geometry can offer pupils an experience of rigour and proof, one which they believe has been lost from the school mathematics curriculum here.

The ways in which pupils should work on shape, space and measures receives attention in the programme of study, where it states: 'Pupils should be given opportunities to explore shape through drawing and practical work using a wide range of materials' (DfE, 1995, p. 16). This highlights the need for pupils to get plenty of 'hands-on' experience to help develop their understanding of and knowledge about shape, space and measures. There is a danger, though, that pupils actually receive only a restricted curriculum in this area, because of the difficulties of organising practical lessons. A useful test of your teaching in this area is to evaluate how much time pupils spend drawing, measuring and constructing 2D/3D shapes. A further way in which shape and space can be explored is through the use of specially designed software packages (see Chapter 8). Interestingly, some of these packages allow pupils to explore some traditional Euclidean topics in a new way.

Task 2.5 Conducting a practical lesson

The purpose of this task is to develop some of the classroom management skills required for conducting a practical lesson. Identify one of your classes that is about to cover some aspect of the 'Shape, Space and Measures' programme of study (or its equivalent). Consider what form of practical work might best promote the desired knowledge, skills and understanding for the topic being covered. Then, in your preparations before the lesson:

- organise sufficient resources that are easily accessible;
- plan how you will manage the resources during the lesson;
- allow time in your lesson plan for the distribution and collection of the resources;
- consider the best way to communicate the practical tasks to the pupils;
- consider how you want the pupils arranged in the classroom.

Talk through your lesson plan with the class teacher, checking that you have made suitable preparations. After the lesson, evaluate its success and consider how you could improve on the classroom management aspect in future lessons. Also, ask the teacher to give you feedback on the lesson.

Handling data

The growing emphasis on both statistics and probability within the mathematics curriculum reflects changes in society, which is increasingly influenced by the way in which data, usually numerical, are handled. Although there have been elements of statistics and probability within mathematics teaching for some time, the breadth of what is now expected by the Mathematics NC is quite new. The programme of study recognises the importance of the whole statistical process (see Graham, 1987, p. 22), including the stages of:

- posing a problem;
- collecting the appropriate data;
- analysing and representing the data;
- interpreting the results of the analysis.

Whilst it may be appropriate sometimes to teach the skills needed for these stages separately, it is also important at times that pupils experience the whole process.

Task 2.6 Questioning the data

Watch a main evening news broadcast. Record all occasions where data are used in the reports. After the programme, try to answer the following questions for each piece of data.

- What was the original reason that the data were collected and who wanted them to be collected?
- How were the data collected and how reliable do you think the methods were?
- In what ways have the data been analysed and presented? How appropriate were these methods?
- How were the data interpreted and what conclusions were drawn from them?

Having worked through this process for yourself, consider what implications this has for the way in which you might teach pupils to 'handle data'.

The aspects of probability required by the programmes of study are also much broader in scope than was often covered prior to the Mathematics NC being introduced. Indeed, many other countries' curricula (including the Scottish one) do not tackle probability until higher secondary level. In the English/Welsh curriculum, there is now an emphasis on more than just theoretical probability, encompassing the use of statistical data and experimental results. There is, however, a need to be cautious here. Concepts underlying probability are subtle, and so there is a danger that, through a superficial treatment of the subject, understanding of key ideas will not be developed.

The teaching of both statistics and probability can be significantly supported by the use of computers to generate, process and present data. The programme of study actually requires pupils to be offered opportunities to 'use computers as a source of large samples, a tool for exploring graphical representations, and as a means to simulate events' (DfE, 1995, p. 18). This raises the broader issue of how much the Mathematics NC requires the use of computers. In the Number programme of study, computer software such as spreadsheets is mentioned. In the Shape, Space and Measures section, using computers to generate and transform graphic images and to solve problems is included. The Scottish guidelines also recommend the use of computers in a range of ways (SOED, 1991, pp. 86–88). Indeed, they emphasise a further importance of computers (see also Chapter 8): 'The [attainment] targets are for all pupils. Those who require personal computers and related devices to aid communication or to provide access to the curriculum should be enabled to use these to demonstrate attainment' (SOED, 1991, p. 11).

Many mathematics curricula overseas suggest the use of computers as a general aid to teaching, but do not prescribe how they are to be used. This was an issue for the NC Mathematics working group, who acknowledged that there was a problem of specifying how computers should be used. They believed that until pupils had ready access to computers, they could only offer suggestions. However, following pressure from the National Council for Educational Technology (NCET), some specific references were included, partly as a stimulus to schools to invest in equipment. The impact of computers on the content of the mathematics curriculum remains very limited, but this will continue to be an issue in the future (see Chapter 8).

SUMMARY

Your Mathematics National Curriculum will undoubtedly have an impact on your teaching. The scope and prescription of the curriculum will influence the extent of this impact and your interpretation of the curriculum will be affected by the way in which it is presented. The way in which standards of attainment are defined will partly shape your practice, particularly how you address the issue of pupils learning at different rates. The programmes of study will not remain static; you will need to continue to refine your understanding of their content and of different possible emphases within them.

You are likely to experience a number of revisions of the National Curriculum during your career as a mathematics teacher. You need to go on thinking about the issues raised in this chapter if you are to engage with and contribute to the important debate that surrounds the revision process.

FURTHER READING

As well as reading a copy of your own Mathematics National Curriculum (see Task 2.1), the following reading is recommended.

ATM (1993b) *Using and Applying Mathematics*, Derby: The Association of Teachers of Mathematics.

This book is designed to give practical help to teachers who are preparing work on Using and Applying Mathematics. It helps to develop an understanding of the strands within this part of the programme of study, and also includes many ideas to use when helping pupils to develop this aspect of mathematics.

Howson, A. G. (1991) *National Curricula in Mathematics*, Leicester: The Mathematical Association.

This book offers a useful general introduction to what mathematics national curricula can address. It also contains a detailed description of the maths curricula in fourteen countries and highlights key points of divergence among them.

Johnson, D. and Millett, A. (eds) (1996) *Implementing the Mathematics National Curriculum*, London: Paul Chapman.

This book gives a broad overview of the policy, politics and practices associated with the development, implementation and revision of the Mathematics National Curriculum. It draws upon a two-year research study evaluating the implementation of the curriculum at Key Stages 1, 2 and 3, and includes results of a study into teachers' perceptions and actions during a period of major curriculum change. It also provides a helpful historical account of the development and revisions of the curriculum itself.

3 Pupils Learning Mathematics

Maria Goulding

INTRODUCTION

As a student teacher, you will probably spend a period of time observing lessons, helping individuals and groups before you gradually move to teaching full classes. You will, therefore, be entering a ready-made social situation, and your growing understanding of how pupils learn mathematics will be strongly influenced by the context in which you see this learning take place. For this reason, I shall approach pupil learning in this chapter by peeling back the layers: looking at the social context first, then moving on to feelings and finally looking at pupils' thinking. This is by no means a typical approach.

For some writers, the mathematics being learned, the conditions under which it is learned and the feelings and attitudes that learners bring to the situation are all but ignored. My own view is that you cannot begin to make sense of what is going on inside the learner's head until these other dimensions are considered. They interact, of course, and the picture is even further complicated by the dynamic relationship between teaching and learning.

The purpose of this chapter is to expose some of the common features of mathematics classrooms, but also to introduce you to some insights from the mathematics education research literature. This will help you to think critically about the circumstances in which learning takes place and the processes that it involves. As you try out the accompanying school-based tasks, you should try to connect what you see in your classrooms with the research and theorising offered here. Making such connections will best be done by sharing your observations with teachers and other students, and by looking for similarities and differences. It is assumed that this will take place for each of the suggested tasks.

This chapter discusses some contrasting theoretical positions about the learning of mathematics. Some of these arise from research. An important summary of recent research in mathematics education is that by Askew and Wiliam (1995). You will find it useful to have a copy to work with as you read this and some later chapters.

OBJECTIVES

By the end of the chapter, you should:

- appreciate the social, emotional and cognitive dimensions of learning, and the importance of context;
- be aware that pupils are both individuals and members of groups at the same time;
- be making links between reading and what you experience in school;
- realise how learning and teaching are intertwined.

THE SOCIAL CONTEXT OF LEARNING

The mathematics classroom

You will probably meet pupils first in a mathematics classroom, so you will immediately see them learning within the frame of this social situation. Typically, there will be one teacher with about thirty pupils in the class, with possibly a support teacher to work with pupils with special educational needs (see Chapter 9). If the pupils are in Years 8–11, then the class will probably be a set based on perceptions of ability, and the numbers of pupils in the sets may vary. Lessons will be about an hour long and there will usually be two or three in the week.

You may find very strong views about the forms of organisation found in the classes you observe. Some of these may highlight the importance of the individual child and the difficulty of catering for individual needs within a class.

> 1. No learner can be expected to think in the same way as his or her teacher.
> 2. No two learners in a class can be expected to think in the same way as each other (possibly excepting twins).
>
> (Backhouse *et al.*, 1992, p. 54)

Some teachers may justify the use of setting by referring to such individual differences and explaining how difficult it is to cater for a very wide spread of individual attainment in a mixed-ability class.

In some schools, however, teachers may use an individualised learning scheme in some or all of the classes to accommodate these differences. Pupils can work at their

Task 3.1 Classroom organisation

As you observe a lesson, note how the class is organised.

- How many teachers are there in the classroom?
- How many pupils are there in the lesson?
- How long is the lesson?
- How is the furniture arranged? Does this correspond to the way in which the children are working (for example, are the pupils sitting in groups but working individually)?
- Do the pupils work as a whole class, in smaller groups or as individuals? Is there a mix of these ways of working? Note how long they work in the different groupings for any one lesson. How are transitions effected?
- Do pupils all do the same tasks? Is there any choice?
- Do pupils make comparisons among different methods of doing the mathematics problems or is everyone expected to use the same method?
- What physical resources are used (for example, texts, practical equipment, calculators, posters, etc.)?

After the lesson, talk to the teacher about the forms of classroom organisation they find most conducive to learning. Which factors influence their decisions (control, the ability of the set, their own preferred style, etc.)?

Reflect on how the organisation of mathematics lessons in this school compares with the school you went to as a pupil. There may be some interesting similarities and differences within the group, depending on when and where you were educated. Write a paragraph in your journal to summarise this.

own pace through commercially produced materials, with periodic tests and reviews to monitor progress; the class can be taught as a mixed-ability group, thus avoiding the potentially damaging effects of labelling pupils by putting them into sets. There is a wide range of tasks in such schemes, including the use of games and practical work, as well as those designed to teach skills and concepts.

For a new teacher, however, keeping track of the pupils can be very demanding, and you may observe teachers simply coping with issues of administration and reacting to pupils' demands rather than initiating interactions. Another potential problem is that pupils working from a text meet a pre-determined sequence of questions, instructions and explanations that may place great demands upon their reading comprehension. This involves far more than simply being able to read the words; it involves extracting the meanings and connections intended by the writer of the materials.

As the Numeracy Project begins to take effect in primary schools and attention turns towards secondary maths, secondary schools are being encouraged to use more whole-class teaching, sometimes apparently regardless of the various interpretations of the phrase. This move has been prompted by comparisons with teaching methods common in countries that appear to perform significantly better on international tests of mathematical content, if not on tests designed to assess the ability to use and apply mathematics (Budge, 1997). David Reynolds (1996) claims that the interactive whole-class teaching methods used in Taiwan are based on the assumption that the pupils will move forward together, in contrast to our Western focus upon individuality. He argues that, by accommodating difference, we may actually *produce* it, with a long tail of under-achievement.

Whole-class teaching, however, can mean different things to different people. In a class selected by ability (a set), the intention may be to produce a homogeneous attainment group. This often entails the class *being taught as if it were an individual.* The teacher may give explanations and demonstrate how to do examples, with the pupils expected to follow a sequence that is in the teacher's head, and to master the material at roughly the same rate.

In contrast, whole-class teaching could also mean that the pupils work on accessible starting points, perhaps initially in small groups, develop their own ideas and strategies with the teacher's help, and then share them with the whole class. Here, difference and diversity are exploited by the teacher rather than ironed out, and the class may work as individuals, small groups and as a whole class at different points in the process. These two models actually amount to very different theoretical positions.

THEORIES OF LEARNING AND KNOWLEDGE

In what follows, there are a number of references to different views and theories of learning (including various forms of constructivism, behaviourism and Vygotsky's socio-cultural theory). For more information on any one of these, read at least the introduction to Wood (1988) or unit 5.1 in Capel *et al.*, 1995.

As you read this section about theories of learning and knowledge, you will need to relate what you read to your own experiences of learning mathematics and to what you see taking place in lessons in your school. Task 3.2 is intended to help you to do this.

The first model of whole-class teaching outlined above, if adopted in its most extreme form, really amounts to a view of learning as copying. In contrast, Barbara Jaworski outlines a *social constructivist* perspective:

> In the classrooms which I have studied, I have regarded the students as meaning makers, and teachers as supporters of the process of meaning making by their students. This does not mean that I see teaching as some wishy-washy process of 'letting it happen', the teacher being no more than a facilitator. This is as simplistic a view as is the image of teacher as the expert who hands over knowledge and skills.
>
> (Jaworski, 1992, p. 13)

Task 3.2 Relating theory and practice

1. Think about your own experiences of learning mathematics. Try to identify two contrasting experiences: one where you were expected to work alone and one where you were encouraged to work with other learners.
2. In the lessons you watch in your school, look out for parts of lessons where the pupils are expected to work alone, and times where pupils are encouraged to work with each other in pairs or small groups.

For each of the cases that you identify in 1 and 2 above, keep them in mind as you read about the theories of learning in this chapter. Keep notes in your journal of your reflections on how the theories relate to the incidents and experiences that you have identified.

Jaworski is stressing the active roles of both teacher and learner, and uses two negative comparisons for emphasis. In the first of these, 'the wishy-washy process of "letting it happen"', we have a very simplified but commonly held version of Piaget's constructivism, in which children learn by passing through a sequence of four stages. No amount of direction and teaching can move a child between stages if the child is not 'ready'. According to this theory, children are often cast as lone discoverers motivated to understand the world around them in terms of previous experiences, but constrained by their particular stage of development. (For a helpful discussion of aspects of Piaget's theory in relation to mathematics teaching and learning, read at least Chapter 5, 'Must we wait until pupils are ready?' in Orton, 1987, pp. 59–80.)

No such active role is available for the learner in Jaworski's second example: 'teacher as the expert who hands over knowledge and skills'. This image describes learners in behaviourist theory, where the teacher's role is to shape and positively to reinforce pupils' responses until they are correct. This theory has its roots in experiments on training animal behaviour and was later applied to human learning, but its effects are still commonly seen in classrooms where the learners' motivation, experiences and understandings are not taken into account and 'rote' learning is achieved through copying and practising until perfect. With an externally imposed curriculum, where much hangs on examination performance, however, it can be very tempting to teach in this way, even for teachers who can see the limitations of this approach.

In acknowledging the importance of action and problem solving in learning, social constructivism has much in common with Piaget's constructivism, but there is a much stronger emphasis on the role of language, communication and instruction. The American psychologist Jerome Bruner is a leading proponent of social constructivism. For him, children do not invent or discover how to adapt their thinking and act intelligently in new situations by themselves. These processes are developed by negotiating and interacting with more mature peers and teachers. In developing this theory, Bruner has been strongly influenced by the Soviet psychologist and socio-cultural theorist Lev Vygotsky, for whom social interaction was a necessary condition for learning: 'Indeed [Vygotsky] defined intelligence itself as the capacity to learn through instruction' (Wood, 1988, p. 9). Instruction here, however, is not the one-directional process involved in behaviourism. It is a much more subtle process in which several important ideas are involved.

1 *The zone of proximal development*
This is the 'gap' between what the learner can achieve on his own, and what he can achieve with help from a more knowledgeable adult or peer.
2 *Scaffolding (or contingent teaching)*
This is the process by which a more knowledgeable adult or peer can help a child move from her actual performance level to her potential level, giving just enough help to move the child from one to the other.
3 *Self-regulation*
In interacting with more knowledgeable peers or teachers, pupils can begin to think about and regulate their own thinking. This could involve questioning their habitual first responses, refining their solutions, asking themselves questions and trying alternative approaches.

Jaworski has illustrated some of these constructs at work with specific examples of negotiation between skilful teachers and pupils in secondary classes, where an investigative approach to mathematics was established and the values behind it were shared. The teachers were enculturating their pupils into a particular way of thinking and acting in mathematical situations. They were doing so by making judgements about the degree of challenge offered to pupils, based on sensitive interactions with the pupils as they pursued lines of enquiry in investigative tasks. These interactions often took the form of the teacher acting as a 'mirror' to the pupils' thinking, subtly probing and asking questions that would help them to clarify their position and to see ways forward.

In another study, Mike Askew, Joan Bliss and Sheila Macrae (1995) have also explored the metaphor of scaffolding. In their observations of 105 lessons of mathematics, science, and design and technology, they found little evidence of teachers using this strategy intuitively. This they attributed to the very special constraints and circumstances in school settings, which make the notion of scaffolding problematic.

> Perhaps the best way to regard scaffolding is as some form of general orientating metaphor, alerting the teacher to watch out for the extent to which pupils can succeed at tasks on their own, suppressing the desire to step in and help too soon, yet being prepared to work alongside the pupil when a genuine need arises.
>
> (Askew *et al.*, 1995, p. 56)

It is important to realise that social constructivism *as a theory of learning* could co-exist with a view of mathematical knowledge as fixed and objective. If you take

Task 3.3 What does it mean to help a pupil?

Try to analyse a situation in which a pupil needs help from you, the teacher or another pupil.

- How does the pupil signal the difficulty? Ask the pupil to describe the difficulty.
- How is the pupil seeing the problem? Write down the pupil's exact words and actions as soon as possible after the event.
- How was the help given? Write down the words and actions as soon as possible afterwards.

Discuss the incident with the class teacher and later with other students. Was there enough/too much/too little guidance? How did you judge? Did the help move the child on or simply solve the immediate problem? Did you see any evidence of scaffolding and what form did it take?

the humanistic view of knowledge of Davis and Hersh (1986), you need to incorporate the idea that unless we negotiate meaning by arguing, discussing and exploring disagreement, we would not be able to communicate with each other. Without this consensus, any one mathematical statement would be as valid as another. Within this paradigm, the classroom could be regarded as a 'community of practice', where ideas are explored, discussed, shared and evaluated. I have already referred to Jaworski's closely observed examples, but you should also read about how this model is illustrated in the research by Jo Boaler (1997, especially pp. 42–45), which features heavily in the next section. In Jaworski and Boaler's work we have social constructivism as a theory of learning together with a theory of knowledge. While we are still thinking about mathematical knowledge, it is appropriate to step outside the mathematics classroom for a moment.

Situated cognition

The Industrial Pragmatists, mentioned in the first chapter, want pupils to be able to apply the mathematics they learn at school to the workplace, but this notion of 'transfer' may not be as straightforward as it seems. American social anthropologist Jean Lave (1988), for instance, has summarised the research on out-of-school uses of mathematics and concluded that all learning is closely tied to the situation in which it is found. She explains that people are unable to use the mathematics they learn at school because it is so closely tied to peculiar and unrealistic practices adopted there. In other words, school mathematics may be useful only in school.

This may be a depressing outlook for anyone starting out as a mathematics teacher, particularly if they share some of the aims of the Industrial Pragmatists. Perhaps this yawning gap is not inevitable, though. We may find that transfer is poor because the common practices of school mathematics need to be questioned, challenged and adapted, so that the 'school' mathematics and 'out-of-school' mathematics have some common ground, not just in the contexts employed, but in the ways of working adopted in the classroom.

Jo Boaler (1997) has used the idea of situated cognition to compare what she describes as *different forms of knowledge* found in two schools, of very similar intake and circumstance, but with radically different approaches to the teaching of mathematics. The first school, which she names Amber Hill, was typical of many schools in that it adopted a conventional textbook-based approach, but despite good relationships between staff and pupils, and controlled classroom conditions, many of the pupils:

> appeared to be disadvantaged in the face of new or 'applied' situations. . . . [They] believed that mathematical success required memory, rather than thought. They had developed a shallow and procedural knowledge that was of limited use in new and demanding situations, and their desire to interpret cues and do the 'right thing' suppressed their ability to interpret situations holistically or mathematically.
>
> (Boaler, 1997, p. 143)

The students in the other school, which she calls Phoenix Park, performed better in the GCSE examinations set at the time. The teaching approach there was based around open-ended projects lasting two or three weeks, with content and techniques interspersed as necessary. Despite a lack of imposed order, most of the pupils responded well to the amount of choice given and were able to adapt flexibly to new situations.

> When the Phoenix Park students encountered a mathematical problem, they believed that they should consider the different variables present and then develop ideas in relation to the specific setting in which they found themselves. They were not disabled by the need to try and remember relevant algorithms. When the students described their use of mathematics, they talked about the importance of thought, the adaptation of methods they had learned and their interpretation of different situations.
>
> (Boaler, 1997, p. 144)

Boaler does not paint a completely rosy picture of Phoenix Park nor a completely negative picture of Amber Hill, and she is wary of generalisations. But she does question the common practices in mathematics classrooms, which many of us have come through, and in which many of you will find yourselves immersed on teaching practice. Her work requires closer reading because of these controversial questions, not just about teaching approaches, but also about ability groupings and gender, the final two sub-sections I discuss in this opening section.

Ability

My own experience of schools supports research evidence (for example, Ruthven, 1987 and Watson, 1996) that mathematics teachers, more than teachers of other subjects, use ability as a major organising principle for their teaching. The view that attainment is mainly determined by some innate ability (Lorenz, 1982), and that it is stable over time, can variously be seen as defeatist, realistic or damaging. In her study, Boaler argues that the practice of setting disadvantaged some Amber Hill students both in the top sets, particularly those who felt anxiety under pressure, as well as those in lower sets, some of whom felt that restrictions were placed on their learning opportunities. In fact, research on ability groupings in this country is surprisingly thin. Askew and Wiliam's tentative conclusion, that 'mathematical attainment groupings can lead to some gains in attainment [and that] contrary to popular belief, setting does not appear to lead necessarily to low self-esteem for low attainers' (Askew and Wiliam, 1995, p. 40) is based largely on research from the United States.

Task 3.4 Setting or mixed ability?

- Are there any mixed-ability classes in your placement school? In which years are they employed? How are they managed? What resources are used?
- Are there any setting arrangements? If so, make a diagram to show the structure of the setting arrangements for the different year groups. Under what circumstances do pupils move between sets?
- Talk to teachers. Find out about the reasons for the organisation, and their own personal preferences. If the classes are setted at your school, compare low sets with high sets for the same teacher. How does she describe differences in practice for these sets?
- Find a way of asking pupils how they arrived in the set they are in and how they feel about it. Note the actual words they use in describing themselves in relation to the set. Has their self-esteem been affected, do you think, and if so, how?

Gender

One aspect of the social dimension of learning mathematics that has had considerable attention over a long period has been the perceived problem of girls' poor achievement in mathematics, largely because of girls' general apparent underachievement and their low level of participation post-16. Explanations arising from biological differences between the sexes have been inconclusive, and have also been undermined by evidence of negligible sex differences in some countries, as well as changes over time (Hanna, 1989). Many of the initiatives designed to improve this situation have focused upon making mathematics 'girl-friendly', for example by widening the contexts, using non-sexist resources, improving careers advice and raising teachers' expectations of girls. Performance is now very even, except for the highest grades at GCSE (Goulding, 1995), but participation post-16 is still unbalanced.

This framing of girls as disadvantaged is very problematic, however, since there may be very positive reasons why they reject mathematics in favour of other subjects that may offer more relevance and interest. From her research, Boaler found that in the face of the traditional practices at Amber Hill, girls did under-achieve and were disaffected, but that neither disaffection nor anxiety was found amongst the girls in the more open, process-based approach at Phoenix Park.

Much of the research on gender has moved from looking at sex differences in performance to looking at the unwritten social rules in play in mathematics class-rooms, and this has thrown light upon the way in which membership of a group, not necessarily of the same sex, can affect an individual's experience of learning. This ability to function effectively in a group, so that the learner's potential is realised, may have a great deal to do with feelings of belonging, of being safe and of being motivated to learn.

Task 3.5 Sex differences in performance?

Find out how your school monitors examination performance in mathematics. Do they look at sex differences? Do they have information on entries at different tiers? Are there any sex differences apparent?

Are there any noticeable differences at Key Stage 3, GCSE or post-16? Are there any differences in other subjects?

Talk to boys and girls about their expectations of success in mathematics. Compare this with their teachers' predictions.

FEELINGS AND MOTIVATION

One of the most striking things to emerge from the Assessment of Performance Unit's (APU) study of attitudes and gender differences was the way in which it connected attitudes with performance. Results showed that feelings ran high when it came to mathematics, and that expressions of enjoyment declined after the age of 11, when 250 out of 500 pupils rated it their favourite subject. By the age of 15, the number of girls finding mathematics difficult was significantly higher than the number of boys, but the link between perceptions of difficulty and actual performance was not straightforward.

> For many other items . . . boys [are] overrating the easiness of an item in relation to their success, that is, many more say it is easy than get it right. Girls tend to overrate the difficulty of more items; more girls produce correct answers for many items than say those items are easy.
>
> (APU, 1988, p. 18)

This means that we must treat work on attitudes and feelings towards mathematics cautiously, whilst still accepting that pleasure and enjoyment are legitimate educational aims in themselves.

By asking 14-year-old pupils to recount good and bad experiences of learning, Celia Hoyles was able to gain insight into pupils' perceptions of their mathematics learning. She found that about one-third of the good stories (42 out of 135) and one half of the bad stories (72 out of 146) were about mathematics learning: 'The stories also showed that anxiety, feelings of inadequacy and feelings of shame were quite common features of bad experiences in learning mathematics' (Hoyles, 1982, p. 362). Although there was considerable diversity, with some pupils enjoying challenge and others simply wanting to know what to do, many of the pupils seemed to want their teachers (in Hoyles' words) to 'make it easy' for them or to 'tell them the way': 'Pupils were appreciative of a secure, encouraging environment in their mathematics lessons and liked teachers to provide a structured logical progression in their work, with plenty of patient explanation, encouragement and friendliness' (Hoyles, 1982, p. 368).

Task 3.6 Good and bad stories about mathematics

Try to replicate some of Hoyles' research; ask pupils to write stories about good and bad learning experiences. Ask them to tell you about the situation in which the event happened, how they felt about it, the reasons why it was good or bad and why they think they reacted in the way they did.

Hoyles' comments about the need for security echo Gordon Pask's (1976) distinction between *serialist* and *holist* learning strategies, by means of which he focuses upon the amount of risk learners are prepared to tolerate. Whereas serialists like to move from certainty to certainty, holists prefer to start working on the whole framework first and then fill in details later. Rosalinde Scott-Hodgetts (1986) uses this distinction to account for the apparent discontinuity of girls' performance at primary–secondary transfer, but concludes that:

> It is the belief of the writer that children who are predisposed to a serialistic approach are less likely to develop into versatile learners within the mathematics classroom, than those who are inclined to adopt holistic strategies; this situation is held to be directly attributable to teacher behaviour.
>
> (Scott-Hodgetts, 1986, p. 70)

Yet another insight into the effect of pupils' preferred learning styles is offered by David Galloway and his colleagues (1996), who emphasise that motivational style may be more a product of situation than a feature of the individual. In their study, they identified one adaptive and two maladaptive styles of motivation. 'Mastery orientation' was considered adaptive because pupils who were faced with the possibility of failure were able to demonstrate perseverance and overcame difficulties. In other words, these pupils were not deterred if they did not always succeed; difficulties were seen as challenges to overcome rather than as insurmountable obstacles. 'Learned-helpless' pupils, however, believed in their lack of ability and believed that failure was inevitable. 'Self-worth orientation' was also considered maladaptive – the pupils here did not necessarily believe in their lack of ability; rather, they were 'not prepared to run the gauntlet of self-exposure in the event of failure' (Galloway *et al.*, 1996, p. 199). The anxiety in their case was a fear of appearing foolish, rather than a fear of failure itself.

Interestingly, these researchers found more evidence of maladaptive motivational styles amongst pupils working on the English comprehension tasks used in the study, with some students debilitated by failure in English but able to rise above it in mathematics. The researchers attributed the differences to receiving less ambiguous feedback in mathematics than in English. In other words, in mathematics pupils were more able to identify clearly what they had to do to improve their future performance, and so they were able to move beyond personal feelings of inadequacy to find practical strategies for success.

In the light of this, it seems vital to: 'foster a view of ability in mathematics as changeable rather than fixed' (Askew and Wiliam, 1995, p. 28). It also appears important to create a classroom climate in which mistakes can be made without shame and where there is clear feedback that students can use to improve their performance.

Before leaving the complex issue of feelings, it is worth listing Laurie Buxton's strategies for overcoming maths anxiety:

- provide students with a high level of success and a level of failure which they can tolerate;
- when approaching a problem, students should be allowed to receive and stabilise the information before being asked to tackle the problem;
- the process of solution to be started with full attention but slowly;
- students encouraged to check their own solutions.

(Buxton, 1981, p. 14)

In the face of all the differences I have covered in this section, I feel that this is a useful general list that acknowledges learners' genuine feelings of inadequacy and fear but does not render them dependent on the teacher to do the thinking for them. In this way, there can be a good mixture of the challenge and support necessary for learning.

THE COGNITIVE DIMENSION

Much of the research and writing on pupils' understanding of mathematics has relied on a conventional framework that links facts, skills and conceptual structures; but there is rather less research on pupils' development of problem-solving strategies

(Askew and Wiliam, 1995, p. 23). This area may well expand in response to the curriculum development work that has been done over the past ten years or so in Britain, and as interest in situated cognition grows. For now, I will concentrate on research and writing about pupils' understandings of conventional aspects of the curriculum.

There can be very few people in the UK mathematics education community who have not been influenced in some way by the work of Richard Skemp. His arguments for the development of *relational* rather than *instrumental* understanding (Skemp, 1976) still have the power to rouse strong emotions and fierce debate. Relational understanding refers to the rich body of interconnected conceptual understandings that a sophisticated thinker can draw upon flexibly, whereas instrumental understanding refers to a set of rules, algorithms and definitions that can be recalled and used accurately in specific situations. He compares these two forms of understanding by using the analogy of a person lost in a strange town. If the person had a map, then there was a good chance of his finding his destination. If the person could only remember a sequence of instructions (turn right at the cross-roads, straight on at the next junction, etc.), then a single mistake in the sequence would leave him stranded.

Task 3.7 Making connections

While you are observing mathematics lessons, look out for pupils who are:

- making connections between different mathematical ideas;
- only able to follow a pre-determined procedure and are thrown when something slightly unfamiliar occurs;
- being taught to make connections;
- being taught a mechanical procedure without reference to meanings or reasons.

South African mathematics educator Michael de Villiers argues that we need to go further and add another desirable category, that of *functional* understanding. This involves: 'understanding the role, function or value of specific mathematical content or of a particular process' (de Villiers, 1994, p. 11). An example of these understandings working in harmony would be when a pupil has a flexible method for solving an equation like

$$\frac{5}{x} = \frac{3}{4}$$

but could also think of a context or situation in which that equation might need solving.

Skemp's distinctions have been identified empirically by his colleagues Eddie Gray and David Tall (1994) who write about a 'proceptual divide', distinguishing pupils who can use the condensed symbolic forms found in mathematics and adapt them flexibly from pupils who constantly return to memorised procedures and

Task 3.8 Functional understanding

Can you think of a variety of ways of solving the equation on the previous page and a context in which it might arise?

Find some other examples in the topics you are going to teach, and try to justify their role, function and purpose.

rules. The latter ended up doing more laborious and memory-intensive mathematical procedures, whilst the former could select and retrieve certain facts and procedures from memory, use them to derive new facts and then add these new facts to their memory store. Common arithmetical examples of non-proceptual thinking would be:

- an over-reliance on counting, for example by counting from 1 and using fingers when doing 1198 + 56;
- continued reliance on repeated addition rather than multiplication even when using a calculator.

The difficulty here is moving children on and helping them to develop more sophisticated strategies, since we know from other research (such as Hart, 1981; Kerslake, 1986; Johnson *et al.*, 1989) that pupils will keep using their sometimes restricted 'own' methods with which they feel comfortable. Other findings from these related studies are that:

- many pupils have restricted or incomplete views of mathematical entities like fractions, or restricted models of operations like multiplication;
- many pupil errors are quite logical and are derived from faulty premises.

Some of these studies produced sustained improvement in pupils' understanding by:

- using situations designed to show the limitations of restricted methods, for example by using $6 \div \frac{3}{4}$ to expose the limitations of the sharing model of division;
- building upon children's own methods and understandings;
- using a wide range of analogies, materials, contexts and language;
- looking out for pupils actively and systematically trying to make sense of their mathematics, and using their errors and misconceptions as starting points for future teaching;
- encouraging pupils to think about and evaluate their methods, that is to regulate their own thinking.

Task 3.9 Thinking about errors

Collect some apparent errors when observing pupils in school.

Try to find out how these pupils have been thinking by talking to them.

Observe the language used by teachers when referring to, say, multiplication or scale transformation. Is a wide range of alternatives used?

Make notes in your journal about the variety of representations and contexts used to embody one mathematical notion (such as fractions).

Discuss this with teachers and other students. Compare with your reading.

It is very useful for the beginning teacher to have some idea of common areas of pupils' difficulties, and there are very good collections (e.g. Dickson *et al.*, 1984) that offer enlightenment. Many of the research reports included in such collections give figures for the percentage of pupils getting test items right or wrong, or they show how the *facility level* of different items (the percentage of those asked who answer correctly) can be radically altered by the context or presentation of the task. For example:

> The item 'Add one tenth to 2.9' elicited the correct answer from 38% of 11/12-year-olds.
>
> (Brown, 1981, p. 61)
>
> 'What is the distance all the way round this rectangle?'

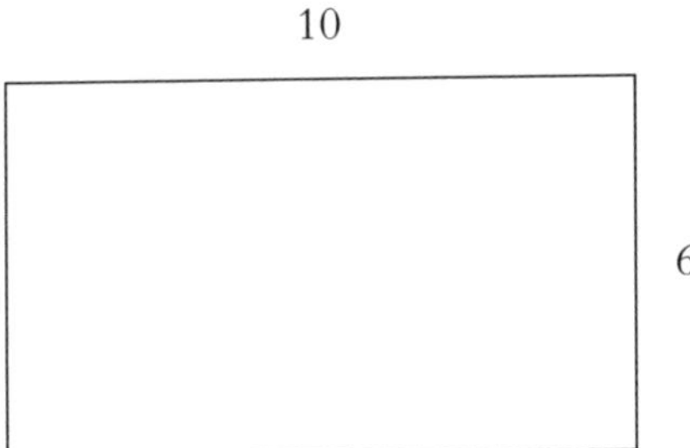

> The correct answer was given by 69% of 13-year-olds whereas 'What is the *perimeter* of the rectangle?' was answered correctly by only 49% of 13-year-olds.
>
> (cited in Dickson *et al.*, 1984, p. 343)

In some cases, we also have evidence from these big surveys of the ways children may be thinking. For instance, when pupils were asked to ring the decimal with the smallest value from the following list: '0.375 0.25 0.5 0.125' (APU, 1986), 34 per cent of 11-year-olds chose 0.375, 43 per cent chose 0.5 and only 17 per cent chose correctly (0.125). The first error was identified as LS, or 'largest is smallest', indicating some confusion about the value of digits in the decimal positions. The second error was identified as DI, or decimal point ignored, and was more common amongst the lowest 40 per cent of pupils (i.e. those pupils scoring overall below the 40th centile).

All this research is of interest, but perhaps the most enlightening work is that which does not just give us results, but also presents a method not unlike that used by the skilful teacher in her everyday formative assessment work. One such example is the clinical interview technique aimed at discovery described by Herbert Ginsburg, amongst others (see Wood, 1988, pp. 194–196): 'The clinical interview procedure begins with (a) a *task*, which is (b) *open ended*. The examiner then asks further questions in (c) a *contingent* manner, and requests a good deal of *reflection* on the part of the subject' (Ginsburg, 1981, p. 6).

Task 3.10 Clinical interviewing

Arrange to speak:

- individually with a pupil;
- with a pair of pupils.

Choose an open task from a familiar topic for them to work through. (There are some good examples of open tasks on page D7 of NCC (1989), reproduced here as Appendix 3.)

Try to probe their understanding without being over-directive. Cued requests like:

- 'Could you explain what this means?'
- 'Would you tell me why you did that?'

may be helpful, but you will need to be sensitive to what the pupils say. Mentally counting to five before 'butting in' can prove another useful strategy.

See if there are any interesting differences that strike you between individual and paired interviews.

It seems to me that not only is this a good research technique but it could inform a potential teaching sequence. The choice of task is crucial, but it should give opportunities for thought and exploration; then the contingent questions would be those that probe and acknowledge the ways in which pupils are thinking, perhaps suggesting further ideas that pupils could pursue. The final element, asking pupils to reflect upon what they have done, would be an opportunity for them to hold up a mirror to their own activity, to think about their own thinking and to evaluate their learning. With the teacher's support and guidance, this could represent a move towards intelligent rather than mechanical learning.

SUMMARY

Pupils often fail to make sense of the mathematics they are taught at school, or develop very insubstantial understandings. They may learn many tricks or routines that are of limited use to them in novel situations. This points to the need for a subtle balance of support and challenge in teaching, plentiful interaction between teachers and pupils and between pupils themselves, and explicit consideration of errors and ways of thinking. There are no blueprints. Teaching for learning is a contingent activity.

FURTHER READING

Boaler, J. (1997) *Experiencing School Mathematics: Teaching Styles, Sex and Setting*, Buckingham: Open University Press.

This is an important book that draws upon very close-grained research into the mathematics teaching and learning in two schools with different teaching approaches. The author uses the insights of situated cognition, which acknowledges that learning is very closely tied to the conditions in which it takes place, and which questions the transfer of school mathematics to out-of-school contexts. Boaler concludes that two different forms of mathematical knowledge were produced in the two schools she studied, and that the school that adopted a less structured, project-based approach produced better GCSE results and pupils who were more able to adapt successfully to unfamilar mathematical situations.

Dickson, L., Brown, M. and Gibson, O. (1984) *Children Learning Mathematics*, London: Cassell.

Research up to 1982 from the UK, US and other countries is summarised. This includes examples of child responses that give valuable insight into the complexities of the process of learning mathematics. Teachers are given some clues as to how children 'fail' to learn mathematics.

Orton, A. (1987) *Learning Mathematics: Issues, Theory and Classroom Practice*, London: Cassell Educational.

Tony Orton acknowledges that teachers making automatic decisions about mathematics teaching in the classroom are guided, albeit unconsciously, by their theories about learning mathematics. He looks at various schools of thought, some of them conflicting, and draws together some of the large amount of research that has informed a considerable body of knowledge about learning mathematics. Although intended as an introduction for higher degree students, much of the book is appropriate for beginning teachers, and each chapter raises an issue of direct relevance to the classroom.

Wood, D. (1988) (2nd edition) *How Children Think and Learn*, Oxford: Basil Blackwell.

This second edition contains new material about children's developmental psychology, but retains the first edition's clarity in synthesising what is known about about how children think and learn. It looks at theoretical debates and outlines the positions of major twentieth-century figures, but it also looks at the problems that teachers face trying to put theory into practice in the classroom. There is a specific chapter on mathematics.

4 Different Teaching Approaches

David Pimm and Sue Johnston-Wilder

INTRODUCTION

This chapter takes a direct look at the range of actions, decisions and intentions that constitute teaching. You will see described a range of different ways of being with pupils in mathematics classrooms, both while you are initially learning to teach and then as an on-going practitioner. Your own repertoire will continue to grow, develop and change as you continue to teach and think about teaching.

It is worth looking out for all sorts of teaching practices, whether formal or informal – sports 'coaching', musical instrument 'tuition', master classes, apprenticeships, individual tutoring – to decide what you wish to appropriate, experiment with, and transform from them into elements of you as a teacher of mathematics. In the words of actor Michael Caine (talking about acquiring from others) 'Steal, steal, steal – but steal from the best!' The people from whom you decide to lift ideas will considerably shape the sort of teacher you become.

What does it mean to teach? The first section of this chapter looks at the complex interrelation between teaching and telling, teaching and asking, teaching and listening. We have then structured the second part of the chapter around three possible levels of classroom organisation: whole-class, small-group and individual ways of working. We look further at some mathematical tasks that might be most appropriately tackled in one of these three settings. In the third part of the chapter, we look briefly at wider resources and strategies for enriching your teaching, including the use of homework. Finally, arising from all the ingredients, we consider a description of a lesson.

OBJECTIVES

By the end of this chapter, you should be able to:

- start to relate various forms of classroom organisation to particular pedagogic intentions and tasks;
- think more deeply about what constitutes mathematics teaching and the roles of exposition, investigation, questioning, listening and explanation within it;
- engage in the current debate around the exclusive merits of whole-class teaching.

TEACHING AS LISTENING, ASKING AND TELLING

> There is a sense in which, in our culture, teaching is talking.
>
> (Stubbs, 1983)

> Who needs the most practice talking in school? Who gets the most? Exactly. The children need it, the teacher gets it.
>
> (Holt, 1970)

There is a fundamental truth to the first observation, made by educational linguist Michael Stubbs: a teacher can teach certain things, at certain times and in certain circumstances, simply by telling. But this is *far* from the whole story. A teacher can teach by asking a question, one that perhaps focuses a pupil's, a group's or a whole class's attention on something or encourages a consideration of alternatives. A teacher can also teach by listening and then engaging directly with what has been heard. A teacher can teach by *not* talking, for instance by withholding what may seem to be an obvious form of help (namely telling a pupil how to do something), by allowing pupils to struggle and think for themselves or by working visually in silence. A teacher can work with pupils' powers of mental imagery, or on conjecturing and convincing – the giving of reasons – for it is answering the question 'why?' as much as 'what?' that lies at the heart of mathematics. A teacher can also significantly facilitate mathematical learning by a range of non-verbal actions such as providing suitable resources, structuring appropriate groupings and offering significant and well-thought out mathematical tasks.

Notice, crucially, that Stubbs does not say that teaching is *telling*, which is a common misinterpretation of current calls to return to whole-class teaching. There are a number of different forms of and purposes for teacher talk, two of which, *exposition* and *explanation*, are distinguished later in this chapter; these forms, at a naïve level, might both be considered *telling*. Before turning to them, here are some comments about teaching and listening from a secondary mathematics teacher, Mark. He was being interviewed about how his teaching had changed over the years, and he commented:

> Listening is part of what I do and I didn't think that it needed to be, other than listening to see if they got it or not. I have to listen more critically now to know what they are saying, to know what they are becoming confused about or what might be an interesting thing to pick up and run with. Before, if I didn't understand what a kid was saying, I needed to help him or her understand what *I* was saying. Then I could hear the way I was thinking about it come back through him or her which was really not the way I thought about it, it was the way the book was doing it. Now I would rather hear about how the kid thinks about it.

Later on in the interview, he added:

> I see my job as something completely different now. Going in [as a novice teacher], I thought it was *telling* kids and doing it in an understanding or clear or creative or fun way – that was what my job was to be. My expectation of what I would consider a good classroom is completely different . . . I see my role as finding ways to put kids into situations where *they* are going to be able to really *talk* about the material and learn.
>
> (Gormas, 1998, pp. 93–4)

Teacher talk in mathematics classes has many important functions, including:

- the giving of instructions and orientation;
- efficient transmission of information;
- focusing a pupil's attention or making an observation of potential significance to the whole class;
- encouraging reflection on what has been done or what could still be done.

However, there are also significant disadvantages to the teacher's voice being the dominant one heard in the classroom every day, as indicated in the quotation from John Holt. Teachers already start out being good at producing and giving mathematical explanations and expositions (it is likely that this is part of the skill you bring to the classroom), and get even better at it as time goes on. How do *pupils* get to acquire such a fluency at speaking mathematically? A significant part of learning mathematics involves learning to speak and write *mathematically*: pupils need many opportunities in various sizes of groupings to hear themselves and their peers speak. (This theme is taken up in Chapter 7.)

One of the more common forms of classroom control is that exercised by the teacher over what is allowed to be said (when, by whom, in what way) and even the manner in which it is to be said. Yet in order to be able to do what Mark is advocating, you have to work on pupils feeling comfortable saying things aloud in class. Achieving this will probably entail you having to give up some of your control of the 'public speech channel' at certain times and in some circumstances, for

Task 4.1 Listening out for listening

Choose a lesson when you are not involved in the teaching and pay attention to the teacher. When do you notice her or him listening to pupils and to what effect? What is done with the pupil's talk? Are the pupils aware of being listened to and do they seem to expect it? Does the teacher encourage them to listen to each other, and if so how? What do pupils do with what they hear from other pupils? Make notes about your observations in your journal.

particular reasons, and with it some sense of control over what is happening, quite simply because you cannot control what pupils will say.

Mathematics educator Mary Boole, writing at the end of the last century, coined a term 'teacher-lust' to describe the desire to control classroom activity. In the following passage, Boole compares teacher-lust with sex-lust and alcohol-lust: heady stuff you might think, particularly bearing in mind the historical context in which she was writing.

> The teacher . . . has a desire to make those under him conform themselves to his ideals. Nations could not be built up, nor children preserved from ruin, if some such desire did not exist and exert itself in some degree. But it has its gamut of lusts, very similar to those run down by other faculties. First, the teacher wants to regulate the actions, conduct and thought of other people in a way that does no obvious harm but is quite in excess both of normal rights and practical necessity. Next, he wants to proselytise, convince, control, to arrest the spontaneous action of other minds, to an extent which ultimately defeats its own ends by making the pupils too feeble and automatic to carry on his teaching into the future with any vigour. Lastly, he acquires a sheer automatic lust for telling people to 'don't', for arresting spontaneous action in others in a way which destroys their power even to learn at the time what he is trying to teach them. What is wanted is that we should . . . not go on fogging ourselves with any such foolish notion as that sex-passion is a lust of the flesh and teacher-lust a thing in itself pure and good, which may be legitimately indulged in to the uttermost.
>
> Few teachers now are so conceited as not to know that they have a great deal to learn, and that their methods need revising and improving, but the majority are seeking for improved methods of doing more of what they are already doing a great deal too much of. The improvement which they most need is to . . . see their conduct, their aims, their whole attitude towards their pupils . . . in the light reflected on them from those of the drunkard and the debauchee.
>
> (cited in Tahta, 1980, p. 11)

Alternative approaches to your teaching may involve you working on the utterances of your pupils, working with the *form* of what they have said: shaping, correcting, reformulating or offering alternatives, probing for more detail or a clearer way of saying something, checking that others have understood what has been said.

Questioning questioning

All questions are not the same, either in their form or in their purpose, and questions can be one of the most subtle instruments available to a teacher. A question can be asked simply by raising your inflection at the end of a sentence (something that cannot be done in print), or by tagging on a phrase like 'isn't it?' or 'do you?' at the end of a statement (which are then, for obvious reasons, called *tag* questions): 'you think it is going to be four, do you?' Then there are the more direct question forms beginning with what are called interrogatives, words such as *who, what, when, which, where, how* and *why*:

- Who hasn't finished their work?
- What is in common between this example and this one?
- When might you choose to multiply rather than add?
- Which algorithm would be better here?
- Where on the figure is the *vertex* of the triangle?
- How could you explain to someone who isn't here how to do that without pointing or touching?
- Why do you think it is cosine?

There are many other ways as well: the English language provides a terrific set of resources for asking questions.

Task 4.2 Listening out for questions

Over the next couple of days, set yourself the task of listening out for the variety of ways in which people ask questions in different circumstances. Try to think about the different purposes for which they are asking. Do this both within lessons and outside, around the school and in your day-to-day life. What forms do people use and how can you tell what they want? Are there any occasions when the responder failed to give the hoped-for response and, if so, what happened next? Record what you find in your journal.

Questions in classrooms are not used just to find things out that the asker does not know (this is perhaps the most common use outside school, and for that reason such questions are sometimes called *genuine* questions); in fact, they are perhaps *least* used to that end. In addition, the words alone are seldom sufficient to find out what the asker intended and what the hearer made of them.

One very common classroom purpose is the *testing* question, in which the intent is not to discover something the asker does not know, but to find out whether the person being asked knows. This need not be carried out in a formal atmosphere of right or wrong, putting pupils on the spot in public. It can also be carried out jointly with a class, more as a form of rehearsal of expected common knowledge present in the class.

Questions can also be used to draw attention to something, to *focus* pupil attention or call their awareness to it. A question can shift the level of a conversation or interaction: 'What might you do next?' (reminding pupils that there is a next, when they are perhaps caught up with this one) or 'What am I about to ask you?' (calling attention to the fact that there are regularities in the questions that you, as teacher, ask, and inviting pupils to notice this, so that they perhaps might take on some of this role of you-as-questioner for themselves).

However, it is also possible to get locked into a series of questions with a pupil, and, when they look blank or cannot answer, for you to feel you have to offer them a simpler question and a simpler one still. John Holt (1964), writing in *How Children Fail*, tells how he questioned a pupil and got 'I don't know' right up to the simplest one to answer. 'I've been had', he thought.

This is, of necessity, the briefest of introductions to questioning. More can be found in an article called 'Telling questions' by Janet Ainley (1987) and also in a monograph on teaching mathematics by Eric Love and John Mason (1992).

Exposition and explanation: two forms of telling

We would like you to consider the difference between *exposition* and *explanation* (for more on this, see Love and Mason, 1992). Explaining often inadvertently turns into exposition, and it can be valuable to be able to decide instead which is the more effective strategy for telling in the circumstances, and to be aware that different effects frequently arise from these two modes of telling.

Exposition involves speaking directly to the pupils from your own mathematical understanding. It is likely that, when you are expounding, you are guided by a desire for completeness and coherence of your account of an area or topic. In some sense, you are talking *to* your class. It may not be important for the pupils to grasp all the detail at first hearing, but they can gain a number of things from listening attentively to your exposition. The rest of their bodies will probably be still and passive (can you imagine a situation in which they would not be still?), so it is important to keep your attention on the pupils' degree of attentiveness and not to get caught up in the joy of your own mathematical fluency.

One possible gain from exposition is that pupils will hear some technical terms used in context and in meaningful mathematical sentences, not as vocabulary items encountered in isolation. Another arises from the educational effect of hearing coherent mathematical expression that they are, as yet, unable to produce for themselves. Exposition could be used to provide an overview of a project, an idea or a procedure. You will probably be able to think of other uses. The point here is that exposition is a valuable tool, but one to be used with care: too much exposition can have a rapidly deadening effect on the attention of your class, and you can end up talking to yourself.

Explanation, whether to the whole class or small groups and individuals within it, involves taking the pupils' current positions as your starting point and making a substantial attempt to shape what you say to their developing understanding, with

Task 4.3 Distinguishing exposition from explanation?

Read the following excerpt from a dinner conversation between Lynn (aged 10), her father Larry, and Laurel (aged 16). Identify where explanation perhaps starts to become exposition. The recipient could have felt left out, and may have lost confidence. Think about why, in this case, this does not seem to happen.

Lynn:	We're doing algebra in math. Give me an algebra problem. But don't use those boring letters like *x* and *y*.
Larry:	OK. Five alpha plus two is seventeen. What is alpha?
Laurel:	What's alpha?
Larry:	The first Greek letter. It's definitely not boring.
Lynn (after a pause):	Three.
Larry:	Wow! How did you figure it out?
Lynn:	Well, I tried alpha as one, then two, then as three, and it finally worked.
Laurel:	There's an easier way. You have the equation five alpha plus two equals seventeen. So you subtract two from each side and get five alpha equals fifteen. Then you divide both sides by five to get alpha equals three.
Lynn:	I don't understand a word you said. (Pause) But I have an idea. What if you subtract two from seventeen to get fifteen and then divide by five. That's just undoing what you did to alpha to get seventeen.
Laurel:	That's just what I said.
Lynn:	No, it's not. You were talking about equations and doing something to both sides. I didn't understand that.

(Pimm, 1995, p. 198)

their responses providing you with feedback. To explain is to talk *with* members of your class, where their understanding and current position are the strongest influences on what you say.

Thus, in explanation, the teacher's words and actions must be subordinated to the pupil's understanding of the situation, and the teacher must make continual effort to obtain whatever information is possible about that understanding. In exposition, the pupil's understanding is temporarily subordinated to the teacher's understanding, giving rise to the account that he or she is producing. The distinction is between finding a way to enter the learner's world and working with them in it and speaking from your (the teacher's) mathematical world to the pupil about it. When working post-16 (see Chapter 11), these two modes are commonly identified with the different forms of action and interaction seen in a typical lecture and tutorial respectively.

One moral is that teaching is not the same as expounding; be sure to work on explanations with your pupils and develop strategies for eliciting a pupil's existing understanding.

FORMS OF CLASSROOM ORGANISATION

> Those to be awarded Qualified Teacher Status must, when assessed, demonstrate that they . . . ensure effective teaching of whole classes, and of groups and individuals within the whole class setting, so that teaching objectives are met, and best use is made of available teaching time.
>
> (DfEE circular 4/98, 1998, p. 13)

A substantial part of teaching involves:

- deciding on the mathematical tasks to offer your pupils (whether made up yourself, absorbed from another teacher, taken from a textbook or other resource – in other words, tasks 'stolen' from the best – tasks involving the pupils' own bodies, physical action, practical materials, work outside school, mental imagery, closing their eyes, communicating without perhaps saying a word or without pointing or touching, making things, . . .);
- choosing how you are going to work with your pupils on these selected tasks, including whether individually, in pairs, in groups, in two or three large groups, or as a whole class;
- choosing what materials or resources to use, with what focus, and with what hoped-for activity on the part of the pupils.

Importantly, these three key components of mathematics teaching are not independent of one another. Certain tasks seem to call out for specific forms of working on them, and conversely certain ways of working in a classroom can enable or hinder particular educational actions. So when you are planning lessons (see

Chapter 5), these components need to be decided on in concert with one another. When looking at a lesson, you will see some ways in which these elements interact in positive or negative ways.

Developing as a mathematics teacher involves developing a repertoire of mathematical ways of being with children in the classroom, and refining your reasons for choosing one way over another in response to a particular topic and a particular group and the strengths and weaknesses of any particular way of working. Paragraph 243 of the Cockcroft Report, although necessarily incomplete and prepared as long ago as 1982, has not been bettered as a short check list for the developing repertoire of a successful mathematics teacher:

> Maths teaching at all levels should include opportunities for:
>
> - exposition by the teacher;
> - discussion between teacher and pupils and between pupils themselves;
> - appropriate practical work;
> - consolidation and practice of fundamental skills and routines;
> - problem solving, including the application of mathematics to everyday situations;
> - investigational work.
>
> (DES, 1982, para. 243)

Notice that although the paragraph is phrased in terms of mathematics *teaching*, it can be read as an entitlement charter for diversity of *learning* opportunities for pupils related to mathematics. However, it is not envisaged that all these opportunities could be available in any one lesson! In the next part of the chapter, we have chosen to focus on what might happen within one lesson; we have chosen tasks that we feel suit a variety of ways of working and we have tried to explain something of how the interaction works.

Whole-class ways of working

There is a difference between the *task* you set a class and the *activity* in which the pupils engage. The activity is produced as a result of the pupils interpreting the task as given. Remember, pupils never have any direct access to your intentions. So if you find some of your tasks going awry, try to listen to what you say when offering the task with the ear of someone who does not know why they are being asked to do the task or what that task is. Pupils always construct their own interpretations and rationale for what they are asked to do, so you could do worse than to ask them from time to time about the sense they are making of and the purpose they are seeing in what you ask them to do. Here is one description of a whole-class lesson.

> I stand by the whiteboard and ask the pupils to be totally silent. I ask them to work inside their own heads. I ask them to watch what I am doing and try to decide what it is. I write

3 4 5

$4 \times 4 = 16$

$3 \times 5 = 15$

on the board. Then I pause and suggest they think about where I started, what numbers I chose, what I did, and what the result is. Then I write

10 11 12

$11 \times 11 = 121$

$10 \times 12 = 120$

> I remind them not to shout out. I suggest that if they think they know what is happening they should construct some similar examples in their heads, or think of a word description of the situation, or think about an algebraic description. Meanwhile I tell them I am going to do another one and they must continue to watch.
>
> (Watson, 1994, p. 52)

The teacher has described the *task*. As Anne Watson writes, she has no control over what goes on inside each pupil's head, which is the resulting *activity*.

A second example of a whole-class task comes from Pimm (1987), who transcribed a videotape of a lesson in which a teacher set up a task to encourage pupils to develop greater precision in speech about mathematical perceptions.

> The pupils (P) are looking at a coloured poster of a great stellated dodecahedron (see Figure 4.1), and are not allowed to point or use their hands. One child is invited to sit in the 'hot seat' (a single chair out front near the poster where the pupil sits to address the class as a whole) and describe something they have seen in this complex picture (T is teacher).
>
> T: Does everyone see it as a three-dimensional object?
> P: Yes. (chorus)
> T: (Invites Jamie to go to the front)
> J: (Taking the hot seat) Well, in the middle, right in the middle, there's a kind of a triangle that kind of points out towards you, and all the fa[ces], the sides of it – there's other triangles that have been kind of broken up from it – say if they was joined to it, and when – by the dark green and the yellow and the light green, the kind of medium green kind of long triangles – and if the ones outside it was moved inwards, they would join the inside one.
>
> (Pimm, 1987, p. 35)

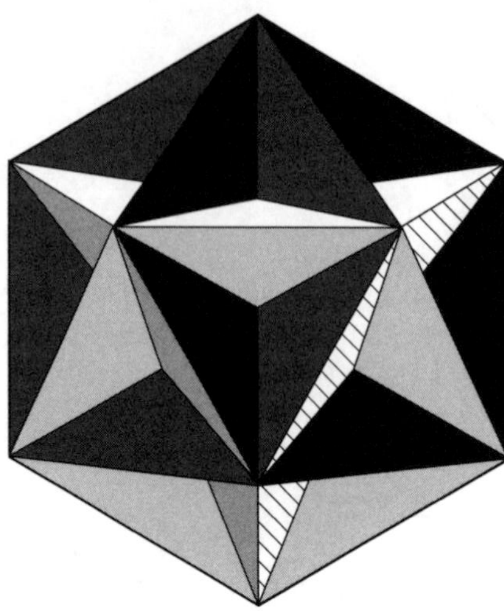

Figure 4.1 Great stellated dodecahedron
Source: Pimm, 1987, p. 35

The pupils were listening and responding to each other. The structure of such a task encourages focused, active listening in order to see whether the person in the hot seat has successfully communicated to the others. The constraints of no pointing and no touching are there to focus the pupil on the use of language to point and the need for language to be more self-contained in mathematics. A further account of this lesson is given by Barbara Jaworski in the journal *Mathematics Teaching* (Jaworski, 1985).

Both the previous two passages describe relatively unusual use of whole-class time. More common whole-class ways of working involve the teacher telling the class something or a pupil responding. The most familiar sight in a whole-class situation is that of a pupil responding to a teacher's question, and the response then being evaluated in some fashion by the teacher. In whatever way you express this response, and possibly despite your best intentions, it is likely to be heard as evaluative; even if you say nothing, the absence of a comment can be interpreted as a negative evaluation. This more usual pattern of teacher-pupil interaction has been named the Initiation-Response-Feedback sequence (see Pimm, 1987 for more details).

Another role for whole-class teaching is that of staging, managing and making use of 'reporting back' after a period of group or individual work. Those who might benefit from the reporting back include:

- *the pupil(s) doing the reporting*:
  they have the opportunity to develop a range of communication and mathematical skills, including reflection on and distillation of events they were involved in for an audience which was not present;

- *the other pupils in the class*:
  they hear about others' difficulties and alternative approaches; they may engage in trying to understand a less-polished presentation of mathematical work than they are usually exposed to;
- *the teacher*:
  he or she has opportunities to make contextually based comments about methods, results and processes, to value publicly the work done by pupils and to broaden the pupils' experience by proxy (other groups working on the same or a similar task).

The teacher's role in reporting back might be one of repeating, rebroadcasting (perhaps with minor editing, for instance by omission) and reinterpreting (anything from reformulating the expression to be more conventionally accurate, providing a different emphasis on what was said, or going further to add points of your own, for example, 'While I was watching them working on this, what I noticed was . . .').

You might work with the class on comparison and evaluation of methods. The class may need to discuss difficulties found in ways of working and strategies used for overcoming them. You may need to set an agenda for future work. You as the teacher will mark certain events or ideas as worthy of the attention of the group. Having allowed the pupils their own voice, you might use an expression such as 'And what struck me about what we've just heard is . . .'.

Task 4.4 Reporting back to the whole class

Try to locate a teacher (not necessarily in maths) who uses report-back sessions and watch one of these sessions with the following questions in mind. If you are able, run a report-back session yourself on an investigative or practical task, ideally with an observer who has the following list of questions (if no observer is available, try a tape recorder). Make notes in your journal.

- Who might benefit from the reporting-back?
- How can you resolve the tension between wanting the pupils to say themselves what they have done and wanting to use what they say to illustrate general points and processes?
- How can you help the pupils develop the skills of selection of and reflection on what to report?
- To whom is the reporter talking?
- What justifications can a teacher make for having the pupils' report back?

The importance of both preserving your pupils' voices *and* allowing yourself your own voice to talk about what has been said is considerable. There is a danger in saying 'What Sally said is . . .', because that might be reinterpretation concealed as repeating. If you assume the pupil is trying to say what you think they are but merely cannot say it right, and you help them by saying it for them, you may also miss out on something novel that the pupil is saying.

Task 4.5 Whole-class variety

Having worked on this section of the chapter, draw up in your journal a list of ways in which you might see a class working as a whole. Arrange to watch a selection of lessons with whole-class elements, both in other subjects and in your own department. What uses do you observe the teacher making of opportunities to work with the class as a whole? What do you observe the pupils doing?

Small-group ways of working

'How can I be teaching if I am sitting on the radiator?'

'I kept wanting to go round and interrupt them.'

A mixed-ability class of 10–11-year-olds are working with their teacher on a mathematical investigation involving movements with a square grid. He starts the lesson with the whole class by having a three-by-three array of mats on the floor and inviting eight pupils to stand on them, leaving one corner mat free. One pupil is asked to wear a red hat and to see whether, by using only sideways and forward-and-back shuffle moves, she can end up in the target square. Having seen that it is possible, the pupils are encouraged to pose questions about this situation. One pupil asks, 'What is the minimum number of moves?' and another, 'what happens with grids of different sizes?'.

The pupils then set off to work in groups, employing a variety of apparatus, and develop a range of forms of recording their explorations, some focusing on the state after each move and others recording the pattern in the moves themselves. Some continue to work on this between lessons and the groups continue in the first part of the second lesson. Later in the second lesson there is a whole-class report-back session.

The same distinction between exposition and explanation holds here as in the whole-class discussion. The difference is that there is a greater opportunity to listen to pupil exposition and to gain some feedback to inform future practice. Group work offers the opportunity for pupils to formulate their own thinking in explaining their ideas to their peers, engaging in exposition and gaining feedback. The pupils listening have an opportunity to reflect upon what they hear and to respond critically but constructively by asking questions to seek clarification, or offering suggestions for improving their account. There is clearly a need for the teacher managing these exchanges to be sensitive to pupils' concerns about being open to criticism from their peers.

It is important to remember that there are times when a class does *not* need you as a teacher. In a group, quite often one or more of the pupils will take on some aspects of the teacher's function: for example, keeping the others focused on the task, sharing out the sub-tasks to be done, explaining or mediating between two other pupils who are arguing unproductively or seem caught in an impasse. If you are there, even if you are not actively talking with the group, you may have a perturbing effect on the group functioning as a self-contained group, so be aware of this possibility.

When the small group is working, it may stop functioning as a small group and temporarily become several individuals, each working independently of the others in their own preferred ways to explore different aspects of a problem, before pooling their data for further communal discussion. The fact that a group has separated out in this way does not necessarily indicate that there is a problem with the group's functioning *as a group*; it could well be simply part of the normal variation in choice about ways of working. Nonetheless, if a group predominantly operates simply as individuals sat at the same table, then you may need to go and work with this group on developing alternative strategies and perceiving strengths when working collaboratively on a task.

The two questions at the beginning of this sub-section reflect a concern about what to do when the pupils are engaged in groups on a task. As you go round the class, you may sometimes find that a useful prompt to get the pupils to engage with you can be to ask them to tell you what they are doing. However, this necessarily pulls them away from working where they are and into the very different role of recount, recall and summary, so you need to use this intervention with care.

Individual working

Whilst giving attention to the broadening of mathematical classroom activity to include purposeful discussion, peer working and practical activity, it is important to remember that a key element in gaining mathematical fluency involves practice: at times this will involve the learner working quietly alone with a piece of mathematics.

When you as a teacher work with an individual pupil, you have an opportunity to tune in more exactly to what that pupil has already understood and thought, and to the pupil's personal preferences. You can look for alternative ways of working, presenting and explaining. However, a simple piece of arithmetic says that you can offer each pupil only about one and a half minutes in a 45-minute lesson, were you simply to move from one to the next. Your attention is one of the most scarce resources in the classroom, and you need to allocate it efficiently. What would the others be doing for the time that you are working with an individual? This is one reason why pupils need to become habituated to asking each other for assistance first, before coming to you.

The issues around teacher purposes for questioning are particularly acute when working with an individual. You will need to be clear about what your aims are and how your questioning contributes to achieving them. For example, in a task where it is an advantage to have a lot of individual data, you might allocate particular cases to different pupils. You might choose indirectly to differentiate by ability here, by knowing which cases are harder and allocating them accordingly.

RESOURCES AND IDEAS FOR ENHANCING YOUR TEACHING

Textbooks and schemes

Textbooks are an important resource for teaching mathematics in many secondary schools, if only because they are so widespread. Very often, the only resource to which all pupils will have access during the lesson, other than the teacher, is a textbook. In many schools, the major determinant of the programme of work taught in mathematics lessons is a commercially produced 'scheme', often consisting of either a sequence of textbooks or a system of individualised workcards or booklets. For years, many mathematics teachers have come to rely heavily on published schemes to provide them with an overarching organisation to the day-to-day work in the classroom, and to provide a source of material and tasks.

Many textbooks contain some excellent ideas for classroom tasks. However, not all the ideas in a textbook are equally good, and the linear presentation of the idea in printed form is very often not the best way to present it to your pupils. It is also worth bearing in mind the importance of the particular knowledge of your pupils that you use in your teaching, knowledge that will not be reflected in a published scheme of work.

The best use of a textbook is selective, adapting the material to suit the needs of individual pupils and classes, and ensuring variety of presentation. There is a risk that the scheme will take over and that activities such as questioning, debating, exposition and whole-class discussion will disappear. It is your responsibility as the teacher to engage fully in the long-term planning of the curriculum and the detailed planning of how to present a topic or a task, as well as to use the full range of approaches available in a classroom.

Practical apparatus

The provision of practical equipment in secondary mathematics classrooms varies widely. At all ages, mathematical equipment can provide tools to think with. Task 4.6 invites you to consider the provision in your school. ICT tools are left to Chapter 8.

Table 4.1 List of possible equipment for a maths classroom

Equipment	*Available*	*Used*	*For use with (topic)*
paper and pencil			
dotty square paper			
geoboards/pinboards			
3D kits (or straws)			
compasses			
protractors/angle measurers			
polyhedral dice			
pie chart scales			
rulers			
scissors			
string			
elastic bands			
playing cards (blank)			
coloured pencils			
isometric dotty paper			
graph paper			
drawing pins			
polar graph paper			
paper fasteners			
polygon stencils			
set squares			
bouncy ball			
weights			
stop clock			
weighing machine			
ATM mats (Pinel, 1986)			
toy cars			
curtain track or shelf			
abacus			
square paper			
card			
mirrors			
paint and potatoes			
glue			
bricks			
Multilink™ cubes			
probability kits			
match sticks			
Sellotape™			

Task 4.6 Maths equipment

Consider the list of equipment in Table 4.1. It includes some of the many items that have been used by secondary mathematics teachers to promote learning. Make a copy of the table, and note in the second column whether the equipment is available in your school, and in the third when you observe it being used.

Discuss with a friend or colleague how each of the items might be used, and for which topic. Make a brief note in the final column.

Homework and parents

The DfEE circular 4/98 speaks of the need for 'well-focused homework' and requires those seeking Qualified Teacher Status to demonstrate that they set: 'tasks for homework which challenge pupils and ensure high levels of pupil interest' (p. 12). A common observation by parents and mathematics teachers is that pupils working on a textbook exercise at the end of a lesson will often be told 'just finish this at home for homework'. However, textbook exercises are usually designed to become progressively harder, so pupils regularly get stuck at home. Since homework commonly involves working alone, often with little support, this does not help the learner's confidence if this is the only homework they are asked to do.

In addition to exercise and practice, pupils can be asked to:

- find out what words mean;
- carry out research for the next topic;
- write *about* the topic in hand;
- write questions for their peers to work on;
- generalise from a sequence of exercises;
- express what is in common between a set of questions or tasks (technique, principle, idea, . . .);
- explain *why* something works the way it does;
- produce some special cases for a general theorem.

The outside world, a world also inhabited by pupils, can also be a source of ideas, data and materials to be brought back into the classroom for discussion and further work. For instance, when working on symmetry with Year 7 pupils, car wheel hub caps could be sketched or a rubbing of a manhole cover could be taken.

Parents and other carers can be an important but unpredictable resource. Some (perhaps many) will find working mathematically at this level difficult and challenging, even threatening. An important role that parents can play is listening to their children explaining what they are doing. This is helpful because acting as a teacher or explainer can enhance the pupil's grasp of what she or he is doing, and may reveal to the pupil some gaps in their own understanding. It can help if the teacher tries to ensure that parents know how important this listening role can be.

Parents and grandparents can assist a project in different ways by providing ideas, materials, past experience, diverse languages and cultures. For example, someone may be able to tell you about different arithmetic algorithms and practices from the past or from different places around the world. One teacher reported:

> We had a parents' meeting when the Year 7 pupils were doing some investigative work within the theme of topology, because many parents did not know what it was. After I had spoken about the main ideas, some parents started contributing. One was an electrical engineer who commented that the idea of looking at connections while ignoring the distances between the nodes was fundamental to electrical wiring. A printer spoke about his need to minimise the number of colours necessary and linked this with the pupils' work on the four-colour map theorem.

Your room

It may seem slightly odd to think of your room as a resource, but it is too easy to think of the room as something given, rather than something over which you can exercise some influence and control and which can assist you in your task of teaching mathematics. Every room has a 'grammar', a structure that goes towards shaping what can take place in it and what cannot. Go into various classrooms in your school. Ask yourself which ones 'feel' welcoming, thoughtful, exciting, open. Identify some of the physical features of the room that contribute to this feeling and atmosphere. It may be the placing of furniture, windows, grouping of desks, or the wall displays or sometimes things hanging from the ceiling. You can experiment with varying your teaching space (if your tutor agrees) to suit the approach and the task and watch for effects on pupils.

The history of mathematics

Much of mathematics can be taught as if it were timeless and detached from any particular culture. One way of remedying this false situation is to make use of the history of mathematics in your teaching. In this way, you can begin to make the study of mathematics as much the study of a story of human endeavour as an abstract exercise. As an example, in Task 4.7 you will study an ancient Babylonian method for finding an approximation to $\sqrt{2}$.

You will find Katz (1992) to be a useful source for extending your knowledge of the history of mathematics. In addition, Eagle (1995) provides some suggestions for worksheets and resource sheets to be used with pupils, with background notes.

Task 4.7 Babylonian mathematics

The 500 or so mathematical Babylonian tablets so far excavated date from between 3200BC and 300BC. The Babylonians approximated √2 as 1:24,51,10 written in their base 60 numeration system; they found other roots accurately to several sexagesimal places. (The transcribed notation reads as follows: 1 whole and 24/60 and 51/3600 and 10/216,000.)

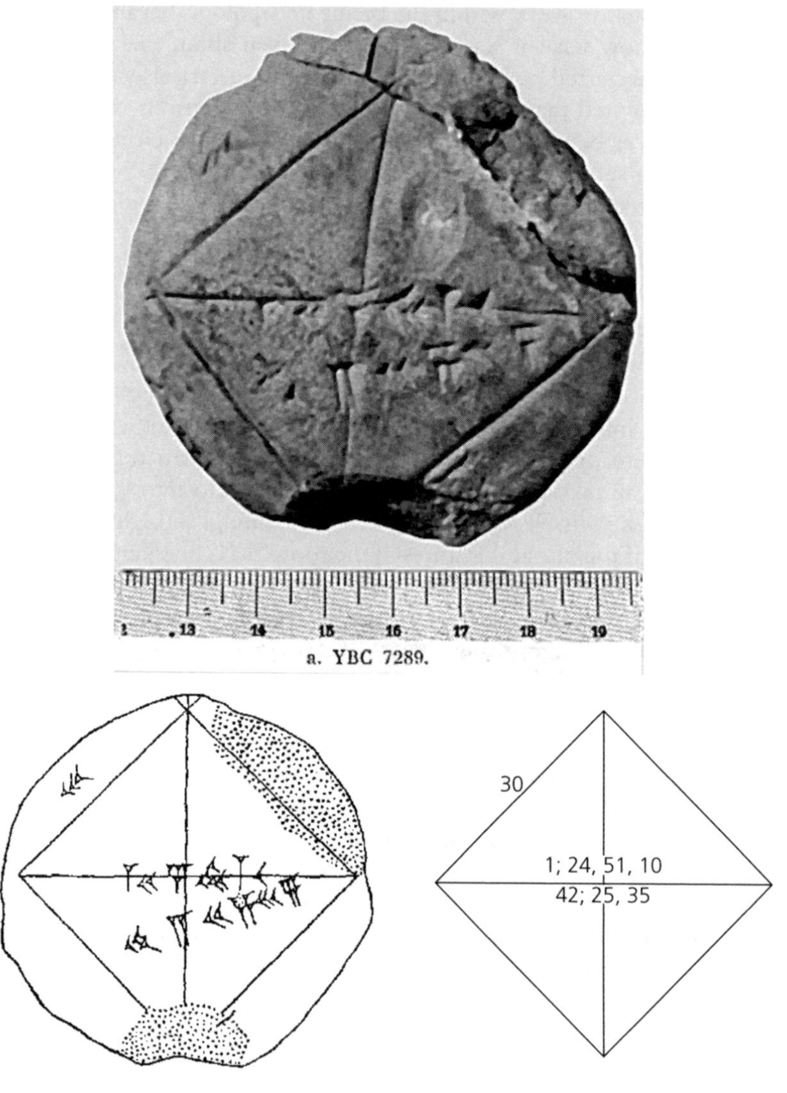

Figure 4.2 A Babylonian tablet and its transcription
Source: Yale Babylonian Collection and Fauvel and Gray, 1987, p. 32

continued . . .

First of all, work out the base ten equivalent of 1:24,51,10 and compare it with a calculator value for √2. In which decimal place does the first deviation between the values occur?

The following may inform your understanding of the Babylonian method for finding √2:

√2 is the length of the side of a square with area 2.

Start with a rectangle that you know has area 2, for example, 2 by 1.

Taking a corner of the rectangle as centre, and the smaller side as radius, draw a quadrant of a circle, and mark off the resulting square.

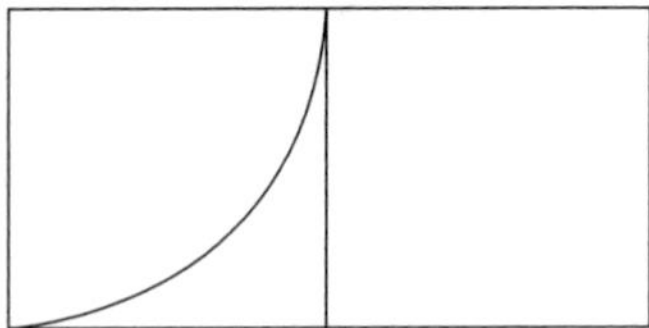

Cut the remaining rectangle (in this example at this stage it is also a square) in half and slide one half under the square, as shown below.

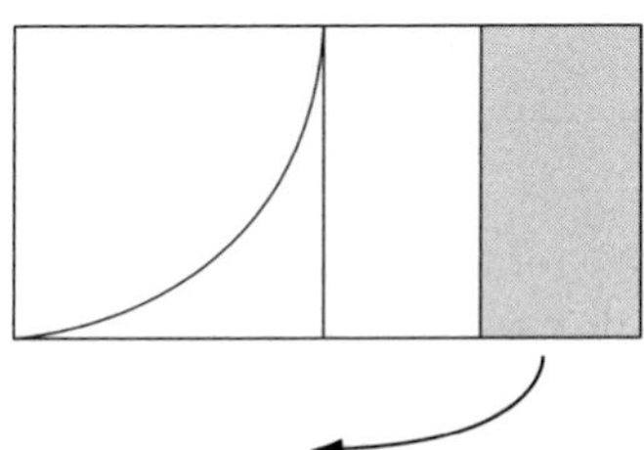

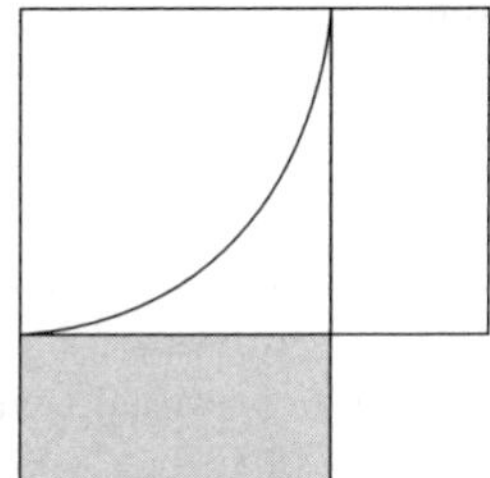

The new shape is a square of side 1.5 with a missing corner.

Use the top of this 'square' as the top of a new rectangle of area 2. The length of the second side of the new rectangle is found by dividing the area 2 by the side 1.5, getting the answer 4/3.

(Note: the Babylonians had methods for calculating divisions of this kind, see Neill, 1994b.)

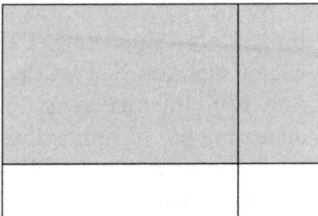

How many times do you have to repeat this process to get an excellent approximation to √2?

Role play

You may find that some teacher colleagues in other subjects in history or RE for example use role play to great effect, but it is an under-used resource in mathematics teaching.

Task 4.8 Play time

Find a colleague in another department with experience of using role play and either talk over the experience or arrange to observe a lesson in which role play is used.

Try the following example with a small group of well-motivated Year 7 students.

> Ask the pupils to work in pairs: one pupil to take the role of a weather forecaster in the winter and the other a member of the public who does not understand negative numbers well. The task is to create a dialogue that covers adding and subtracting of negative numbers.

After your experiment, think hard about how the use of role play could help to make you a more effective teacher. Remember that some pupils can connect particularly well to mathematical ideas when they can see them embedded in a human setting or when they approach them through the pupils' own strengths.

A second suggestion for a starting point for a role play is Leibniz' argument that the probability of throwing 12 with two dice is the same as that of throwing 11, and half that of 10. He reasoned that there is one way of scoring 12 (6 and 6) and one way of scoring 11 (5 and 6), and there are two ways of scoring 10 (6 and 4 or 5 and 5). Further ideas for role play emerge from an exploration of the history of mathematics.

Simulation

Some real-world situations are very complex, and it is sometimes difficult or time consuming to collect data about them. Simulating a real-world situation means setting up a simpler, easier or safer situation that will produce a similar pattern of data more easily or more quickly. With the increasing power of technology to help, many industries are making increasing use of simulations to solve hitherto intractable problems. For pupils, simulation of a real-world situation can help to bring insight or understanding of how mathematics can be used to model the world. The following examples of classroom simulations illustrate this.

> Prepare a large, transparent plastic jar full of beans, a known number of which have been painted yellow. Each pupil takes a turn to draw a sample of beans from the jar using a small plastic cup. In each case, the number of yellow beans in the sample is recorded as is the number of beans altogether. The idea is to obtain from the samples an estimate of the proportion of yellow beans in the whole jar and to use this, together with the known number of yellow beans in the jar, to estimate the total number of beans in the jar. This simulation illustrates how capture–recapture methods are used in biological investigation to estimate the populations of some forms of wildlife. A sample of the population is captured and marked (like the yellow beans) and then released into the wild. Later, a second sample is captured and the proportion of marked creatures in the population is estimated.

A second example of a classroom simulation is to simulate the flow of traffic at a road junction controlled by traffic lights:

> Collect data beforehand about the time interval between changes of a set of traffic lights and about the number of cars arriving per minute on the road at the junction. Arrange the desks and chairs in the classroom to resemble a road junction, so that the gaps between the chairs represent the road. The pupils can then pretend to be cars, arriving at times determined by a spinner. In this way, the effect of different timings can be explored.

You can find further examples of simulations to use in the classroom in the professional journals: see, for example, Selkirk (1983a and 1983b).

Video and TV

Video is an under-used resource in mathematics teaching. There are possibilities afforded both by published videos and by taping programmes from the television. Your school may already have some video resources. To start your collection of published videos, contact the London Mathematical Society (see Appendix 2) and ask for their current list of Popular Lectures. These are aimed at sixth-form pupils.

School libraries

The school librarian is another under-used resource for most maths departments. Librarians are often highly trained professionals who can be of great help to the maths department. There is often a budget for mathematics library resources that is not fully used.

Task 4.9 Maths library resources

Visit the school library. Carry out an inventory of the materials that could be used for teaching mathematics; include encyclopaedias, and material with data, such as Key Data, an annual publication from the Government Statistical Service (see Appendix 2 for a contact address). The librarian may be able to help you with this task, provided you make the effort to go at a convenient time.

- Make a note of books that pupils would enjoy.
- What dictionaries are there?
- Look up 'right angle' and 'algebra' in any available dictionary and reflect on what light is shed on the meaning.
- Ask the librarian about CDs available in the library. There may be a CD encyclopaedia at the very least. Check to see what maths there is in it.
- Plan a homework using the library resources.

Maths clubs

You might be lucky enough to be in a school that already has a maths club, but it is more likely that you are not. So now is the time to collect ideas. A maths club is relatively easy to start but harder to maintain. Some ideas that you might use to sustain a maths club are:

- enlist the help of the pupils;
- conduct surveys;
- collect resources;
- ask colleagues about their own experiences;
- talk to teachers who run other clubs;
- find out whether any parents have relevant expertise and will help.

One possible way to start is with a maths homework club or maths workshop where you provide practical resources and activities that pupils do not usually see in their maths lessons. You will find ideas for such activities in such catalogues as the Tarquin and the ATM catalogues (see Appendix 2 for addresses).

Books by Martin Gardner, Ian Stewart, Brian Bolt and other writers can be a rich source of stimulating mathematical ideas for a maths club, and copies are often to be found in second-hand book shops. Why not start your own collection of interesting and enriching books? There are also many useful references on the World Wide Web. One particularly good source of ideas for a maths club is the NRich web site, run from Cambridge University. An article about one teacher's experience of using this resource is in *Micromath* **14**(2) (Dadd, 1998). An article about the experiences of four teachers who are running maths clubs can be found in *Mathematics in School* **25**(5) (Cocker *et al.*, 1996).

Maths trails

The idea of a mathematics trail is to encourage pupils to see mathematics in the world around them. It is possible to adapt the notion of a maths trail to fit the circumstances and to conduct one within the classroom, within part of the school building, outside the school grounds, or as part of a more adventurous field trip. Look around the room you are in for a moment. You could either start from a particular topic, such as measurement or shape, or you could take a general approach, depending on your objectives. Suggestions for questions include:

- estimate the height of the blue shelf from the ground;
- sketch the window frames;
- how many rectangles are there?
- estimate how much paint it would take to paint the ceiling if 1 litre covers 2.5 square metres;
- find a cylinder.

When setting a trail for the town, which could then be used as a homework activity, you might ask questions like:

- how old are the black railings outside the Town Hall, in the cathedral?
- find the grave of the Lord Mayor by the east door. How old was he when he died? How long ago did he die?

For the more ambitious, the following idea might be thought provoking. In a forest in Norfolk is a dinosaur park, where a forest trail leads past life-size tableaux of dinosaurs 'grazing' or hunting. A maths trail here might include questions about scale; estimating heights, lengths and weights; and about time.

Task 4.10 Devise a maths trail

Read further about maths trails. For example, you might read Selinger and Baker (1991), Morris (1986) and Blair *et al.* (1983). Devise a maths trail of your own around the school or the school grounds. Try it with a couple of volunteer pupils, and ask for their comments and ideas.

Task 4.11 Reflecting on a lesson

Before you move on, consider the following account of a mathematics lesson. This is an unusual lesson in lots of respects. Mathematics teachers go about providing diversity for their pupils in many different ways. What works for one teacher may not work for another. As you read the account, make notes in your journal about:

- the environment in which the lesson takes place;
- the ways in which pupils are involved with and given responsibility for their own learning;
- the role of written dialogue with pupils.

A lesson observed

I got to the room before the class or the teacher. It was furnished simply with groups of tables and chairs informally arranged. A couple of grey filing cabinets stood at the back, their half-open drawers bulging with SMILE cards. The wall displayed pupils' work. One large poster declared 'the puzzle of the week', while another invited pupils to contribute their own matchstick puzzles. On one side of the board was pinned a statement on cheating yourself, while on the other was a pupil-composed policy on equal opportunities. Three-dimensional solids hung from the ceiling. Pupils began to arrive, first a trickle, then a rush. Some sat, others stood. A few busied themselves giving out folders. One boy cleaned the board and then wrote his name alongside number 1. Others followed, adding to the list. A girl entered, writing her name next to 15, leaving a large gap in the list. As a pupil approached to ask me whether the teacher was away and was I there to take them, in walked Jill. I had counted by this time 29 pupils: fourth years, 15 boys, 14 girls.

'Sorry I am late,' she said, 'thanks for getting yourselves organised,' and 'Oh, hello,' turning to me. Turning back to the class she continued. 'I've got your books here. They have all been marked. Now remember, your first job before you do anything else is to read my comments and write at least one or two sentences by way of reply to me on what I've said, OK?'

The books were given out. Pupils opened their exercise books and read the comments, some reading them out loud to their neighbours. By now they were all sitting in groups. After writing their replies, they all got down to work. I roamed the room to find out what they were doing. One group was designing a board game. Another group was working on graphs, taking the British Telecom charge leaflet and trying to turn it into something more easy to understand. Another group

continued . . .

seemed to be working on a textbook exercise, whilst yet another was doing some paper folding from a SMILE pack.

The rest of the class appeared to be working individually, mostly from SMILE cards. A few left their places to get cards or equipment from filing cabinet or cupboard. The room hummed with purpose. Jill joined a group and got into conversation. I followed suit.

'Why the list of names?' I asked, pointing to the board.

'Oh that's the help list,' a boy replied. 'You put your name down and she comes around in the order of the list. It stops queue jumping by shouting out.'

For the first time I noticed that there was no teacher's desk, just a group of cupboards in the corner of the room, stacked with papers.

'Why did Hannah put herself down at 15 when she could have got in at 7?' I asked.

'Ask her.'

So I went to Hannah. Hannah had her head down and was hard at work.

'What's that?' I asked.

'ShSh! I'm trying to finish it off,' she said. 'It's English.'

'Is it homework?' I asked.

'No, I started it off last lesson and I want to finish this bit off before I forget what I want to say.'

I left to disturb others before returning to Hannah. She now appeared to be on mathematics. I asked her about the list. She explained that she knew that she needed some help with her maths project but had wanted to finish off her English first. She also wanted to have another look at her maths work before Jill got to her. I asked her about her project and whether she liked maths.

'It's all right,' she told me, but she didn't think she was very good at it. The project had been hard initially but it had got easier after she had 'learnt up about sines, cos and tangents and things'. She got stuck a couple of times, but with the help of the teacher and one or two other pupils which she 'chatted up' she had got herself sorted out. She now needed some advice on how to write up her conclusions. I helped her as much as I could. I asked if I could look at her exercise book and I read an interesting dialogue between her and Jill throughout the book. Jill was now sitting alongside another pupil and was in no hurry to move on. I asked if I could help and she told me to help the next person on the list.

(John Hibbs, personal communication)

SUMMARY

This chapter has offered you many principles, ideas and starting points for beginning to teach. You read at the beginning of the chapter about the complex interrelation between teaching and telling. You will need to work out how this interrelationship will operate in practice in your own teaching. There are different possible levels of classroom organisation: individual, group and whole class; and you have begun to think about how you might take advantage of the differing strengths of these various ways of organising work in a classroom. Furthermore, you have begun to think about a range of resources and about the use of homework to develop and extend the tasks that give rise to pupil activity in the mathematics classroom. Finally, at the end of this chapter you have read and reflected on a description of a lesson in which pupils were given a lot of responsibility for their own mathematics learning.

Your task as a mathematics teacher will require you to use teaching methods which sustain the momentum of your pupils' work and keep your pupils engaged through (amongst other things):

- stimulating intellectual curiosity;
- communicating enthusiasm;
- matching the approaches you use to the mathematics being taught and to the pupils being taught;
- effective questioning;
- selecting and making good use of resources;
- and exploiting opportunities to contribute to the quality of pupils' wider educational development.

(DfEE, 1998, p. 13)

What you need now is to consider thoughtfully how to weave these ingredients into lessons. This you will work on in Chapter 5.

If teaching and learning are seen only in terms of lessons, you might be tempted to think about what 'the perfect lesson' might be, a lesson that is to be repeated endlessly through time in all its perfection. When looking at issues of balance, diversity and entitlement (which is how we started this chapter), you have to look beyond the constraints of the single lesson and think about the overall experience of the pupils.

Although you will inevitably focus on the lesson as the unit of teaching and planning, you will need to think of both the larger and the smaller scale. This means, on the one hand, long-term planning of sequences of lessons and schemes of work for larger-scale structure, and on the other hand, detailed short-term planning of smaller sections within a lesson when different things are happening.

FURTHER READING

ATM (1994) *Teaching, Learning and Mathematics*, Derby: Association of Teachers of Mathematics.

ATM (1998) *Teaching, Learning and Mathematics: Challenging Beliefs*, Derby: Association of Teachers of Mathematics.

These two collections of timeless articles taken from *Mathematics Teaching* and *Micromath*, as well as other contributions, have been put together as a PGCE reader.

Katz, V. J. (1992) *A History of Mathematics*, New York: HarperCollins.

A well-written, accessible and comprehensive history of mathematics book, originally written for American teachers. It includes accounts of mathematics and mathematicians from all over the world, and provides exercises for pupils to work on inside and outside the classroom.

LAMP (Low Attainers in Mathematics Project) (1994) 'Schemes', in Selinger, M. (ed.), *Teaching Mathematics*, London: Routledge, pp. 29–37.

In this article, the authors discuss the role of published schemes, home-grown schemes and resources. They draw on evidence from LAMP.

Open University (1989a) *Preparing to Teach*, Milton Keynes: The Open University.

This pack develops a framework for thinking about and researching a mathematical topic in preparation for teaching it. Three topics are used as examples: angle, ratio and probability. In each of the three topics, the pack explores ideas and activities; standard techniques; context; root questions; standard misconceptions; language patterns; and the imagery of the topic.

5 Planning for Mathematics Learning

Keith Jones

INTRODUCTION

Effective planning is fundamental to the successful teaching of mathematics. This means that learning to plan successful lessons is one of the most important skills you will acquire. It is also, it has to be said at the outset, a far from straightforward thing to do. For the most part, this is because learning to plan involves co-ordinating a range of skills with different areas of knowledge.

There is little doubt that planning is a complex and demanding task that involves teachers generally, and mathematics teachers in particular, in interpreting and transforming a significant range of knowledge (John, 1993, 1994; Simon, 1994). Given the demands that it places on experienced teachers, planning is undoubtedly one of the most difficult tasks you will encounter. The important thing to remember is that effective lesson planning is closely linked to the equally demanding but often more overt issue of effective classroom management. A good lesson plan, which actively involves the class, boosts your confidence and gives you a sound basis for managing the class successfully. A good plan can go a long way towards *preventing* classroom problems.

Reys *et al.* provide a useful summary of some of the well-established reasons for planning lessons. They suggest that planning:

- establishes definite goals for each lesson and helps you to ensure that essential content is included;
- helps you to schedule work in feasible units of time and in a sensible sequence;
- helps you to ensure that your lessons begin interestingly, maintain a good pace throughout and have a satisfying ending;
- helps you to hold the pupils' interest and attention;
- helps you to avoid unnecessary repetition;
- creates a feeling of confidence for you, the teacher.

(Reys *et al.*, 1995, pp. 39–40)

Perks and Prestage look rather more widely than the usual reasons for stressing the importance of planning. They also point out that, in addition to encouraging you to articulate what you think will happen in a given lesson, and enabling you to rehearse aspects of the lesson, planning:

- makes you more likely to be receptive to the ideas of others;
- can act as a basis for discussion and evaluation;
- can be a basis for negotiation with teachers and tutors;
- provides a history of your thinking.

(Perks and Prestage, 1994, pp. 66–67)

OBJECTIVES

By the end of this chapter, you should be able to:

- understand some relationships between the mathematics curriculum, a scheme of work, the choice of teaching strategies and your individual lesson plans;
- select appropriate teaching strategies and mathematical tasks;
- plan mathematics lessons and units of work identifying clear objectives and content;
- set appropriate and demanding expectations for pupil learning.

In enabling you to meet these objectives, this chapter examines a range of related issues including the mathematics curriculum, teaching strategies, differentiation, progression, motivation, relevance, the use of contexts and examples from everyday life, pupil grouping and equal opportunities. This chapter begins by considering what a lesson is and then moves on to examine how experienced teachers plan their lessons.

TEACHERS PLANNING LESSONS

What is a lesson?

The conventional unit of teaching is the lesson, or period, although in any given school this might last anywhere from thirty to seventy minutes. In contrast, there is no conventional unit of learning. Learning can take place at any time, day or night, and does not necessarily occur only in the presence of the teacher. There is a useful aphorism coined by John Mason that summarises this phenomenon: 'teaching takes place in time, learning takes place over time'.

Whilst there are aspects of planning that are both larger and smaller than the lesson, it remains important to think in terms of the lesson as a unit. Mathematics educator Alan Bishop refers to this arrangement as 'lessonising' the curriculum. He suggests that this *can* result in a fragmentation of topics and ideas if teaching is solely thought of in terms of individual lessons. For example, without careful planning, pupils may never appreciate the connections between fractions, decimals and percentages, particularly if these are all treated separately at different times. Another form of fragmentation can happen with investigative tasks when this leads to pupils needing substantially more than the allocated time to pursue their enquiries properly.

An alternative way of thinking of lesson structure is to see it as subordinate to the mathematical aims of your teaching. Investigative work, for instance, has its own structures and rhythms. Such work might start with a whole-class posing and discussing a problem, move into small-group exploration, and subsequently return to further whole-class work with groups reporting back on their findings. Other lesson structures might suit other teaching and learning intentions.

One way of thinking about how you will develop as a mathematics teacher involves you developing a repertoire of mathematical ways of being with children in the classroom (some possibilities for which were outlined in the previous chapter). This also entails you refining *your* reasons for choosing one way of working over another in response to a particular classroom topic or task and a particular group of pupils. This, in turn, means becoming aware of the strengths and limitations of any particular way of working.

How experienced teachers plan

Whenever you observe effective teachers of mathematics, you can see the results of their planning. This planning is based on their accumulated professional knowledge of mathematics and of effective teaching strategies. What you see in the classroom is a reflection of this accumulated knowledge and, more immediately, of their evaluation of previous lessons with this and other classes, their established routines and their personal teaching qualities.

Much of this planning you can observe. It is, for instance, contained within departmental documents, particularly the scheme of work (something considered later in this chapter). It occurs whenever such schemes of work are evaluated and reviewed. Yet some planning will inevitably occur away from the department (and so may be hidden from you) or it occurs during conversations between teachers within the department. This can mean that whilst the planning carried out by experienced teachers is detailed and complex, some of their lesson plans may appear to consist of only phrases or illustrations, which, while they are likely to be fully meaningful to the teacher concerned, may not conjure up a complete lesson for you (John, 1991, 1993; Wragg, 1995).

In constructing lessons, an experienced teacher draws on a range of experiences and knowledge in an attempt to fit the anticipated and observed needs of a particular lesson or set of lessons. Research evidence suggests that successful teachers often start with tasks or pupil activity: that is, they start with the context, the content and the tasks being set for their classes. The objectives of the lesson may be hidden in the planning process or occur at various points within it (although such objectives can, when necessary, be made more explicit). Wragg (1995), for example, reports a research study showing that experienced teachers may have a mental outline of what they intend to do rather than a complete written plan.

For experienced teachers, in many instances, such apparently sparse lesson outlines are entirely appropriate. But there will also be times when a more explicit lesson plan may be appropriate: for instance, when a new or seldom-taught topic is scheduled. Full lesson plans can also be a useful basis for dialogue with teacher colleagues such as yourself. Yet, in the normal course of events for experienced teachers, full lesson plans would necessarily need to be rather complex and could be costly, in terms of time, to produce. Furthermore, given the flexibility to respond to pupil input that is demanded by experienced teachers, such plans may well not accurately reflect what takes place during the actual lesson.

This preference for a more fluid mode of planning by experienced teachers can appear to pose a difficulty for you. It could be that the more skilful the planning or the more it happens at unscheduled times, the more difficult it is for you to understand how successful lesson planning is achieved. What is more, the requirement for you to produce detailed written plans may seem oddly at variance with the practice of established teachers: a case, perhaps, of doing what I say rather than what I do. *Nothing could be further from the truth. Planning is carried out by all successful teachers and remains of critical importance.* It is how you begin to plan, and how your planning changes as you develop professionally, that you should keep in mind. Likewise, you need to reflect on your lesson plans as you use them. Detailed written plans should be designed to give you the confidence to begin teaching well. As your confidence grows, and as you make progress with your classes, you might begin to negotiate the appropriate amount of detail to include in your plans.

Task 5.1 How teachers plan

1. Ask your tutor or a class teacher if they can take you through the process involved in planning a lesson. What are the important aspects of this process? What aspects of the plan get recorded? How are they recorded?
2. See if you can observe or take part in the lesson and then discuss with your tutor or the class teacher how the lesson went in practice. Try to identify how and why it may have deviated from the planned lesson.

You should find there are key elements in a lesson plan. These can include:

- practical details such as date, class, time, room;
- references to topic, module or scheme of work;

- aims, objectives or learning outcomes;
- teacher and pupil activity arising from chosen tasks;
- timings for elements of the lesson;
- homework.

However, which of the above elements occur and how they are arranged in an individual lesson plan can vary quite considerably.

Task 5.2 The variety of lessons

1 The mathematics lessons you observe are likely to differ in style and approach from each other. From your observations of different teachers and different mathematics lessons, record as many different formats as you can. How might the lesson plan (and the lesson planning) be different for different forms of lesson?

2 Devise a way of analysing all the mathematics lessons that you have observed using the categories of teaching given in the Cockcroft Report (DES, 1982), paragraph 243 (you may well find that some lessons contain examples of more than one category). How much variety in strategy is there? How does this variety vary over time and with different classes? Does your analysis suggest that some teachers have favoured strategies?

3 Talk to teachers who use a variety of teaching strategies about how they have come to use those particular strategies in the way they do. Is it the case that any piece of mathematics can be introduced to pupils in any way you choose, or can you detect influences that guide teachers in their choice of teaching strategy?

There can be a number of reasons why the mathematics lessons you observe may differ in style and approach. This may be partly due to individual teacher style, but there can be other underlying reasons.

Jones (1997) reports how research into the way in which mathematics is taught in different countries indicates that the typical Year 9 Japanese mathematics lesson:

- is with a mixed-ability class;
- begins with a complex problem;
- focuses on developing mathematical thinking;
- devotes most time to mathematical reasoning and understanding;
- makes explicit links between concepts.

It is also the case that Japanese pupils scored amongst the best in the world in mathematics in a recent large-scale international survey of mathematical achievement (England and Wales, Scotland and the USA all scored about the same, and considerably lower than Japanese pupils). This suggests that what may influence how successful UK pupils are in mathematics is both how mathematics is taught (that is, the teaching strategies used) *and* what form of mathematical knowledge is taught. It is likely that the teaching strategies used will depend on the form of mathematical knowledge taught, and so it is the curriculum that is addressed next.

Task 5.3 The structure of lessons

Below are examples of the structures of mathematics lessons from a study of typical lessons in the USA and in Japan on the topic of the area of triangles.

Typical US lesson

- review concept of perimeter (1 minute);
- explanation of area of rectangle plus practice examples (8 minutes);
- explanation of area of triangles plus practice examples (25 minutes);
- pupils work individually on an exercise (11 minutes).

Typical Japanese lesson

- presentation of a complex problem (3.5 minutes);
- students attempt to solve the problem on their own or in groups (14.5 minutes);
- student presentations and class discussion of student solutions to the problem leading to general formula (29 minutes);
- students work on practice problems (5 minutes).

(Stigler *et al.*, 1996, p. 153).

From your observations, are the lessons you see more like the typical US lesson or more like the typical Japanese lesson?

PLANNING WITH THE MATHS CURRICULUM

There are two aspects of the current structure of the Mathematics National Curriculum for England and Wales that are of central importance to your planning: the programme of study and the level descriptions for the Attainment Targets. One way to think about the relationship between the two is to consider the programme of study as indicating what you should plan to teach, whilst the level descriptions allow you to judge what your pupils have learned. What happens during your lessons provides the link between the two.

A further important use that you can make of the level descriptions is to provide some indication of what you can expect from pupils. This can be especially helpful in planning your lessons. There is also a range of exemplary material available (SCAA, 1995a and 1995b).

The current version of the England and Wales Mathematics National Curriculum is, of course, only one vision of how the curriculum can be specified. Another conception might be to arrange the curriculum around what are sometimes referred to as the 'big ideas' in mathematics. These 'big ideas' might include such notions as place value, variable, function, invariance, symmetry, proof, and so on. The resulting curriculum might well appear to be very different from the current model, and, as a consequence, may be taught in a different way. This illustrates the idea of the curricular shaping of teaching: that is, how the specification of the curriculum directly influences the teaching strategies used.

Another way to look at the mathematics curriculum is to consider the approach taken by Her Majesty's Inspectors of schools in their discussion document on mathematics 5–16 (DES, 1985). In the HMI account, the aims of mathematics teaching are considered in terms of facts, skills, conceptual structures, general strategies and personal qualities. As the document acknowledges, 'placing objectives in categories helps to highlight the different elements in mathematics activities'. Yet the danger in doing so is 'the development of classroom approaches which place different objectives in watertight compartments and deal with them separately' (DES, 1985, pp. 7–8). This is a danger that should not be underestimated. Indeed, it is also a danger with the current version of the Mathematics National Curriculum.

According to the HMI document:

- *facts* are terms, notation, conventions, results;
- *skills* include performing operations, sensible use of calculators and computers, practical skills, communicating skills;
- *conceptual structures* focus on building concepts and links between concepts, selecting data, using mathematics in context, interpreting results;
- *general strategies* include estimation, approximation, trial-and-improvement, simplifying, looking for pattern, reasoning, hypothesising, proving;
- *personal qualities* include good work habits, and a positive attitude.

(DES, 1985, pp. 8–25)

Task 5.4 The structure of the curriculum

1. Examine your Mathematics National Curriculum in terms of the HMI list of facts, skills, conceptual structures, general strategies and personal qualities. Which aspects occur most often? What might be missing and why?
2. Choose some statements from the programme of study for Key Stages 3 and 4 mathematics and see how these are reflected in the level descriptions. Are statements in the programme of study equally reflected in the level descriptions? Are there some statements in the programme of study that do not seem to be mentioned in the level descriptions?

The relationship between the programme of study and the level descriptions is one to become familiar with. It is likely to be the case that in planning your lessons you need to refer to both the programme of study and the level descriptions.

In many ways, the form of the curriculum directly influences the way in which mathematics teachers teach. The current form of the Mathematics National Curriculum, particularly the level descriptions and the associated testing, can suggest teaching strategies that give prominence to a fragmented view of mathematics and an instrumental view of learning. The result is lessons that are similar to the US format given above, with teacher demonstration followed by individual student practice. A richer, more connected view of mathematics is possible for pupils if appropriate attention is paid to teaching strategies. The departmental scheme of work can also help by providing guidance on issues such as continuity and progression.

SCHEMES OF WORK

The department in which you are learning to teach will have a scheme of work: a long-term plan for pupil learning. It may be very detailed and provide the basic outline of every lesson taught to every class, including the learning materials that are needed. Alternatively, it may be relatively brief and give no more than an outline of the topic headings for a particular year group. The intention of the scheme of work is to provide the basis for the teaching of mathematics in that school. It is designed to provide:

- continuity of mathematical content and teaching approach as pupils move from class to class up the school;
- progression over time of knowledge, skills, understanding and attitudes to work;
- advice about resources, including what texts and practical equipment are recommended;
- guidance on assessing, recording, and reporting pupil achievement.

Task 5.5 Getting to know the scheme of work

Choose a topic or an area of work from the scheme of work in your school. Find out what the topic or area of work is designed to achieve, what the pupils were taught before, what length of time is devoted to it, what resources are suggested, how the work is assessed, and what the pupils will do next.

Now that you have considered the structure and design of the mathematics curriculum, the different forms of teaching strategy, and the guidance provided by the scheme of work in your school, you have built a firm foundation with which to begin planning for mathematics learning.

FIRST STEPS IN LESSON PLANNING

A good place to begin your first steps in lesson planning is with a reasonably self-contained part of a lesson. This could involve some or all of the following:

- seeing the class into the room and calling the register;
- going over homework;
- going over a test the class has taken;
- introducing a new topic or new problem-solving or investigative task;
- presenting an agreed segment of a lesson;
- concluding the lesson and dismissing the class.

All of these starting points will need to be negotiated and agreed with the class teacher. All are designed to boost your confidence in speaking to a whole class and may help you to get to know their names. All require you to use, and practise, your presentation skills.

Presentation skills can be divided into verbal and non-verbal elements. Verbal skills include:

- use of voice;
- effective explaining;
- effective questioning;
- directing discussion.

Non-verbal skills include:

- use of blackboard/whiteboard/OHP;
- use of equipment and apparatus;
- gesture;
- posture;
- facial expression.

Remember, presentation skills can be learned, but they take practice. It is vital that you get feedback on what you do. This also takes planning on your part!

You now know that learning to plan involves the co-ordination of many areas of knowledge and a wide number of skills. The following sections serve to build on your knowledge of the curriculum and of teaching strategies and show how this is linked to presentation and organisational skills. Important next steps are selecting mathematical tasks and identifying learning objectives.

Task 5.6 Presenting parts of lessons

Negotiate to take a reasonably self-contained part of a lesson. Discuss your plan for this lesson segment with your tutor and/or the class teacher. What aspects of the lesson segment would you like feedback on? Discuss how the chosen element went in practice. Which aspects of your presentation skills do you need to work on?

Selecting mathematical tasks

A vital skill in planning is being able to recognise good tasks that will work with your classes. The class teacher is a good source of ideas, but you need to develop such skills yourself. Find tasks that you think will provide a stimulus for pupils to think about particular mathematical concepts and procedures, their connections with other mathematical ideas and their applications to real-world contexts. Good tasks can be ones that help students to develop skills in the context of their usefulness. Tasks that require students to reason and to communicate mathematically are usually more likely to promote their ability to solve problems and to make connections. Your aim should be to find tasks that illuminate mathematics as an intriguing and worthwhile domain of enquiry.

As part of the Low Attainers in Mathematics Project (DES, 1987), a group of mathematics teachers attempted to draw up a list describing the necessary ingredients for 'rich mathematical activities'. They suggest that a rich mathematical task:

- must be accessible to everyone at the start;
- should not restrict pupils searching in other directions;
- needs to allow further challenges and be extendible;
- should promote discussion and communication;
- should invite children to make decisions;
- should encourage originality and invention;
- should involve children in speculating, hypothesis making and testing, proving or explaining, reflecting, interpreting;
- should encourage 'what if . . . ?' and 'what if not . . . ?' questions;
- should have an element of surprise;
- should be enjoyable.

Such a definition is similar to the one for 'worthwhile mathematical tasks' contained in the US National Council of Teachers of Mathematics *Professional Standards for Teaching Mathematics* (NCTM, 1991). This suggests that teachers of mathematics should pose tasks that are based on:

- sound and significant mathematics;
- knowledge of students' understandings, interests and experiences;
- knowledge of the range of ways that diverse students learn mathematics;

and tasks that:

- engage students' intellect;
- develop students' mathematical understandings and skills;
- stimulate students to make connections and develop a coherent framework for mathematical ideas;
- call for problem formulation, problem solving and mathematical reasoning;
- promote communication about mathematics;
- represent mathematics as an on-going human activity;
- display sensitivity to, and draw on, students' diverse background experiences and dispositions;
- promote the development of all students' dispositions to do mathematics.

This suggests that you should choose and develop tasks that are likely to promote the development of pupils' understandings of concepts and procedures in a way that also fosters their ability to solve problems and to reason and communicate mathematically. Good tasks tend to be ones that do not separate mathematical thinking from mathematical concepts or skills, that capture students' curiosity and that invite them to speculate and to pursue their hunches. Many such tasks can be approached in more than one interesting and legitimate way; some have more than one reasonable solution.

Task 5.7 Selecting mathematical tasks

Review some of the mathematical tasks that you have available. How many can you describe as 'rich' or 'worthwhile'? For each such task you find, what is the main learning intention?

Once you are able to select good classroom tasks, identifying the main learning intentions will aid you in deciding the objectives for the lesson.

Objectives for mathematics learning

Peter John claims that: 'virtually all major guide books on curriculum and lesson planning begin with the importance of laying down at an early stage, the educational and learning goals that will guide the lesson' (John, 1993, p. 30). This reflects the view that the way to introduce student teachers to the complexities of lesson planning is to use a framework based around the 'rational planning model' first outlined by Tyler (1949). This model asserts that planning a lesson or a sequence of lessons involves:

- specifying objectives;
- specifying knowledge and skills;

- selecting and sequencing learning activities;
- evaluating the outcomes.

In this model, the specifying of objectives comes *before* the selecting of tasks. This is in stark contrast to what is known of how experienced teachers plan their lessons. For them, the objectives come out of the chosen tasks, rather than the objectives determining the tasks. This may well be an important distinction.

The assertion that *starting* with objectives is the most common approach used with student teachers is supported by evidence from the many published texts for student and beginning teachers, some of which you may have seen. Certainly, most do contain advice about lesson planning, and most emphasise the requirement to consider learning objectives very early in the planning process. To be fair, a few published texts do deal with some of the advantages and disadvantages of focusing on the explicit formulation of lesson objectives. The suggested advantages of specifying objectives include that they:

- are measurable;
- are easily communicated;
- help to clarify thinking and planning;
- make assessment and evaluation clearer.

Amongst the disadvantages are that specifying objectives:

- makes planning rigid;
- inhibits opportunist learning;
- trivialises learning;
- encourages a 'technicist' rather than 'creative' view of teaching.

Task 5.8 Specifying objectives

1 Review some of the successful lessons you have seen. How easy was it to specify the objectives for each one? Are some sorts of objectives easier to specify than others? How can you tell to what extent objectives have been met?
2 Select some 'worthwhile' mathematical tasks. Think about what each one demands in terms of the HMI categories of *facts, skills, conceptual structures, general strategies* and *personal qualities*. Would you say that these are the *main* learning outcomes for each (if you think there is more than one)? How might the main learning outcome you choose vary according to the context in which you are using the task (for example, the particular class you are planning for)?

Approaching planning whole lessons

The research undertaken by John (1991) suggests that as you embark on your course of initial teacher education, you do so with a set of beliefs about teaching that clearly influences a great deal of your learning on the course. In particular, your perceptions of mathematics appear to have a strong influence on your ideas about planning. For example, John found that mathematics student teachers who saw mathematics as a predominantly hierarchical subject were heavily influenced by their own vision of how they should plan and teach the subject. As a result, they planned lessons consisting of a pattern of exposition (by the teacher), examples and practice. Evidence from international comparisons of mathematical achievement suggests that such a format may not necessarily develop the forms of connected knowledge necessary for long-term success in mathematics (Jones, 1997; Stigler and Hiebert, 1997). This is why you need to ensure that you consider other approaches to your lesson plans.

One way to approach planning whole lessons is to use different *pro forma* plans. These usually contain the following elements, which were explored earlier in this chapter:

- practical details such as date, class, time, room;
- references to topic, module or scheme of work;
- aims, objectives or learning outcomes;
- teacher and pupil activities;
- timings for elements of the lesson;
- homework.

Task 5.9 Using lesson-planning *pro forma*

1. Review some of the lesson *pro forma* plans that you have seen or have been given. How suitable are they for the lessons you will teach? How might they aid the planning of your lessons? In what ways might they restrict what you do with your classes?
2. An alternative to using pre-printed *pro forma* plans is designing your own. Design some *pro forma* plans for your own use. How can these vary according to the format or learning intentions of the lesson?

Whichever *pro forma* plans you use, whether pre-printed or ones designed by yourself, you will certainly need to learn how to work creatively with objectives. Unless you do so, the disadvantages of specifying objectives, such as making your planning too rigid or inhibiting opportunist learning, can outweigh any benefits (Jones and Smith, 1997). One way to ensure that you remain creative is to plan the lesson around interesting and meaningful pupil activity, and, once you are happy with your plan, decide what the main learning outcome will be.

An important aspect of successful lesson plans (and thence successful lessons) is careful consideration of the various stages in a lesson. It can be useful to think of lessons as having a beginning, middle and end, just like many successful books, films and plays. Hence, you need to devote time and creativity to developing and sequencing lesson steps.

Often the most crucial step is the lesson opening. Use this to grab the attention and interest of the class. You can do this by using an interesting object or problem, a poster, a video extract, and so on. Within this stage it is also useful to inform the pupils of the main point of the lesson and how this fits in with both previous and forthcoming lessons.

The main part of your lessons almost certainly consists of activity involving you and your pupils. Whilst this can take various forms (selected by you so as to meet the needs of the class), an important issue to consider is the timing of the various elements. As you begin planning lessons an important source of information on timings comes from lessons you have observed. Whilst you will inevitably find it difficult to be precise, it can be useful to include estimations of timings in your lesson plans and then modify these in the light of your experience.

The end of the lesson is also very important, as this can influence the impression or image that your pupils take away with them. You can use the end of the lesson not only to provide your pupils with a summary of the lesson and what they will do in the next lesson, but also to provide yourself with some feedback on how successfully you addressed the main learning points in the lesson. For example, you might end with asking one or two pupils to summarise the main idea of the lesson, or you could pose some questions that address the main learning idea. It is also a sensible time to set or remind the class of the homework.

It is certainly likely that some lesson segments will take more time than you expect, whilst others may take considerably less. Clearly, you need to adjust your plans to account for both eventualities. This involves working flexibly with your

Task 5.10 Beginning planning whole lessons

1. Negotiate to plan a complete lesson *with* your tutor (and/or class teacher) that your tutor (or the class teacher) will take. During the lesson, make notes on the opening and closing segments of the lesson, the timing of each segment and any deviations from the set plan. Discuss how each segment went and the reasons for any changes.
2. Negotiate to plan further lessons with your tutor (and/or class teacher) of which you will take agreed elements. For example, you could start the lesson, or conclude it. Discuss the extent to which the learning outcomes were achieved. How can you build assessment opportunities into your plans and use the outcomes to inform your future planning?

lesson plan and having more ideas at hand in case you need them, but also being prepared to jettison some ideas if need be. Always ensure you finish on time, and avoid rushing things if they are taking longer than you expect.

Reflection on all the points raised in this section will provide you with the basis for sound evaluation of your work and of your progress as a developing teacher.

Your early experience with lesson planning will confirm that the most important consideration to take into account is what the pupils already know. As you take more lessons, your role in the lessons can increase with your confidence until you are taking responsibility for teaching the whole of your lessons.

PLANNING TOPICS OF WORK

Being confident about planning and taking individual lessons is a good start. Building on this so that you can plan and teach a coherent series of lessons alleviates some of the problems associated with the 'lessonising' of the curriculum, mentioned near the start of this chapter, when mathematics can seem fragmented and incoherent for your pupils. This section looks at how you can ensure the continuity and progression of pupil learning in your classes so that learning does indeed happen over time.

In this context, a topic of work is a coherent series of lessons on perhaps a mathematical topic such as fractions, or solving equations, a 'big idea' in mathematics such as invariance or symmetry or, indeed, a piece of project work such as an investigation or a substantial problem. As was mentioned earlier, the scheme of work in your department may well specify quite precisely what each lesson contains. On the other hand, it may provide no more than a title and a list of resources. No matter what you find you have in your current circumstances, there are inevitably going to be times when you want to plan or review a topic of work.

A good source of advice on topic planning is contained within the original non-statutory guidance for the England and Wales Mathematics National Curriculum (NCC, 1989, pp. B8–B11). Although this advice is directed at schemes of work as a whole (rather than individual topics within a scheme of work), many of the issues have direct relevance to planning a series of lessons. Among these are suggestions that:

- tasks should be balanced between tasks that develop knowledge, skills and understanding and those that develop the ability to tackle practical problems;
- tasks should be balanced between the applications of mathematics and ideas that are purely mathematical;
- tasks should, where appropriate, use pupils' own interests or questions either as starting points or as further lines of development;
- tasks should, where appropriate, involve both independent and co-operative work;

- tasks should be both of the kind that have an exact result or answer and those that have many possible outcomes;
- pupils' activity should be balanced between different modes of learning: doing, observing, talking and listening, discussing with other pupils, reflecting, drafting, reading and writing, etc.

You can use the above both to inform your planning and to evaluate current topics within the scheme of work. The practical issues involved in planning a topic include:

- deciding aims and objectives (or learning outcomes);
- breaking down the topic into lesson-sized chunks;
- making assumptions about capability, timing, appropriateness, style, variety . . . (and then checking on these assumptions).

In terms of aims and objectives, it is probably wise to determine *an aim for the topic* and, subsequently, to determine *objectives for each lesson*. Selecting these objectives involves:

- separating a topic into distinct elements or aspects;
- designing a sequence through these elements.

Research suggests that this is the most demanding aspect for a beginning teacher. Deciding how to select objectives, in a way that satisfactorily meets the pupils' needs, demands:

- good subject knowledge;
- skill at separating and sequencing the elements of a topic;
- awareness of pupil needs.

One way to begin is to rely on established practice (for example, the scheme of work, or a textbook scheme or equivalent). But remember that an objective is *not* which exercise the pupils are to do, or what they are going to draw, or the fact that they are going to have a class discussion: these are the tasks and related pupil activity used to promote learning. *Objectives say what is to be learnt. A major pitfall in planning a topic is to neglect objectives and to see planning as simply organising activity.* There is much more to it than that.

When selecting learning tasks, it is a good idea to return to the advice given above. Consideration here includes deciding about:

- context ('real-life', 'pure', . . .);
- single outcome/many possible outcomes;
- ways of working;
- exposition;
- discussion (in small groups, whole-class);
- solving problems;
- investigating.

In terms of monitoring and assessing pupils' progress, it is worth asking yourself if this is to be formal (say, through a test) or informal, or a mixture? It certainly needs you to be *active and purposeful in the classroom* (not just waiting for hands up) and involves you observing, probing, questioning, checking, assessing, and so on.

Your evaluation of your teaching should focus on answering some or all of these questions:

- were the objectives of each lesson clear?
- did you select the most appropriate way of achieving these objectives?
- was the lesson staged in a logical way?
- was the material appropriate and relevant?
- were the instructions clear?
- were the pupils involved in the lesson?
- was the timing right?
- was the level right?
- what did the pupils learn?

Planning for equity and differentiation

The promotion and realisation of equity of opportunity for your pupils to learn mathematics need to be integral to your planning. Take care to promote pupil experiences, resources and content that do not reinforce, and, wherever possible, positively counteract, stereotypical thinking. Ensure that you provide the best for *every* pupil, irrespective of gender, social class or ethnicity.

Differentiation is not solely about helping slow pupils or stretching the bright ones – it is about the educative inclusion of all children. *Diversity* refers to the range of individual abilities and aptitudes; *differentiation* is the planned process of intervention in the classroom to maximise potential based on individual abilities and aptitudes (Stradling *et al.*, 1991; Dickinson and Wright, 1993). Individual abilities and aptitudes can vary in terms of attainment, motivation, interest, skills, and so on.

You can *differentiate* in a number of ways:

in planning:

- by employing an appropriate variety of tasks;
- by identifying outcomes of tasks;
- by ensuring elements of pupil choice.

in task design:

- through type and design (text, worksheet, poster, tape, video, computer, etc.);
- through ease of use (for example, reading level).

in providing support:

- from you as the teacher;
- from other adults or pupils;
- in terms of materials or technology.

in expected response:

- having accessible aims and objectives;
- making assessment criteria explicit.

Planning for homework

When planned well, homework experiences provide a valuable supplement to classroom activities. For example, you can use homework to reinforce and consolidate classroom learning, or to gather information that you will then use in classroom activities. Homework is one way in which parents come to know about what their child does in your lessons. Amongst the things you can investigate are the use of home–school contracts and how mathematics departments in particular, but schools more generally, involve parents in supporting pupil learning.

One particular issue to consider in your planning is whether you can use homework as an opportunity to practise skills or for widening the perceptions of mathematics. Perhaps you can aim to do both over time.

SUMMARY

Your success in teaching depends crucially on the effectiveness of your planning and how well you put your plans into action. Your planning needs to be explicit and detailed, particularly in the early stages of taking over classes. This takes good organisation and it also takes time. Develop a range of lesson structures and match these to what you want to achieve in your lessons. Spend time getting to know the structure of the curriculum and the departmental scheme of work so that you can begin to work creatively within the statutory framework. Practise your presentation skills, both verbal and non-verbal. Get to know what your classes can do and what motivates them. Build up a collection of classroom tasks that you are confident will engage the attention of pupils. Review and evaluate your work, and both seek and act on advice. Always expect a high standard of work.

Do not forget that there are others around in the school who may well be able to assist you: in particular, various support and technical staff. Plan to draw on their expertise and availability as well.

Successful planning entails preparing a rich mathematical diet for your pupils. Your efforts will be rewarded with the quality of pupil learning you are able to engender.

FURTHER READING

ATM (1993c) *In Our Classrooms: Strategies for the Teaching of Mathematics*, Derby: Association of Teachers of Mathematics.
A thoughtful collection of accounts of teachers working in their classrooms to develop their pupils' mathematics.

Harris, J. (1995) *Presentation Skills for Teachers*, London: Kogan Page.
A helpful guide to many of the skills involved in developing a good presentation style in the classroom.

John, P. D. (1993) *Lesson Planning for Teachers*, London: Cassell.
A practical guide to many of the general issues involved in planning lessons. A range of useful *pro forma* lesson plans are included that can be photocopied.

Neill, S. and Caswell, C. (1993) *Body Language for Competent Teachers*, London: Routledge.
Despite having a rather odd-sounding title, this useful book shows how to use non-verbal skills such as gesture, posture and facial expression to establish good relationships with classes. Contains many illustrations of classroom situations.

6 Assessment and Public Examinations

Peter Johnston-Wilder

INTRODUCTION

Every teacher needs to make judgements about pupil attainment in order to evaluate the effectiveness of their teaching and to inform their planning. In mathematics, it is particularly important to assess what pupils already know because, to an extent, mathematical understanding is hierarchical. It is always possible that some pupils will have already acquired deep-rooted misconceptions about, or difficulties with, certain mathematical ideas. Such misconceptions can have serious implications for these pupils' ability to comprehend new topics. So teachers assess:

- to inform their planning;
- to help diagnose the sources of pupils' difficulties.

In addition, teachers assess:

- to provide a basis for reporting progress to pupils themselves and their parents;
- to meet the requirements of external public assessments.

Each of these varied purposes for assessment may require a different approach.

This chapter is in two parts: the first is focused on formative (on-going) assessment, and the second on public and summative assessments. Considering these separately is a device to structure the chapter, but in practice these two purposes of assessment are often closely related. Your first tasks in this chapter will be to consider more closely how you can develop your ability to assess pupils during the school year in your lessons. You will be asked to consider the different methods of assessment that are available to you and the resources for assessment that you will probably find in your school. You will also need to consider how to interpret and make use of the information forwarded to you about your Year 7 pupils' attainment in the end of Key Stage 2 assessments. After this, you need to make yourself aware of the elements that make up public assessment of mathematics at ages 14 and 16. An important part of the professional work of a teacher is to be aware of the requirements of public examinations, as they have important implications for the mathematics curriculum and for what you teach and how you teach it.

Throughout this chapter, the assessment requirements of the England and Wales National Curriculum for Mathematics are considered as an example of how a national system affects your practice as a classroom teacher.

OBJECTIVES

By the end of this chapter, you should:

- have used a range of different methods of assessment in mathematics and considered when they are appropriate;
- have considered the manageability of assessment in your everyday classroom practice;
- be aware of the importance of a departmental assessment policy;
- be aware of the requirements of public assessment in mathematics at Key Stages 3 and 4.

FORMATIVE ASSESSMENT

In Chapter 6 of the core book in this series (Capel *et al.*, 1995), you were introduced to various purposes of assessment, particularly the difference between formative and summative purposes. Formative assessment has the purpose of informing your planning of the teaching and learning experiences for individual pupils. In contrast to this, the purpose of summative assessment is to summarise the pupil's attainment at the end of a stage of learning, or at the end of a module or course of study. The outcome of summative assessment is often for public consumption, and is used to select and order individuals, whereas formative assessment is intended to help learners to learn more effectively.

The distinction between formative and summative purposes is not always clear-cut, particularly in terms of being able to say clearly that any given form of assessment is definitely one or the other. For example, class test results can be used to inform teacher decisions about where to go next, but may also be taken home to inform parents about current progress.

At the time of the Cockcroft Report (DES, 1982) in England, public assessment in mathematics was entirely 'norm-referenced', as was almost all formative assessment by teachers within their classes. This means that each pupil's achievement was assessed by how it compared with that of other pupils in the same age cohort, or, in the case of in-class formative assessment, by comparison with performance of other pupils in the class. In recent years, there has been a greater emphasis on 'criterion-referenced' assessment, where pupils' achievement is assessed against specific curricular criteria. Criterion-referenced assessment is now acknowledged as an essential feature of good assessment practice in the classroom. However, norm referencing is still a strong feature within public assessment, particularly in some aspects of GCSE and A level.

Formative assessment might include evidence of what pupils can do and understand, gathered in various ways. Sometimes the evidence you obtain is in a permanent form that can be reviewed again later, such as written evidence recorded in the pupil's exercise book. However, the evidence can often be ephemeral, such as when you observe a pupil choosing to use a ruler to measure appropriately, or when you hear one pupil explain her reasoning to another pupil. The list below summarises some forms of evidence that are important in the formative assessment of mathematics:

- marking exercises;
- class tests (end of unit, end of module or end of year);
- aural and mental maths;
- open and extended work;
- oral assessment;
- questioning (both open and closed questions);
- observation.

Task 6.1 Taking in pupils' books

Find a class that has done two contrasting tasks: an exercise and an open-ended task. Collect mathematics work books from a group of about six pupils. Look closely at their work on these two contrasting tasks and consider carefully what the evidence recorded in the pupils' books tells you about:

- what the pupils know and can do;
- what the task allows and encourages the pupils to show of their ability, and hence what information the task does *not* give you about the pupils' abilities;
- what the pupils need to do next to follow up the work you have looked at;
- what the teacher might do next.

Try to be very precise in your responses to each of the points above. You may find it helpful to identify particular aspects of pupil attainment from your National Curriculum assessment framework (in England and Wales, this will be the level descriptions for each Attainment Target).

When you observe teachers at work in your school, you will see many of the elements of formative assessment used in practice in classrooms. Written tests and exercises have been commonplace assessment practices in mathematics classrooms for generations. However, these alone will not tell you all that you need to know as a teacher about the present understanding and abilities of your pupils and their potential to go further. The assessment method chosen needs to be fit for the purpose of assessing a specific kind of ability. For example, if you are assessing the pupils' ability to 'communicate mathematically', then you will be looking for the pupils' ability to discuss what they are doing, and to explain why they are doing it. For this purpose, there would be no point in setting a test consisting only of short-answer questions that need to be given only right or wrong answers.

Content and process

The *content* of the Mathematics National Curriculum in England and Wales is broadly what is specified in Attainment Targets 2, 3 and 4; on the other hand, mathematics Attainment Target 1 specifies *process*. In mathematics, assessment of content can require assessment methods different from those required for the assessment of process. The content of mathematics has been described as consisting of facts, skills and concepts (see, for example, the Cockcroft Report [DES, 1982] and the HMI discussion document on mathematics 5 to 16 [DES, 1985]). This classification of content was discussed in Chapter 5, and it can be helpful when considering how to teach or assess a particular topic. Learning facts involves memory, and the assessment of this will be a test of 'recall'. Mathematical skills often involve the ability to perform algorithms quickly and efficiently, which might require regular practice and might also sometimes be assessed by some form of written test.

By contrast, Attainment Target 1 specifies the processes involved in working and thinking mathematically. These involve applying mathematical knowledge and understanding in unfamiliar contexts, or making decisions about what mathematical techniques will be helpful or appropriate to solve a particular problem. Processes such as these cannot be effectively assessed through short exercises, where the pupil knows which skills or concepts are required. On the contrary, they require the pupil to engage with a problem or a task at a deeper level and over a longer period.

Extended work in mathematics

To appreciate fully what your pupils can achieve in using the processes of thinking mathematically (Attainment Target 1 in the National Curriculum for England and Wales), it is important that you include opportunities for the pupils to engage with open-ended and investigational tasks from time to time, and that these are allowed to extend over several lessons. Open-ended work is also a very important learning experience: it is where pupils learn to take responsibility themselves for working mathematically and to make decisions about how to use their mathematical skills to work productively on unfamiliar problems.

Assessment of open-ended work is very different from the assessment of exercises and tests. Mathematics teachers usually assess open-ended work by outcome. This involves judging the pupil's level of achievement by the work attempted and by what specific examples and generalisations the pupil has discussed. Higher-level attainment will include some explanation, justification and perhaps proof of the generalisations made.

Assessment by outcome is an informative way to assess a pupil's attainment on Mathematics Attainment Target 1 (Ma1: Using and Applying Mathematics). Indeed, this is what underlies the assessment of GCSE coursework. The issue of assessing extended work by outcome is discussed further in the sub-section on GCSE coursework later in the chapter.

The example in Task 6.2 is intended to illustrate very briefly how different pupil responses to the same task might be indicative of differing levels of understanding and attainment.

Task 6.2 Assessing open-ended tasks

Example: A class is set the following task:

If the answer is 10, what could the question be?
Show as much different mathematics as you can.

Look at the following extracts from two pupils' responses to this task and consider what each pupil has demonstrated that they know and can do. You might try to assess these two outcomes against your own National Curriculum assessment framework.

A $3 + 7 = 10$, $13 - 3 = 10$

B $2^3 + 2 = 10$, $\sqrt{9} + \sqrt{49} = 10$

When you have considered the extracts, discuss your ideas with your tutor in school. With the help of your tutor, find a Key Stage 3 class that has completed an open-ended task. Arrange to discuss the work of about six pupils from this class on their open-ended task. Spend some time working for yourself on the open-ended task completed by the pupils, and identify the content areas of the curriculum that might reasonably be addressed by a pupil working on the task. Assess the work done by each pupil in the various content areas of the curriculum. For each pupil, you should aim to identify the highest level demonstrated in each content area of the curriculum.

Oral assessment, questioning and observing

The following are examples of classroom interaction.

- During an exercise on expansion of brackets, a pupil claims that $(x + y)^2 = x^2 + y^2$.
- In solving the equation $2x = x + 2$, a pupil suggests taking away 2 from each side to give $x = x$.
- In an exercise on solving equations, a pupil faced with $\frac{(4x + 2)}{6x} = x$ suggests taking away the x from the numerator and denominator to give $\frac{4 + 2}{6} = x$, and hence $x = 1$.

Each of these examples shows that the pupil has not understood something; or perhaps the pupil knows that there is a rule that can help but has not understood when this rule applies. In the third example, the problem is compounded by the fact that the pupil's incorrect reasoning has led to a proposed solution, $x = 1$, which just happens to be a true solution to the original equation.

In such situations, the teacher needs to assess the situation and adapt the teaching accordingly. An important method for making a diagnostic assessment of the pupil's difficulty in such situations is to use carefully targeted open questions.

Task 6.3 Assessing for understanding

In each of the examples above, consider what the pupil has understood and what has gone wrong. Decide how you would follow up the situation described. What questions could you ask the pupils to help you to diagnose the nature of the pupil's problem? What action might you take to help develop the pupil's understanding in each situation?

Discuss your ideas with your tutor in your school.

Look out for examples of teachers using questioning to find out about pupils' understanding. Try to identify some general principles about questioning pupils to diagnose the sources of difficulties.

The examples above were taken from a situation in which the teacher was observing the pupil working on a task, or listening to the pupil explaining his or her work, or asking questions in a whole-class question-and-answer session. These are important aspects of formative assessment in the classroom. Such methods are part of the teacher's basic skills to focus on improving the pupil's understanding.

What the pupil needs is *not* to hear a repeat of some explanation he or she has heard before, but to have new explanations to help explain why the rule, as he or she has learned it, does not apply in these cases. The teacher's task is to encourage and enable the pupil to modify existing conceptions in particular respects. Recognise in yourself, and guard against, the tendency just to repeat the answer if it was not understood straight away.

As teacher, you need to pay careful attention to the questioning strategies you adopt to elicit the pupil's existing conceptions and explanations (recall the brief discussion of forms of questioning in Chapter 4). When a pupil gives a wrong answer, it may be quite unhelpful to the pupil if you simply say 'No, that's wrong', and then give the 'right' answer. It may be more helpful to ask the pupil to explain how he or she arrived at the wrong answer. When required to do this, the pupil will often see errors in reasoning for him- or herself and correct them. However, from the pupil's explanation, you may be able to infer much more about what he or she has understood, and about the source of the misunderstanding. Pupils' existing conceptions may have been adopted because they work in some instances. Therefore a pupil may be able to give an answer that seems correct, but may have arrived at this answer through incorrect or limited reasoning. The questions you ask to encourage the pupil to explain the reasoning that led to the wrong answer can help you to uncover problems of this kind, and can sometimes help the pupil herself to recognise and correct the problems.

Aural and mental mathematics and tests

In aural assessment, pupils are given spoken instructions and questions, and are usually required to interpret the problems posed without further written information. Such tests are therefore a test of the pupils' abilities to interpret and process information mentally. Success in these tests requires careful concentration, and pupils often enjoy the task for short periods at the beginning or end of a lesson.

In setting tests of this kind, or tests for end of unit, end of module or end of year, teachers need to be creative. If all your tests look the same and are predictable, there is a danger that pupils will learn to perform well without necessarily improving their understanding. As well as providing assessment information, assessment activities, including tests, can be used to motivate your pupils and to direct their attention towards those ideas, skills and practices that you want them to develop. Pupils can be asked to find different ways of solving a problem, or to explain their reasoning. Setting effective tests, which will engage your pupils and motivate them, takes persistent practice and requires careful preparation.

Providing appropriate feedback to pupils

When you make a formative assessment of a pupil's work, you need to consider what to tell them about how they have done, and how to present the information. It is helpful to think about what types of feedback are available and when each might be appropriate. Consider under what circumstances it would be appropriate simply to give 9/10 as the feedback on a pupil's work. If the pupil did make any mistakes, it is often worth considering what these tell you about the pupil's understanding. Pupils need informative comments about how to improve and what to pay attention to; this requires time and careful consideration on your part. Sometimes it is effective to provide brief written comments to the individual pupil at the end of the exercise. However, if the pupil has a substantial difficulty, or if you are not sure what is the source of the pupil's difficulty, it may be better to ask to speak to the individual during the following lesson. If there are several pupils with the same, or similar, difficulties, it will be a more efficient use of your time to speak to the group in the next lesson, or to take some time to give a new explanation to the whole class.

Task 6.4 Providing constructive feedback

A class of Year 11 pupils preparing for GCSE were given an exercise on substitution. One pupil's attempt at the exercise is shown in Figure 6.1 below.

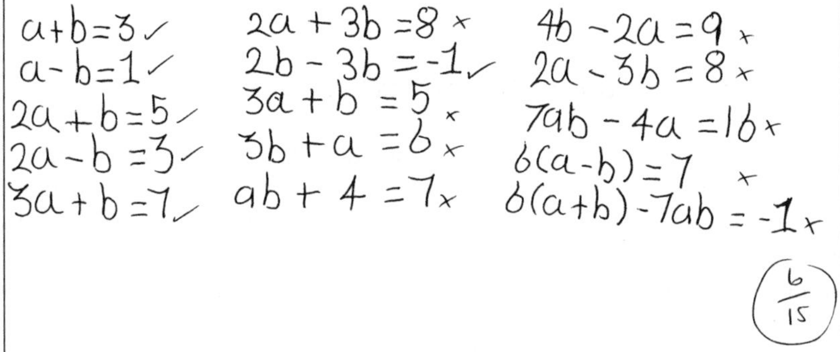

$a+b=3$ ✓	$2a+3b=8$ ✗	$4b-2a=9$ ✗
$a-b=1$ ✓	$2b-3b=-1$ ✓	$2a-3b=8$ ✗
$2a+b=5$ ✓	$3a+b=5$ ✗	$7ab-4a=16$ ✗
$2a-b=3$ ✓	$3b+a=6$ ✗	$6(a-b)=7$ ✗
$3a+b=7$ ✓	$ab+4=7$ ✗	$6(a+b)-7ab=-1$ ✗

$\frac{6}{15}$

Figure 6.1 Pupil script

Discuss in your journal the merits of each of the following forms of feedback.

A 6/15

B You have made a systematic error in questions 8 to 15. Look at your work again and see if you can identify the error. If you have difficulty, you might discuss this with other people in the class. See me after the next lesson to discuss what you have found out.

C In an algebraic expression, $3a$ means $3 \times a$.

You might consider that none of the suggestions above is ideal, or that some combination of more than one of them would be suitable. What do you think is the most appropriate feedback to give to this pupil? Consider what factors would help you to decide how best to respond. Don't forget that you may have thirty other pupils' scripts for this exercise to mark, just from the one class. You will need to be aware not only of the demands on your time, but also of the ultimate time saving in the lesson when you give appropriately focused feedback to enable pupils to correct their own misunderstanding.

Recording and reporting

It is important that you develop systems to record the results of your assessments of pupils. Your records may be required for several different purposes, and it is important that they are kept up-to-date and in a form that can be understood by other professionals. Some of the purposes to which your assessment records might be put are:

- passing relevant information on to subsequent teachers at the end of a school year, or when the pupil moves to another class or another school;
- passing relevant information on to the parent through regular reports to parents or at parents' consultations;
- informing your teacher assessment of each pupils' progress in each attainment at the end of each year, especially at the end of Key Stage 3 (Year 9);
- informing special assessments of particular pupils, such as the assessment for special educational needs.

In the following paragraphs you will consider first some contrasting systems for record keeping, and then some of the different purposes for which your records might be used.

Recording progress

Teachers are required to keep records of each pupil's progress. In mathematics, the recording systems adopted by schools in England have sometimes taken the form of very detailed tables of each pupil's achievement of each identifiable item in the National Curriculum level descriptions. This is a consequence of the way in which the Mathematics National Curriculum in England and Wales evolved from a detailed list of criteria in the 1989 and 1991 versions (DES/WO, 1989a and 1991) to the more general level descriptions that we see in the 1995 version (DfE, 1995). Such detailed recording systems have sometimes become difficult to manage, and some teachers have found themselves perpetually ticking boxes. With the present framework of National Curriculum assessment, it may no longer be necessary to keep such detailed records, but some detail is clearly desirable to provide a systematic basis for planning, and to provide the basis for effective reporting to other teachers, to governors and to parents.

A useful set of characteristics for a formative assessment scheme is given by the British Educational Research Association (BERA).

> We suggest that a formative assessment scheme should provide information that is:
>
> - gathered in a number of relevant contexts;
> - criterion-referenced and related to a description of progression;
> - disaggregated, which in this context means that distinct aspects of performance are reported separately and there is no attempt to combine dissimilar aspects;

- shared by both pupil and teacher;
- a basis for deciding what further learning is required;
- the basis of an ongoing running record of progress.

(BERA, 1992, p. 6)

You will need to find out precisely what records of pupils' progress will be expected of you within your school. However, you should also look at other systems of recording progress. Table 6.1 shows a recording sheet based on the system used in one school. The top part of the table shows information about the pupil and records the pupil's progress through the teaching scheme. The bottom

Table 6.1 Pupil National Curriculum record sheet

Name ______________ Form ______ Set ______ Staff ____

Year 7 Units
Year 8 Units
Year 9 Units
Year 10 Units
Year 11 Units

	Attainment Target															
Level	1 Using and Applying			2 Number			3 Algebra			4 Shape, Space and Measures			5 Data Handling			Level
8+																8+
7																7
6																6
5																5
4																4
3																3
2																2
1																1
Year	7/8	9	10/11	7/8	9	10/11	7/8	9	10/11	7/8	9	10/11	7/8	9	10/11	Year

part of the table is a record of the pupil's attainment in each Attainment Target in each of Years 7 to 11. Every time a piece of work is marked for assessment against the National Curriculum, the teacher records the highest level demonstrated in that piece of work in each relevant Attainment Target, and marks this with a cross on the appropriate column of the table. The result is that a picture is built up of the pupil's progress through the National Curriculum.

Many commercial teaching schemes in mathematics have their own recording system tailored to the scheme. These often relate very closely to banks of question and other assessment material published with the scheme. It is worth obtaining information about some of these from the publishers, and comparing them with the system used in your own school.

Task 6.5 Recording assessments

Obtain some examples of assessment recording systems from some of the major published mathematics teaching schemes for Years 7 to 11. Some examples are:

- *SMP 11–16*, published by Cambridge University Press;
- *Oxford Mathematics*, published by Oxford University Press;
- *Key Maths*, published by Stanley Thornes.

Try also to obtain copies of some other recording systems used in nearby schools.

Arrange a meeting with your tutor to discuss the departmental recording system in your school. Compare the recording system in your school with the published systems and with other school systems that you have obtained, and with the system shown in Table 6.1.

Evaluate each of the assessment schemes you have against the BERA criteria. In particular, try to identify explicitly what are the distinct aspects of performance in mathematics that need to be reported separately, and see to what extent the various assessment schemes succeed in achieving this.

Reporting to parents

Parents are often particularly concerned about how their child is progressing in mathematics. Your school and your mathematics department will have established practices for producing regular reports to parents. This will usually include a programme of parental consultations, in which parents have the opportunity to meet teachers, as well as the regular written reports on each subject. These practices will often be formalised as part of the school and departmental policies for assessment, recording and reporting. It is important that you learn to use the established framework to communicate effectively with parents. You need to be aware of the various backgrounds that parents will have in mathematics, and to tailor your comments appropriately.

In writing your comments, you should aim to encourage dialogue between parent and pupil about the pupil's learning. There are many ways in which parents can be encouraged to contribute to their child's progress in mathematics. However, because the school mathematics curriculum has changed significantly during the last twenty years, many parents rely on the advice of their child's teacher to know how best they can help. The report to parents and the parental consultations can each play a part in this by giving parents suggestions about ways in which they can help their child to learn.

Transfer from Key Stage 2 to Key Stage 3

All local education systems involve transitions from one phase of education to another. In some areas, schooling is organised into three stages: lower, middle and upper; whilst in others it is in two stages: primary and secondary, with transition at age 11. If transition from primary schools or middle schools to secondary or upper schools is not managed well, then pupils can lose up to a year of useful progress in mathematics. In this section, you will consider the value and use of information from the Key Stage 2 assessments at the transfer between Key Stage 2 and Key Stage 3. This information can support the planning and teaching in Year 7. In secondary schools, where the end of Key Stage 2 is also the transfer from primary to secondary school, this is particularly significant information. In middle schools, the issues are

Task 6.6 Interpreting Key Stage 2 levels

For this task, you need the National Curriculum programme of study for Key Stage 2, and some Key Stage 2 SATs. Your school may be able to show you some KS2 SATs, or you may be able to borrow some from a neighbouring primary school. Some major bookshops are selling books of past SAT questions for KS2. Otherwise, you can obtain past SATs from QCA at the address given in Appendix 2.

Look at the Mathematics National Curriculum for Key Stage 2 (age 7 to 11), and at the level descriptions that describe the likely attainment at age 11 (levels 1 to 6 in England and Wales). In each curriculum area (Attainment Target), reflect on what you would expect a pupil to know, understand and be able to do for each level of attainment at age 11

Look at some Key Stage 2 SATs for mathematics. Levels in the SATs are awarded according to the total number of marks gained in the test. Reflect on what you can expect to learn from knowing the level achieved by an individual pupil in the KS2 SATs.

Talk with teachers in the department about how they make use of the data that come to them from the feeder schools.

slightly different, but the Key Stage 2 results may still provide an important basis for the information passed from middle schools to upper schools.

Two publications from SCAA may be useful references when you think about this issue: *Promoting Continuity between Key Stage 2 and 3* (SCAA, 1996b) looks at whole-school planning issues to do with promoting continuity in pupils' learning, whilst *Making Effective Use of Key Stage 2 Assessments* (SCAA, 1997c) discusses methods being used in some schools to inform planning of teaching in Year 7 lessons. It is likely that these publications will be superseded by new publications from QCA in the near future, so you should keep aware of the catalogue of publications from QCA as it is updated.

In Task 6.6 you will look more closely at the Key Stage 2 curriculum and at the nature of the information available at the end of the Key Stage.

PUBLIC EXAMINATIONS

The results of public assessment of school mathematics have been the subject of considerable attention in the UK during the late 1980s and the 1990s. Some of this attention has centred on a concern that the standards of mathematics achieved by young people in schools in the UK are not as high as those achieved in other countries. This debate has been fuelled by the publication of results from the Third International Mathematics and Science Study (TIMSS) in 1996 (Keys *et al.*, 1996); these also appeared to show that results from England and Wales were not as good as those from competitor nations. The level of concern and attention given to standards in school mathematics has led to some significant changes and developments in the methods used in the public assessment of mathematics.

There has been a move since the Cockcroft Report (DES, 1982) to introduce criterion referencing into public assessment. This was very noticeable within the early assessment framework for the National Curriculum in England (DES/WO, 1989a and 1991), where the assessment criteria were tightly specified statements of what a pupil would be able to do. The latest revision of the Mathematics National Curriculum (DfE, 1995) has broader level descriptions, which give, for each level, a description of the kinds of achievement that a child might be expected to show.

In the next sub-section, you will look closely at the mathematics assessments in the Key Stage 3 SATs; in a later section, you will look at the GCSE.

Key Stage 3 SATs

The assessment of each pupil at the end of Key Stage 3 is made using two distinct elements: the SATs and teacher assessment. The SATs are administered to pupils in Year 9 during May. For most pupils, the SATs are conducted under examination conditions. The written papers are organised in overlapping tiers, with each set of papers addressing three National Curriculum levels: 3 to 5, 4 to 6, 5 to 7, and 6 to 8. The idea is that a pupil who is expected to attain level 5 should be entered for the tier assessing levels 4 to 6. At each tier, there are two papers, each lasting one hour. In addition, each pupil takes a mental test, in which the focus is on the Number curriculum.

There are special mathematics assessment tasks for pupils in Year 9, who are expected to achieve at levels 1 or 2 of the National Curriculum. These tasks may be

Task 6.7 SAT tests

SATs exam papers

In your school, look at the SAT material for the end of Key Stage 3. If you need to obtain more examples, they are available from QCA.

Look at the structure of the tests, as tiers of overlapping papers. Look at one question that appears in different forms on different papers. Notice how the content to be assessed is arising out of a context.

Take a topic in the Mathematics National Curriculum for Key Stage 3 that you have taught or are going to teach soon. Construct your own set of three overlapping questions, like those in the Key Stage 3 SATs, to assess your pupils' understanding of this topic across four National Curriculum levels, after you have taught them. Discuss your questions with your tutor before you try them on the children. Try out your questions on your class a few weeks after you have taught the topic.

Consider what are the difficulties of writing questions for the Key Stage 3 SATs. What difficulties will your pupils have with the questions in the SATs? What experiences can you give to your pupils to help them to maximise their achievement in the SATs?

Consider the range of abilities of the children who take these tests. Is the language used in the questions suitable for the least able pupil at level 3, and for the most able pupils working at levels 7 and 8?

Mental tests

Look at the mental test samples for KS3. Compare them with the GCSE mental maths tests: what is similar, what is different? Consider what experiences pupils need of similar activities to prepare them for these.

Level 1 and 2 assessment materials

Find out what special provision is made in your school for the assessment of lower attainers in KS3 maths.

Speak to your tutor to obtain some KS3 maths tasks for levels 1 and 2. Otherwise, order some from the QCA catalogue.

Consider what these tasks suggest about the mathematics curriculum for low attainers at KS3. How do these tasks differ from the standard KS3 assessments for level 3 and above?

administered at any time from early January to the end of the summer term. Pupils complete three tasks to obtain a task level, and teachers can integrate these tasks into the normal classroom activities as they wish. Teachers are expected to use their professional judgement to present the tasks appropriately for their pupils.

Teacher assessment

Teacher assessment at Key Stage 3 is the second component of the end of Key Stage assessment. Teachers are required to make an assessment of each pupil on each of the Attainment Targets. This assessment is made in the final term of Year 9, based on work done in class across the Key Stage. Each school may have a different approach to this requirement, but one approach is to build a portfolio of the pupil's best work, providing written evidence of attainment. Some of the work in the portfolio needs to be open-ended work to provide evidence of achievement in Attainment Target 1. Assessment of the portfolio is made using the level descriptions in the National Curriculum for Mathematics. Guidance for teachers in making these judgements is provided in a document produced by SCAA in 1995: *Exemplification of Standards* (SCAA, 1995a and 1995b).

In Task 6.8, you will assess the work done by a class of Key Stage 3 pupils on an open-ended task you have set. You will need to have a clear idea of how to interpret the level descriptions in each Attainment Target. If you can obtain a copy of each exemplification document (SCAA, 1995a and 1995b), then you will find them useful. You will also need to discuss the task with your tutor.

Teachers develop their own practice for identifying the level achieved in a piece of open-ended work. One possible approach is described in this paragraph. Look first at the process Attainment Target (Ma1 in the National Curriculum for

Task 6.8 Using level descriptions

Arrange to carry out an open-ended task with a Key Stage 3 class, preferably in Year 9. You need to choose a task that will provide opportunities for the most able in the class to be challenged, but will also be accessible to the least able, so that every pupil will be able to achieve something. You may wish to consult your tutor for advice about a suitable task to use. Some ideas about open activities are given in Appendix 3. You will need to allow the pupils at least a whole lesson, and you may wish to give them a homework and perhaps another lesson as well to complete their report on their work.

When you have collected in the pupils' work, use the level descriptions to assess the work done by each pupil. Look first particularly for evidence of attainment in Ma1 (Using and Applying Mathematics). Then revisit the scripts to look for evidence of achievement in the content Attainment Targets. Discuss the results of your work with your tutor.

England and Wales). Start at level 1 and work up the levels, looking for evidence at each level. When you have identified the level whose description is the best fit to the evidence in the piece of work, look at the description for the next level up, to what is missing from this piece of work that makes it miss the next level. Then look at the description for the level below to identify what is the evidence in this piece of work that marks it out as better than that. In this way, you can rigorously check the evidence of achievement. Then look at the content Attainment Targets that are relevant to the work done, and note where there is evidence of any content at a level surrounding the level identified for Ma1.

GCSE ASSESSMENT

Key Stage 4 of the National Curriculum in England and Wales is assessed through GCSE (the General Certificate of Secondary Education). The assessment arrangements for GCSE are administered by independent examination boards, with approval from the Qualifications and Curriculum Authority (QCA). GCSE mathematics syllabuses are designed to assess Key Stage 4 of the National Curriculum in Mathematics, but some are also designed to meet the needs of post-16 students and mature adult learners. Some GCSE syllabuses are written specifically for use with a particular teaching scheme. Within your school, you may find that all pupils are entered for the same mathematics syllabus, or you may find that different syllabuses are used with different groups of pupils, or with different year groups. It is quite common for a school to use a different syllabus for sixth-form students who want to retake GCSE mathematics to improve their grade.

All GCSE mathematics syllabuses now have three elements to the assessment process: written papers, aural test and coursework. Within the written papers, all syllabuses have a common structure of three overlapping tiers of assessment, with different content specified for each tier. The intention of the different tiers is to provide a fair assessment for pupils of different abilities. The tiers of entry allow achievement at different grades, as shown in Table 6.2.

Table 6.2 Tiers of entry for GCSE

Tier	*Grades attainable*
Foundation	D E F G
Intermediate	B C D E
Higher	A* A B C

The examining groups are required to follow the GCSE Revised Subject Criteria for Mathematics (SCAA, 1995c). These include grade descriptions providing a general indication of the standards of achievement represented by particular grades. They are not prescriptive but indicative. There are grade descriptions for grades A, C and F, which are used by the exam board in arriving at candidates' grades. These descriptions are published in the syllabus documents, and can assist schools in deciding which is the appropriate tier of entry for particular pupils. Tables 6.3 and 6.4 show extracts from the revised subject criteria for mathematics: Table 6.3 is the aims and assessment objectives for GCSE mathematics, and Table 6.4 is the description of performance at grade C.

Schools have to decide which tier of papers is appropriate for each pupil. This decision is sometimes made in Year 9, and certainly in Year 10. Most schools teach mathematics in ability groups during the GCSE years, and prepare whole ability groups for one tier of entry. Some schools are able to keep the decision flexible, and will allow pupils to be moved from one group to another during Years 10 and 11, but the flexibility to move a pupil to a higher group inevitably reduces during Year 11. Clearly, the decision about which tier of entry a pupil should be prepared for is an important one, with serious consequences for the pupil, and it must be made with care.

Non-calculator tests

Most syllabuses now include a non-calculator test. This is usually an aural test, in which a teacher reads the questions to a group of pupils, and pupils have to answer using mental mathematics, estimation and approximation strategies, and sometimes using pencil-and-paper methods for arithmetic. These tests are intended to be given to pupils in their normal teaching groups, but not all schools do this.

Exam boards for GCSE

At the time of writing, there has been a reduction in the number of groups providing examinations for GCSE and A level, as well as vocational qualifications. There are now three groups, but there may be a further rationalisation in the next two or three years. At present, the examination groups for GCSE are:

- Northern Examination and Assessment Board (NEAB), which operates as part of the Assessment and Qualifications Alliance (AQA);
- Southern Examining Group (SEG), an offshoot of the Associated Examination Board (AEB), which also now operates as part of the AQA;
- Midland Examining Group (MEG), which is centred in Cambridge and now operates as part of the Oxford and Cambridge Examinations and Assessment Council (OCEAC);
- EDEXCEL, the result of a merger between the University of London Examination and Assessment Council and the Business and Technician Education Council (BTEC).

Table 6.3 GCSE criteria for mathematics

Aims

The aims of all syllabuses must be consistent with National Curriculum requirements.

Assessment objectives

A syllabus must require candidates to demonstrate their ability to:

i *Using and Applying Mathematics*
- make and monitor decisions to solve problems
- communicate mathematically
- develop skills of mathematical reasoning

ii *Number and Algebra*
- understand place value and the decimal number system
- understand and use relationships between numbers and develop methods of computation
- solve numerical problems
- understand and use functional relationships
- understand and use equations and formulae

iii *Shape, Space and Measures*
- understand and use properties of shape
- understand and use properties of position, movement and transformation
- understand and use measures

iv *Handling data*
- collect, process, represent and interpret data
- estimate and calculate the probabilities of events

Using and Applying Mathematics must be assessed in contexts provided by the other assessment objectives.

Schemes of assessment

Externally assessed components must have three tiers of assessment:

- a Foundation tier awarding grades G–D
- an Intermediate tier awarding grades E–B
- a Higher tier awarding grades C–A

Source: SCAA, 1995c, p. 57

Table 6.4 GCSE grade C description

Using and Applying

Starting from problems or contexts that have been presented to them, candidates introduce questions of their own which generate a fuller solution. They examine critically and justify their choice of mathematical presentation, considering alternative approaches, and explaining improvements they have made. Candidates justify their generalisations or solutions, showing some insight into the mathematical structure of the situation being investigated. They appreciate the difference between mathematical explanation and experimental evidence.

Number and Algebra

In making estimates, candidates round to one significant figure and multiply and divide mentally. They solve numerical problems involving multiplication and division with numbers of any size using a calculator efficiently and appropriately. They understand the effect of multiplying and dividing by numbers between 0 and 1. Candidates evaluate one number as a fraction or percentage of another. They understand and use the equivalences between fractions, decimals and percentages and calculate using ratios in appropriate situations. They understand and use proportional changes. Candidates find and describe in symbols the next term or the *n*th term of a sequence, where the rule is quadratic. They solve simple polynomial equations by trial and improvement and represent inequalities using a number line. They formulate and solve linear equations with whole number coefficients. They manipulate simple algebraic formulae, equations and expressions.

Shape, Space and Measures

Candidates solve problems using angle and symmetry properties of polygons and properties of intersecting and parallel lines. They understand and apply Pythagoras' theorem when solving problems in 2-D. Candidates find areas and circumferences of circles. They calculate lengths, areas and volumes in plane shapes and right prisms. Candidates enlarge shapes by a positive whole number or fractional scale factor. They appreciate the continuous nature of measurement and recognise that a measurement given to the nearest whole number may be inaccurate by up to one half in either direction. They understand and use compound measures such as speed. They use sine, cosine and tangent in right-angled triangles when solving problems in 2-D.

Handling Data

Candidates construct and interpret frequency diagrams. They specify hypotheses and test them. They determine the modal class and estimate the mean, median and range of a set of grouped data, selecting the statistic most appropriate to their line of enquiry. They use measures of average and range with associated frequency polygons, as appropriate, to compare distributions. They draw a line of best fit on a scatter diagram by inspection. Candidates understand relative frequency as an estimate of probability and use this to compare outcomes of experiments.

Source: SCAA, 1995c, pp. 59–60

Each examining group may have two, or even three, syllabuses for mathematics, so there is still some considerable choice available to schools. Each GCSE mathematics syllabus has to be approved by the QCA, so the various syllabuses have much in common with each other, but there are still some significant differences.

Task 6.9 Comparing different syllabuses

In this task, you will find out which GCSE mathematics syllabuses are used in your school and which GCSE Examining Groups are used. You will consider the syllabuses, their content and the different methods of assessment, and the reasons for choosing a particular syllabus.

1 Ask your tutor if the school can give you a copy of each of the syllabuses available for mathematics. (If necessary, contact the GCSE Examining Group used in your school to obtain copies of the mathematics syllabuses.) Study these carefully to identify what are the similarities and differences between the requirements. Look particularly at the elements that make up the assessment package: module tests, mental or aural tests, coursework, end of Key Stage examinations.

   As an extension of this, to enrich your own awareness of the range of options available, you might like to contact each of the GCSE examining groups to ask for a copy of each of the GCSE mathematics syllabuses they offer.

2 Arrange to talk to the Head of Mathematics in your school about the GCSE syllabuses used. Discuss the reasons for choosing the examining Group and the syllabus. Try to identify how the departmental work in Years 10 and 11 is affected by the chosen syllabus.

3 What boards do other subjects use? Ask some other Heads of Department in your school how they choose between exam boards and syllabuses; try to find out some of the reasons behind the choices they make.

The final preparation for public examinations brings a different set of priorities. Revision for examinations and the development of exam technique are important aspects of your work with GCSE groups in the final months of Year 11. Pupils need help to maximise their performance in the examination. They need to be totally familiar with what is expected of them in the exam, with the style of questions, and with precisely what is in the syllabus. The teacher is clearly responsible for ensuring that the pupils have covered the whole syllabus, but in the final weeks it is appropriate to focus closely: to show pupils the syllabus; to study past papers; and to look at past exam questions that address particular syllabus topics.

Coursework

The examining groups offer a choice between syllabuses that provide for coursework tasks to be set and marked by the examining group, and syllabuses that require the school to set and mark appropriate tasks using general coursework assessment criteria provided by the examining group. Coursework tasks are to be carried out under normal classroom conditions, with sufficient supervision to allow the teacher to be sure that the work is that of the individual pupil. The examining groups encourage teachers to create their own tasks, and the school has to ensure that the tasks chosen will allow the pupils to perform to their potential against the coursework assessment criteria. Some syllabuses provide suggestions for suitable tasks and task-specific marking guides.

Coursework tasks in mathematics usually require pupils to engage in some extended work of an open-ended nature for between one and three weeks of lesson and homework time. Achievement at the higher grades of GCSE is likely to require more persistent effort over the period of the task.

The main purpose of coursework tasks is to assess the pupil's attainment in Ma1; the assessment criteria are taken from the level descriptions for the Mathematics National Curriculum for England and Wales. A pupil's work is assessed in terms of three strands, which correspond to the three areas in the programme of study for Using and Applying Mathematics at Key Stages 3 and 4:

- Making and monitoring decisions to solve problems;
- Communicating mathematically;
- Developing skills of mathematical reasoning.

The table of nationally agreed assessment criteria for coursework tasks in mathematics is shown in Table 6.5.

There are two important factors that the teacher needs to consider when selecting an appropriate task for pupils to work on as a GCSE coursework task. First, the task needs to provide a fair opportunity for pupils to achieve at different levels; there must not be a ceiling level of achievement that will be achieved by many pupils, beyond which it is difficult to go. Second, the task needs to provide opportunity for achievement in each of the three strands of Ma1. With experience, you will be able to identify appropriate tasks more readily. However, it is always valuable to consult with members of the department about the choice of coursework tasks.

It is the responsibility of the teacher to ensure that the work submitted by each pupil is genuinely the pupil's own. There are strategies that can help to monitor this. One idea is to use a standard planning sheet on which each pupil has to submit their plan for how they will tackle the task. In addition to monitoring each pupil's work on the task, this has the added benefit of helping to ensure that each pupil has a realistic approach to enter the task. Further monitoring can be conducted through a progress sheet that always accompanies the pupil's coursework. This sheet can be used to record ongoing dialogue between the teacher and pupil as the work progresses, and pupils can be required to keep a record of any progress they make on the task outside school, and of any resources used or consulted in the work.

Sometimes a pupil will need significant help with the task to make any progress. When this is the case, it is important that the pupil is enabled to get started. However, it is also important to keep a record of the specific help given

Table 6.5 Coursework assessment criteria for GCSE mathematics

Mark	*Making and monitoring decisions to solve problems*	*Communicating mathematically*	*Developing skills of mathematical reasoning*
1	Candidates try different approaches and find ways of overcoming difficulties that arise when they are solving problems. They are beginning to organise their work and check results.	Candidates discuss their mathematical work and are beginning to explain their thinking. They use and interpret mathematical symbols and diagrams.	Candidates show that they understand a general statement by finding particular examples that match it.
2	Candidates are developing their own strategies for solving problems and are using these strategies both in working within mathematics and in applying mathematics to practical contexts.	Candidates present information and results in a clear and organised way, explaining the reasons for their presentation.	Candidates search for a pattern by trying out ideas of their own.
3	In order to carry through tasks and solve mathematical problems, candidates identify and obtain necessary information; they check their results considering whether these are sensible.	Candidates show understanding of situations by describing them mathematically using symbols, words and diagrams.	Candidates make general statements of their own, based on evidence they have produced, and give an explanation of their reasoning.
4	Candidates carry through substantial tasks and solve quite complex problems by breaking them down into smaller, more manageable tasks.	Candidates interpret, discuss and synthesise information presented in a variety of mathematical forms. Their writing explains and informs their use of diagrams.	Candidates are beginning to give a mathematical justification for their generalisations; they test them by checking particular cases.

continued . . .

Table 6.5 Coursework assessment criteria for GCSE mathematics (continued)

Mark	*Making and monitoring decisions to solve problems*	*Communicating mathematically*	*Developing skills of mathematical reasoning*
5	Starting from problems or contexts that have been presented to them, candidates introduce questions of their own, which generate fuller solutions.	Candidates examine critically and justify their choice of mathematical presentation, considering alternative approaches and explaining improvements they have made.	Candidates justify their generalisations or solutions, showing some insight into the mathematical structure of the situation being investigated. They appreciate the difference between mathematical explanation and experimental evidence.
6	Candidates develop and follow alternative approaches. They reflect on their own lines of enquiry when exploring mathematical tasks; in doing so they introduce and use a range of mathematical techniques.	Candidates convey mathematical meaning through consistent use of symbols.	Candidates examine generalisations or solutions reached in an activity, commenting constructively on the reasoning and logic employed, and make further progress on the activity as a result.
7	Candidates analyse alternative approaches to problems involving a number of features or variables. They give detailed reasons for following or rejecting particular lines of enquiry.	Candidates use mathematical language and symbols accurately in presenting a convincing reasoned argument.	Candidates' reports include mathematical justifications, explaining their solutions to problems involving a number of features or variables.
8	Candidates consider and evaluate a number of approaches to a substantial task. They explore extensively a context or area of mathematics with which they are unfamiliar. They apply independently a range of appropriate mathematical techniques.	Candidates use mathematical language and symbols efficiently in presenting a concise reasoned argument.	Candidates provide a mathematically rigorous justification or proof of their solution to a complex problem, considering the conditions under which it remains valid.

to the pupil. This record can then be consulted and considered when assessing the work.

Some of the exam groups distinguish between different types of coursework task. One classification is: pure maths investigation; statistical task; and design task. Essentially, these differ in the area of mathematical content that they relate to: investigations usually relate to number and algebra; statistical tasks are usually related to data handling; and design tasks relate mainly to shape, space and measures.

When the work is marked, it is important that the teachers in the mathematics department work together to moderate each other's work. When you mark a piece of work, it is often helpful to annotate the pupil's script to show where you have found the evidence to justify the mark awarded. When the marks are agreed by the members of the department, a sample of the scripts will be sent to the exam group for external moderation.

Entry policies

Pupils with special educational needs – whether those with specific learning difficulties or the exceptionally gifted – may need special treatment in assessment, especially in public assessment such as GCSE. There is a small proportion of pupils amongst the most able and the least able, whose needs are not met by the standard National Curriculum assessment arrangements. Some schools have policies for early GCSE entry of high attainers in mathematics. This can have the benefit of ensuring that the able pupils are challenged, but it can also be divisive and sometimes leads to an environment in which pupils are encouraged to enter early for the GCSE when it may not be desirable. The tiers of entry in GCSE can have a similar result at different levels of ability, as pupils who may be best entered for the Foundation or Intermediate levels of entry experience pressure from peers, parents or teachers to enter a higher tier. Remember that the intention of GCSE is to optimise attainment and to enable pupils to experience success. When pupils are entered inappropriately for higher levels, they are likely to experience failure, which can be demotivating.

In many schools, pupils who are not entered for GCSE at age 16 follow courses leading to GNVQ or NVQ. These are part of a curriculum for ages 14 to 19, and they are discussed in Chapter 11. However, there are some assessment schemes run by the GCSE examination groups that are intended for the lower attainers at age 16. These awards are called 'Certificate of Achievement: Mathematics', and are intended to provide appropriate assessment for pupils at Key Stage 4 who are achieving at levels 1 to 3 of the National Curriculum.

Issues of fairness

Within any system of selection and grading in a school, it is very important that every care is taken to ensure that no individual is disadvantaged for any reason. Unfortunately, this high ideal is often challenged in unexpected ways, so it is important that teachers remain alert to the possibility of inequity in their classrooms. In mathematics, pupils for whom English is a second language may experience difficulties with understanding what is required of them in assessed tasks, because of their difficulties in understanding English.

Schools often have a significant role in deciding which tier of GCSE mathematics a pupil will be entered for, and this decision is sometimes made several years before the GCSE examination. The basis for these decisions is often assessments made by the mathematics teachers during Key Stage 3. Hence, even assessments made in the classroom during Key Stage 3 need to be monitored to ensure that they are being made fairly and equitably.

Task 6.10 Departmental entry policy at age 16

Talk to the Head of Mathematics in your school about the policy for assessment of mathematics at age 16.

- What levels of entry in the assessment are pupils entered for?
- How does the department decide, for each pupil, which level of entry to enter?
- What assessment arrangements are made for pupils at the extremes: those who will struggle with the lowest level of entry at GCSE, and those for whom GCSE is too easy?

SUMMARY

A particularly relevant issue for you, as a future mathematics teacher, is how to manage your time effectively. Assessing pupils' work in mathematics can become a full-time job on its own if you attempt to mark and correct in detail every piece of mathematical work ever done by a pupil. On the other hand, inadequate marking often leads to poor planning of lessons, poor motivation on the part of pupils and under-achievement. It is therefore very important that you learn how to decide which pieces of work to assess, and in how much detail. 'There is no statutory requirement to keep detailed records or evidence on every pupil' (SCAA, 1995a and b, p. i). This means that you need to be clear about your purposes in assessing, and tailor the feedback you provide to meet your purposes.

What is required is a decision as to which of the level descriptions best describes the overall performance of an individual pupil in each Attainment Target. However, you do need to be able to discuss a pupil's mathematical work with parents and with other teachers, so it is advisable to keep reliable and manageable records.

FURTHER READING

Ollerton, M. (1991) 'Teaching versus assessment', *Mathematics Teaching* **135**, 4–6.
In this article from the early days of the National Curriculum, Mike Ollerton argues the case for a holistic approach to assessment.

QCA (1998) *Standards at Key Stage 3 Mathematics: Report on the 1997 National Curriculum Assessments for 14-Year-Olds*, London: School Curriculum and Assessment Authority.
In recent years, SCAA, and now QCA, have published reports on the National Curriculum assessments of 14-year-olds at the end of Key Stage 3. This document is the most recent at the time of writing, and they give a useful analysis of how the questions on the SATs were answered by pupils across the country. There are indications of the common errors made by pupils at different levels of attainment, and suggestions about the implications for teaching and learning. These reports are worth following.

SCAA (1995a) *Consistency in Teacher Assessment, Exemplification of Standards, Mathematics: Key Stage 3, Levels 1 to 3*, London: HMSO.

SCAA (1995b) *Consistency in Teacher Assessment, Exemplification of Standards, Mathematics: Key Stage 3, Levels 4 to 8*, London: HMSO.
SCAA has produced these two booklets to show what the standards set out in the level descriptions mean in practice, and how to use the level descriptions to make accurate and consistent judgements. Examples of pupil work are included.

SCAA (1997a) *Standards at Key Stage 3 Mathematics: Report on the 1996 National Curriculum Assessments for 14-Year-Olds*, London: School Curriculum and Assessment Authority.
This book provides a commentary on the national assessments for England in mathematics at the end of Key Stage 3 in 1996. It is similar to QCA (1998), which is described above.

Webb, N. L. (ed.) (1993) *Assessment in the Mathematics Classroom; 1993 Yearbook of the National Council of Teachers of Mathematics*, Reston, VA: NCTM.
This is the 1993 yearbook of the National Council for Teachers of Mathematics (NCTM). It contains chapters that discuss many important issues relating to assessment of mathematics. The chapters consider the assessment of pupils from age 5 to 18. The main focus is on assessment methods that can be used by teachers to assess the pupils in their own classes. Many of the chapters are from North American authors, but they are still of interest in other contexts.

7 Communicating Mathematically

Candia Morgan

INTRODUCTION

Most of the activities involved in the teaching and learning of mathematics involve some form of communication: between teacher and pupil(s), between pupils, between pupil and text, between pupil and computer. There is oral communication (speaking and listening) and written communication (reading and writing). Much the same might be said of teaching and learning in many other subject areas, but there are special features of mathematics classrooms and mathematical language that make communication a particularly significant issue for mathematics teachers. Whilst all teachers have a responsibility for enhancing pupils' general use of spoken and written language, as a mathematics teacher you have a particular responsibility to help pupils to learn to speak and write *mathematically*.

Many beginning teachers see an ability to explain mathematical concepts and procedures clearly as the most important quality of a teacher. Being able to make good use of language yourself is, of course, an essential skill for a teacher. It is important, however, to remember that you cannot assume that when you tell a child something, however clearly, they will necessarily hear and understand what you intended to communicate. Similarly, it is always useful to bear in mind that a child may not find it easy to communicate their state of mathematical understanding to you.

Learning mathematics is sometimes compared with learning a foreign language. Certainly, it can be mystifying for those who are unfamiliar with its vocabulary and grammar, whilst becoming fluent at speaking and writing as well as listening and reading can open up new possibilities for creating and communicating mathematical ideas.

OBJECTIVES

By the end of this chapter, you should:

- have considered the special nature of mathematical communication and the ways in which the use of language in the classroom may help or hinder the learning of mathematics;
- be aware of some similarities and differences between speech and writing in relation to the mathematics classroom;
- be able to think about the special nature of the language that is used to talk, write and think about mathematics;
- have encountered some ways in which children may be helped to learn to communicate effectively about mathematics.

THE NATURE OF MATHEMATICAL LANGUAGE

Task 7.1 Reflecting on experiences of mathematical language

Think back to your own experiences as a learner of mathematics. Try to remember some of the different ways in which you were involved in communication – listening, speaking, reading and writing.

- What was particularly mathematical about the language used?
- When you first encountered new terms or forms of language, how did you feel?
- What did you find difficult or challenging?

Like other specialised areas of human activity, mathematics has special forms and ways of using language that make it possible to communicate specifically mathematical ideas. As mathematics has developed through history, mathematicians have developed new words (or new meanings for old words), new notations and conventional styles of argument with which to think about and communicate new mathematical ideas and ways of thinking. This process of linguistic creation is still continuing; *fractal* (a newly invented word) and *fuzzy logic* (a new application or extension of old words) are but two relatively recent examples. Learning to understand and to use this mathematical language is an essential part of learning mathematics. For those of us who have succeeded in becoming competent mathematicians, it is often difficult to realise how unfamiliar and confusing this special language can seem to those who are still struggling to learn how to use it. Reflecting on the nature of mathematical language can provide you with some insight into the problems it may cause your pupils. It is therefore worth taking a look at some of its characteristics and at its relationship with the everyday knowledge of language that pupils bring with them into the classroom.

Mathematical English

One of the most obvious places to start is with the *vocabulary* of mathematics. Mathematics educator David Pimm (1987) distinguishes between words that are unlikely to be encountered outside the mathematics classroom (e.g. *quadrilateral, parallelogram, hypotenuse*) and those that have been 'borrowed' from everyday English (e.g. *face, power, product, rational*). Unfamiliar words may cause difficulties for learners simply because of their unfamiliarity; moreover, they are often long, multi-syllabic and difficult to pronounce and spell. Few pupils (or teachers?) nowadays have the familiarity with the Latin or Greek roots of many of these words that might help in constructing and remembering their meanings (e.g. *isosceles* from Greek *iso* – equal and *skelos* – leg; *tangent* from Latin *tangere* – to touch).

Borrowed 'everyday' words, whilst apparently more familiar, can bring with them their own problems, simply because their mathematical meanings are subtly different from their everyday meanings. In some cases, pupils' ability to come to terms with specialist mathematical uses of language may be further complicated by the emotional charges associated with words such as *odd, vulgar, improper, irrational.* The negative connotations of such terms can prevent a pupil from attending to their 'pure' mathematical meanings alone.

To give a common example of the ways in which everyday meanings may interfere with precise mathematical usage, many secondary pupils will understand *straight* lines to be those that are drawn straight up and down or straight across the page (i.e. vertical or horizontal). For such pupils, *straight* may be seen to be opposed to *diagonal.* This can lead to further problems when dealing with the *diagonals* of polygons. Thus, Pimm (1987, pp. 84–85) describes the work of a girl who saw one rectangle as having no diagonals whilst claiming that another had four (Figure 7.1).

It is not only less-able learners who have such difficulties with mathematical language. A study of sixteen high-attaining Year 9 pupils, working on a problem

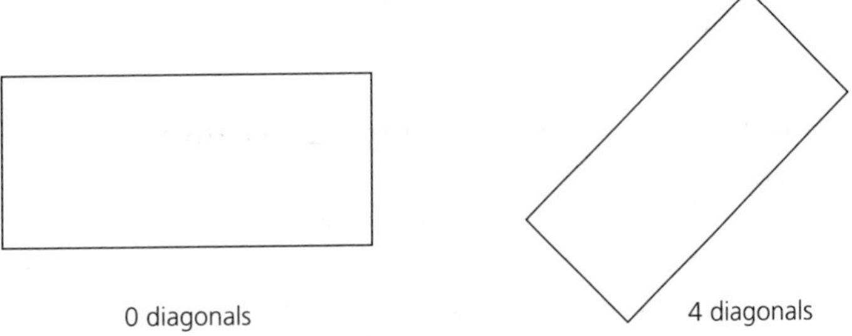

Figure 7.1 How many diagonals?

about the diagonals of polygons (Morgan, 1988), revealed that, between them, they interpreted the word *diagonal* in at least six different ways, only one of which was the conventional mathematical meaning.

A particular area of potential difficulty is in the precise ways in which mathematical logic uses 'little' words like *and, or, some, all* or *any*. For example, when faced with a problem like: 'Show that the sum of any two odd numbers is an even number', some pupils will believe that they have answered satisfactorily if they give an example such as $3 + 5 = 8$. This may indicate that the pupil giving such an answer believes that a single example is enough to prove a general statement. On the other hand, it may be that they have understood the problem to be asking them to provide *any* example that confirms the statement. In mathematical discourse, the convention is that *any* is used to indicate generality, whereas in everyday discourse it tends to indicate mere arbitrariness (e.g. 'any old one will do'). When evaluating pupils' work, it is important for you to consider how they may have understood the question. In this case, you cannot know (without further investigation) whether the problem lies in the pupil's understanding of the nature of mathematical proof or in their understanding of the conventions of mathematical language.

Task 7.2 Identifying mathematical language

Take a chapter in a textbook or a set of workcards on a topic that you will be teaching to one of your classes in the near future, and consider the following questions.

1 What specialist mathematical vocabulary or special uses of familiar words are employed in the text?
2 How much of this would you expect all pupils in the class to be familiar with before starting the topic? What specialist vocabulary and uses of language would you expect to be new or unfamiliar to the pupils? What sort of problems in understanding might this cause for your pupils? How important is it to their learning of this topic at this stage that they should learn this new language?
3 How does the textbook or workcard introduce new language to the pupils? How might you help pupils to develop the necessary language when you are teaching this topic?

Non-verbal forms of written communication

As well as the specialised use of verbal language discussed above, much written mathematical communication is characterised by its use of symbolism and graphic components such as diagrams and graphs. Whilst such forms of communication are very powerful for expressing mathematical ideas, they can also be obscure or confusing for learners who are not familiar with the conventions of the system.

Algebraic symbolism

It is not possible here to give a detailed analysis of the characteristics of the mathematical symbol system or of the difficulties for learners that it may cause. Such an analysis may be found in Pimm (1987). I will, however, highlight a few of the issues of which mathematics teachers need to be aware.

1 Reading text that includes mathematical symbols involves different skills from those needed for ordinary verbal texts (Shuard and Rothery, 1984). Whereas ordinary English text can be read, in order, from left to right, some arrangements of symbols require the reader to attend to the components in a non-linear way. For example:

$$\left(\frac{3}{4} + 5\right)^2 \text{ or } \int_1^6 \frac{1}{x^2}\,dx \text{ or } \frac{6x + 4}{7x^2 - 3}$$

2 It is also important to remember that some learners will find it difficult to cope with symbols if they do not have any way of articulating them – reading them aloud to themselves or to others. The introduction of Greek letters (e.g. α, θ, Σ) should not, therefore, be seen as a simple extension of pupils' existing familiarity with algebraic symbolism. It may be necessary to pay attention to helping pupils to develop ways of talking and thinking with these symbols.

3 The commonly used 'metaphor' that algebraic symbols are 'shorthand' (e.g. *a* stands for apples, *b* for bananas) does not provide a sound conceptual base for the idea of letters as variables, and may contribute to some of the common difficulties that pupils have with algebra (Nolder, 1991).

Ways of working in the classroom to develop pupils' use of symbolism will be discussed later in this chapter.

Task 7.3 Reading symbols in words

To add to pupils' difficulties with symbolic expressions, there is not always even a single 'correct' way to say them aloud. Ask some pupils and teachers to read these expressions aloud to you, and listen carefully to the words each of them uses:

$$2(x + 3), \quad \frac{(3x - 4)}{2}, \quad (A \cap B) \cup C, \quad \sin^2 2x$$

What implications might such diversity have for learners and how might you deal with it in the classroom?

Graphs and diagrams

Although many other kinds of texts include graphical elements, in most cases these are used to supplement or illustrate information contained in verbal form elsewhere in the text. In mathematics, however, graphs, tables and diagrams are often used independently to communicate information that may not be available in any other form. Again, we cannot assume that pupils will naturally pick up the skills needed to make sense of such diagrammatic forms. Indeed, there is considerable evidence that many secondary pupils do not read graphs in the conventional mathematical way. For example, the CSMS study (Concepts in Secondary Mathematics and Science – see Hart, 1981) found a substantial proportion of 13–15-year-olds who read distance–time graphs as if they were pictures of a journey. Thus, the journey shown by the graph in Figure 7.2 was described as 'climbing a mountain' or 'going up, going down, then up again' (Kerslake, 1981). As well as learning to read and interpret the values of separate points on a graph, pupils also need to learn how to interpret its overall shape.

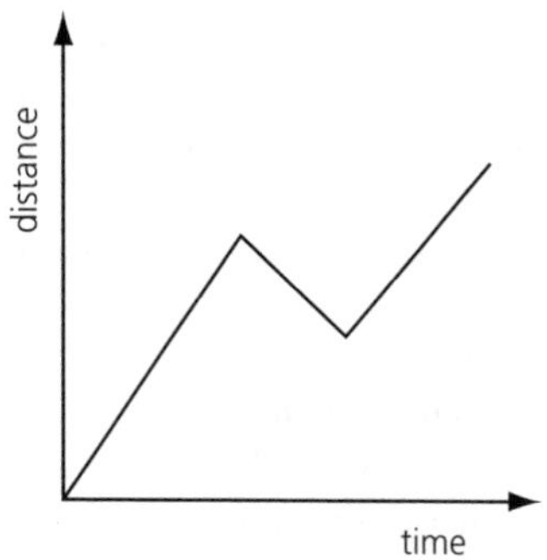

Figure 7.2 A distance–time graph

Mathematical diagrams, too, need to be read in specialised ways. Remember the girl who saw one rectangle as having no diagonals whilst another had four? For her, the different orientation of the diagram seems to mean that the two rectangles are different kinds of objects with different properties. The conventional mathematical way of reading such diagrams, however, assumes that, unless otherwise specified, orientation and size (and often other characteristics such as angle) are irrelevant.

Task 7.4 Analysing diagrams

Find a geometric diagram in a textbook you are using (e.g. a diagram illustrating a circle theorem).

Which characteristics of this diagram are essential and which are irrelevant, i.e. could be changed without affecting the mathematics?

How might you help pupils to see the diagram the same way that you do?

The reader is supposed to attend to only a subset of the physical properties of the diagram – it is not a picture of a concrete object, but a representation of an abstract idea. Again, pupils need to be helped to learn how to make sense of mathematical diagrams.

TALKING MATHEMATICS

A lot of talking goes on in many mathematics lessons, as in lessons of other subjects. It is important to ask, however, how much of this talking is likely to be productive for pupils' learning of mathematics and of mathematical language. Much of the talking is done by teachers. As we have seen, there are many areas in which it is possible for teachers' talk to be misunderstood, so we should look at how teachers may try to ensure that pupils do understand and improve their knowledge of spoken mathematical language. It is also relevant to consider ways in which pupils may themselves be involved actively in speaking mathematically, through conversation or discussion with the teacher or other pupils.

One of the main ways in which many teachers try to ensure that pupils are listening actively and making sense of what is being said is through the use of questioning or teacher–pupil discussion, expecting pupils to contribute to the joint construction of the exposition of a topic. It is widely recognised that discussion can play an important part in the mathematics classroom. The Cockcroft Report included 'discussion' as one of the ways of working that all pupils should experience, seeing it as a means of developing the precision needed for communicating mathematical ideas:

> The ability to 'say what you mean and mean what you say' should be one of the outcomes of good mathematics teaching. This ability develops as a result of opportunities to talk about mathematics, to explain and discuss results that have been obtained, and to test hypotheses.
>
> (DES, 1982, para. 246)

Moreover, discussion between pupils or between pupils and teacher can be a good way of exploring and developing pupils' concepts and their awareness of relationships between different areas of mathematics.

At the same time, however, there is not a clear consensus among teachers about what it might mean to 'discuss' in the mathematics classroom. Some seem to interpret *any* verbal interaction as discussion, including conventional question-and-answer sequences. Sometimes, however, the pupils' side of such interaction consists only of 'guessing what is in the teacher's mind', and can be little more than 'filling in the gap' left by the teacher. This may be useful for the teacher to check that pupils are following the lesson, and may be effective for reinforcing the use of correct vocabulary, but it is less likely to involve pupils in higher-level thinking or to encourage them to use and develop other aspects of the language needed to express more complex mathematical ideas and reasoning.

For such purposes, the questioning teacher needs to create opportunities for pupils to think and to formulate contributions in their own words. This means asking more searching questions that demand higher-level thinking rather than straightforward recall (for example, questions that ask for observations, comparisons, explanations). It also means allowing pupils time to think about their answers. If an answer is not volunteered straight away, the silence that ensues can seem threatening to both teacher and pupils, and it can often then be tempting to make the question less demanding or to provide one's own answer. More searching questions, however, need to be thought about before an answer is given, in order to work out not only what needs to be said but also the words with which to say it. One way of dealing with this is to develop a culture in your classroom that values thinking before talking. One teacher, described by Jaworski (1992), achieved this by introducing the idea of a 'hands-down think' after such a question had been posed; the pupils knew that they were then expected to think seriously about the question and that their contributions would be valued.

Task 7.5 Observing classroom language

Arrange to observe another mathematics teacher's lesson. Focus on the ways in which they use questioning. Note how they use questions:

1 to assess pupils' understanding or knowledge;
2 to prompt exploration of an idea or problem.

What sort of responses are expected of pupils? How long does the teacher give pupils to formulate their responses? What opportunities do they get to develop and practise their use of mathematical language?

Reflect on your observations of other teachers (including those of other subjects). What similarities and differences are there between teachers in the ways they use questioning? Why might this be?

Communication between teacher and pupil, whilst an essential component of every classroom, is not always the best way to develop pupils' use of precise mathematical language. The pupil usually feels that the teacher has a good knowledge of what they are trying to say, and the teacher usually works quite hard to understand what the pupil is saying, drawing on expectations of mathematical correctness and past experience. A joint understanding of what is being said may thus be constructed *without* the pupil having to produce a complete and exact verbal statement.

In order to develop more complete verbal communication skills, it can be helpful to create situations in the classroom where the pupil is trying to communicate with someone (often another pupil) who does not have this sort of prior knowledge of what is being communicated. For example, when working with three-dimensional shapes, one pupil may be asked to construct an object using eight interlocking cubes and then describe it (without showing it) to a partner who must construct the same object from the verbal description. This task includes its own automatic feedback: the partner will ask for further clarification if necessary, and the match or mismatch between the two objects will reveal whether or not the communication has been successful.

The poster lesson using a poster of the great stellated dodecahedron, which was described and discussed in Chapter 4, is a whole-class task requiring the same sort of precision of language.

Task 7.6 Discussion to develop use of language

Plan a lesson for a small group of pupils that will involve them in discussion with you or with each other and that will require them to use mathematical language correctly and with precision (some useful suggestions may be found in the Mathematical Association (1987) publication *Maths Talk*).

You will need to consider:

1 what the topic of discussion will be;
2 what sorts of things the pupils might be expected to say;
3 the social context of the discussion – what is the purpose for the pupils of communicating with each other or with you?
4 providing a *context* that requires correctness and precision in order to communicate (not just as an arbitrary requirement on the teacher's part).

After the lesson, reflect on the extent to which the activity you designed succeeded in encouraging the pupils to use mathematical language effectively.

WRITING MATHEMATICALLY

Until relatively recently, very limited writing took place in secondary school mathematics classrooms. The situation has changed, however, since the introduction of coursework for GCSE examinations in England and Wales and the requirement introduced by that National Curriculum for all pupils to be able to demonstrate their mathematical processes of Using and Applying Mathematics (Attainment Target 1), including explanation and justification. Most secondary pupils are now expected to produce quite lengthy pieces of writing, reporting on their work on mathematical tasks. Many find this a difficult task; even some of those who are otherwise very successful in mathematics may have difficulty constructing effective reports of their mathematical activity.

Writing explanations and justifications is particularly challenging for many pupils, including those who might be able to construct an adequate explanation in a verbal dialogue with their teacher or another pupil. The analysis of pupils' answers to the 1996 Key Stage 3 tests (SCAA, 1997a) reported that few pupils responded adequately to those questions that demanded written description or explanation, and that many left these sections out completely. Whilst explanation and justification may be difficult in themselves, the requirement to write about them seems to make the task even harder. In this section, some of the more troublesome characteristics of mathematical writing will be outlined, together with some discussion of ways of supporting pupils as they learn to write mathematically.

Task 7.7 Writing mathematically

It is likely that you yourself will have had little experience of mathematical writing of the sort your pupils may be expected to do. Here are some suggestions of different kinds of starting points for writing. Try some of them for yourself and, when you have done so, reflect on:

- how this mathematical writing is different from other kinds of writing you do;
- the mathematical thinking you had to do in order to write effectively;
- how these starting points might be adapted for use with pupils in the classroom.

1. Write interesting statements starting 'Circles . . . '.
2. Factorise the expression $7x^2 - 62x + 48$. Explain how you did this. Describe your general strategies for factorising quadratic expressions efficiently.
3. 'The mean is the most useful measure of central tendency.' Discuss.
4. Explain why the sum of three consecutive integers is always divisible by three.

If you can work with another mathematics student teacher, read each other's pieces of writing, identify similarities and differences, and consider how your writing might be improved by redrafting; alternatively, a colleague in your school might help.

It is sometimes argued that it is the English teacher's job to teach pupils to write – mathematics teachers have neither the time nor the expertise. It might be convenient to believe this; however, it is clear that English teachers do not on the whole have the expertise themselves to teach pupils how to write mathematically (nor the time to devote to the specialised needs of every area of the school curriculum). The forms of language needed to construct a concise and precise mathematical definition or a rigorous justification are different from those required in everyday or literary writing or, indeed, in other subject disciplines. Moreover, it is not possible to judge the complete effectiveness of a written definition or justification without the sort of mathematical content knowledge that belongs to the mathematics teacher's expertise. This is not to say that the English teacher has nothing to offer. Indeed, collaboration with language specialists can be a very valuable experience both for the pupils and for the teachers involved. See, for example, Lawson and Lee's (1995) description of the support provided by an English teacher during a mathematical investigation, and the account of partnership teaching by a mathematics teacher and a language support teacher given in the Association of Teachers of Mathematics booklet *Talking Maths, Talking Languages* (ATM, 1993a).

An example of the way in which learning about the forms of language needed to express definitions can happen alongside learning about the concept being defined is offered by American maths educator Raffaella Borasi (1992) in her book *Learning Mathematics Through Inquiry*. She collected definitions of the concept *circle* from her students, getting typical responses like the following.

- All the possible series of points equidistant from a single point.
- πr^2 area formula, = radius, an exact centre, 360°.
- Round – 3.14 – shape of an orange, coin, earth – pi.
- Circle = something whose area is = to πr^2.
- A closed, continuous, rounded line.

The students were then asked to discuss and produce a critique of the written definitions, identifying which were precise enough to make a distinction between circles and non-circles. The discussion with the teacher also addressed the difference between a definition and a list of properties. One outcome of such discussion can be an agreed, revised definition that is acceptable to all the students as well as to the teacher. Because all the students have been involved in the writing and rewriting of this definition (rather than merely reading or copying a definition given by their textbook or teacher), they are not only more likely to understand and remember the concept itself but are also likely to have learnt something about the ways in which mathematical definitions ought to be written. You cannot assume that children will learn to write mathematically merely by engaging in writing. Talking together with other pupils and/or with a teacher, and drafting and redrafting in a group can provide much needed support and feedback and increase awareness of the requirements of effective communication.

Communicating using algebraic notation

If you ask adults who have not been successful at learning mathematics about their experiences and feelings in the mathematics classroom, you will often get a response that refers to *x*s and *y*s as a major source of mystification. In some cases, the introduction of algebraic notation early in the secondary school is felt to have been the turning point at which an otherwise academically successful student started to fail in mathematics. To many people, symbols appear to have little meaning, and attempting to work with them may be a frustrating and anxiety-inducing activity. At the same time, however, algebraic symbolism is enormously important in mathematics, not only as a means of expressing generalisation but also as a means of thinking about and manipulating problems that might otherwise prove intractable. It is, therefore, important to help pupils to develop meaning for symbols and to see them as useful means of communicating mathematical ideas.

One way of demystifying symbolism is to introduce it as a natural development of pupils' own attempts to record their generalisations of patterns. James and Mason (1982) describe the process by which some children's verbal explanations of how to build square 'picture frames' out of interlocking cubes were converted, via the introduction of a 'thinks cloud' standing for the variable size of the picture, into a more conventional algebraic expression (Figure 7.3).

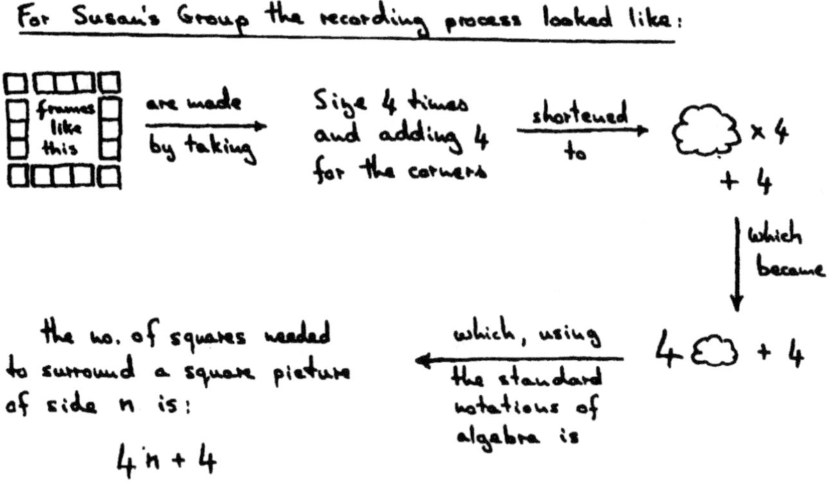

Figure 7.3 Progression towards conventional recording
Source: James and Mason, 1982, p. 257

The teacher's role is crucial here in introducing appropriate forms of notation at a time when the pupils can appreciate a need for them. Through having struggled to produce their own means of recording, and to interpret others' attempts, pupils are more likely to see the usefulness of a standard notation. In this case, an obvious further benefit that the pupils would be able to see is the possibility of comparing different ways of building the picture frames through the use of a common descriptive notation. Such an introduction, building on pupils' own patterning and generalising, should enable pupils to attach meaning to algebraic symbols and to see them as a useful addition to their repertoire of means of communicating mathematical ideas.

COMMUNICATION AS THE KEY TO ASSESSMENT

One very important type of communication that goes on in classrooms is that involved in assessing pupils' understanding. Most of a teacher's knowledge about pupils' achievement is gathered through listening to them talk and reading their written work. When the classroom is full of pupils talking and/or writing about mathematics, one major benefit is the opportunities provided for teachers to listen and read and hence to gain some access to the pupils' understanding of the mathematics. (This is another reason for not spending too much time talking yourself!)

Miller (1992) suggests that the use of short 'writing prompts', getting pupils to write briefly about a specified topic, can not only encourage the pupils to reflect on and hence reinforce what they have learnt, but can also provide the teacher with valuable insight into what pupils have learnt and where they may still have difficulties. For example, you might ask pupils:

- to explain *how* (to add fractions, factorise an algebraic expression, . . .);
- to write *what* they know about a topic (triangles, equations, . . .);
- to explain *why* (a quick way of multiplying a decimal number by 10 is to 'move the point', 50 ÷ 2 is not the same as 2 ÷ 50, . . .).

You must, however, be cautious about relying too much on written forms of communication in order to assess pupils' understanding. Children's written work may not always fully represent what they can do, not only because they lack full familiarity with the necessary forms of language, but also because they may be unsure of what aspects of their work and their thinking need to be recorded.

MacNamara and Roper (1992) describe how they listened in as a pair of children discussed how they should write about their work on a problem. They found that the children decided to omit some of their findings, because they realised that

Task 7.8 Attending to pupils' attempts to communicate

(a) Listening to pupils

Plan to work for one lesson with a pair or small group of pupils working on a problem or investigation (e.g. 'How many different shapes can you make with five cubes?'). Give the pupils some time at the end of the lesson to write about what they have done. If possible, tape record the lesson or take notes about what the pupils say.

After the lesson, listen to the recording and compare this with the pupils' written records. To what extent does their writing give you a full picture of what the pupils achieved during the lesson?

(b) Reading pupils' writing

At the end of a lesson or sequence of lessons, ask pupils to write a few sentences about what they have learnt and what questions they still have about the topic.

What do their responses reveal about (a) their understanding of the topic, and (b) their grasp of mathematical forms of language?

others in the class had also found the same results and felt that they were therefore no longer interesting enough to be communicated. If the teacher had not been near the pair at the crucial moment, their moment of insight into the problem would never have been noticed. It may happen by chance that the teacher is present and listening at such a moment, but think how many conversations between pupils take place out of the teacher's hearing and, in consequence, how many such decisions may be taken unnoticed. It is probably useful, therefore, for the teacher to plan deliberately to talk with small groups of pupils about their on-going work and to provide them with some help in making better decisions about what should be recorded in writing.

SUMMARY

In this chapter, you have been asked to think about the special nature of the language that is used to talk, write and think about mathematics. It is necessary to be aware of the difficulties that mathematical language may cause to learners in the classroom as they struggle to understand their teacher's speech and to read and make sense of the written materials they are expected to respond to during a lesson. As you plan your lessons, one of the factors that should be considered is the language demands on the pupils: how familiar or comfortable are they likely to be with the language they will encounter, and how will you help them to become more fluent in understanding and using it themselves?

The conciseness and precision of mathematical notation, vocabulary, definition and argument are not merely conventional but play important roles in mathematical thinking. You have been introduced to some ways of working with pupils in the classroom to help them to develop mathematical ways of speaking and writing and to appreciate the reasons that mathematical language has developed in these ways. There is, however, a tension between the wish to introduce pupils to conventional mathematical means of communicating and the need to avoid the mystification and consequent anxiety or dislike of the subject that can be induced by using language with which pupils are unfamiliar. It is this tension that you are asked to reflect on in the final task for this chapter.

Task 7.9 Your reflections on the use of 'correct' language

Should we insist that children use 'correct' mathematical language?

Make a list of the reasons why it is important that pupils should learn to use mathematical language.

Make a second list of reasons why it might be better to allow pupils to use non-mathematical language in some circumstances. Give some instances of such circumstances.

Compare your lists and discuss with another student teacher or with a practising mathematics teacher.

FURTHER READING

ATM (1993a) *Talking Maths, Talking Languages*, Derby: Association of Teachers of Mathematics.

This book looks at issues involved for mathematics teachers working in multilingual classrooms. It contains discussion, classroom ideas, case studies and a useful resource list. Although there is a focus on the needs of multilingual learners, there is much here that is equally relevant for all those involved in learning to communicate mathematically.

Connolly, P. and Vilardi, T. (eds) (1989) *Writing to Learn Mathematics and Science*, New York, NY: Teachers College Press.

This is a collection of papers written by teachers (mostly in the United States) who have introduced writing into their mathematics (or science) classrooms. There are lots of ideas of writing activities to use and some useful discussion of ways in which pupils may be helped to write more effectively.

Mathematical Association (1987) *Maths Talk*, Cheltenham: Stanley Thornes.

Although originally aimed at primary teachers, most of this book is equally relevant to mathematics teachers at secondary level. It discusses developing spoken language skills, including issues related to classroom organisation, and offers ideas for starting mathematical discussions.

Pimm, D. (1987) *Speaking Mathematically: Communication in Mathematics Classrooms*, London: Routledge and Kegan Paul.

This comprehensive book provides a thorough analysis of mathematical language and discusses the many ways in which spoken and written language are used in mathematics classrooms and the ways in which this may affect pupils' learning of mathematics.

8 Using Information and Communications Technology (ICT)

Sue Johnston-Wilder and David Pimm

INTRODUCTION

> A new teacher, interested in the possibilities afforded by emerging technology, made no headway until she had a computer of her own at home. She was later loaned a graphic calculator, but it sat in the cupboard until she attended an inspiring workshop; the workshop gave her a vision of possibilities and enabled her to overcome the initial hassle of starting with a portable, but less friendly, piece of technology.

Personal access is a major advantage in allowing teachers the time and space to make good progress in the use of technology. As well as access, you need inspiration to see possibilities for yourself and your class before you can start to make progress along what can at times be a frustrating road. Happily, these days access is relatively easy, and there are inspirational leaders and resources to help you along the way.

In this chapter, you will consider the role of new technologies in the mathematics curriculum. Important resources, whose role you will consider, include: calculators, graphic calculators, graph plotters, spreadsheets, dynamic geometry, small programs (such as the SMILE programs) and programming languages such as Logo. Computer algebra is considered in Chapter 11, although you will see it has possibilities for younger pupils. Throughout the chapter you will look at some important general features of working mathematically with computers:

- learning from feedback;
- observing patterns;
- seeing connections;
- working with dynamic images;
- exploring data;
- teaching the computer.

As in Chapter 4, you will consider different organisational structures for working with ICT in the classroom, such as whole-class, small-group or individual ways of working, whether structured or exploratory. You will be asked to compare and contrast different kinds of software use, some appropriate and some inappropriate, in relation to your pedagogic goals. Some research evidence will also be presented in order to support the development of your critical thinking.

The chapter ends by considering some implications for mathematics teaching of some important current ICT developments, including: CD-ROMs; the Internet; rapidly increasing access to home computing (according to the 1997 statistics from DfEE, 45 per cent of school-aged children had a computer in their home bought within the last two years, a figure which has sharply increased recently).

As you read the chapter, do not allow more experienced users to put you off. ICT is only easy when you know how, and you have the right to take time to learn.

> An experienced ICT presenter went to run an INSET session and the computers were not logged on. She found the computer specialist and asked him to log on for her. 'Oh, that's easy,' he replied. Nevertheless, she asked him to come and do it for her. It turned out that a secret password was needed and he had forgotten that he was the only person available who knew what it was.

OBJECTIVES

By the end of this chapter, you should be able to:

- understand and discuss thoughtfully the contribution that ICT (including calculators and computers) can make to learning and teaching mathematics;
- provide an appropriate environment (including tasks) that will enable pupils to learn from feedback, observe patterns, see connections, work with dynamic images, explore data and 'teach' the computer;
- develop your knowledge of particular software to enhance your mathematics teaching, including getting access to available resources and support for using ICT in the maths classroom.

BACKGROUND MATTERS

The England and Wales National Curriculum for Mathematics states: 'Pupils should be given opportunities, where appropriate, to develop and apply their information technology (IT) capability in their study of mathematics' (DfE, 1995, p. 1). The free NCET (1995) leaflet, *Mathematics and IT – a pupil's entitlement*, describes six major ways in which IT can provide opportunities for students learning mathematics (see Table 8.1). By the end of the course, you should be able to bring to mind examples of your own use of ICT that illustrate these six ways. You will also have seen some examples of pupils learning from feedback, observing patterns, seeing connections, working with dynamic images, exploring data and teaching the computer.

Table 8.1 A pupil's entitlement to IT in mathematics

1 Learning from feedback

The computer often provides fast and reliable feedback, which is non-judgemental and impartial. This can encourage students to make their own conjectures and to test out and modify their ideas.

2 Observing patterns

The speed of computers and calculators enables students to produce many examples when exploring mathematical problems. This supports their observation of patterns and the making and justifying of generalisations.

3 Seeing connections

The computer enables formulae, tables of numbers and graphs to be linked readily. Changing one representation and seeing changes in the others helps students to understand the connections between them.

4 Working with dynamic images

Students can use computers to manipulate diagrams dynamically. This encourages them to visualise the geometry as they generate their own mental images.

5 Exploring data

Computers enable students to work with real data, which can be represented in a variety of ways. This supports interpretation and analysis.

6 Teaching the computer

When students design an algorithm (a set of instructions) to make a computer achieve a particular result, they are compelled to express their commands unambiguously and in the correct order; they make their thinking explicit as they refine their ideas.

CALCULATING DEVICES

Throughout history, various invented devices (such as mathematical tables, abaci, slide rules and mechanical or electronic calculators) have been devised to assist with the performing of calculations. With each one, there are practices and conventions to be learned concerned with how to *use* the device to implement an algorithm

Task 8.1 ICT Audit

Look at the audit chart in Table 8.2. There are seven different technological tools, each of which will be covered in this chapter. For each tool, there are columns for four levels of experience. These levels have been designed to help you audit your present experience and identify where you need to develop your experience of technology in your mathematics teaching. If any of these tools is new to you, there is an introductory description in Appendix 4.

The first level, 'Acquainted', represents having met and used the tool enough to know what it is. This is the level assumed in this chapter.

Level 2, the 'Personal User' level, describes someone who has used the tool to explore some mathematics for themselves and who is aware of some of the processes involved.

Level 3, the 'Classroom User', describes someone who has ideas for appropriate use of the tool with pupils learning mathematics at school level, and who has had the opportunity to work through and reflect on a variety of activities designed to explore the power of the tool for enhancing the teaching and learning of mathematics.

Finally, level 4, the 'Critical User', refers to someone who feels able to identify some pitfalls and problems that may arise when using the tool with pupils, and who has some knowledge of educational research findings related to the tool. This chapter and your background reading will help you to consider some of the important issues that the use of the tool raises. These range from specific curriculum issues through to questions about teaching and learning styles and issues of equality of opportunity.

Make a copy of the audit chart in Table 8.2. Use it to record your current level of experience with each of the tools shown. You should return to the table and review your progress at intervals during the year.

Table 8.2 ICT self-audit chart

	Level 1 Acquainted: have used and know what it is	*Level 2 Personal User: have used reflectively for own maths*	*Level 3 Classroom User: have ideas for use with pupils*	*Level 4 Critical User: have critical awareness of research issues related to use*
Calculator				
Graphic calculator				
Spreadsheet				
Dynamic geometry				
Logo and Microworlds				
CD-ROMs				
Internet				

(such as when and how to move beads or change rows, or how to read off from the cursor, or which buttons to press and in which order).

In addition, with each device there are questions about what service they may be in *learning* mathematics directly (rather than merely helping it to be done). What images are offered implicit in the way numbers are represented; what understandings about operations or the numeration system do they support, as we become more fluent users; what sort of devices are they? One might reflect on the usefulness of the 'borrow and pay back' cover story for a way of undertaking written subtraction; to what extent does it promote understanding of the process?

'Slide of hand'

We start with neither an account of the abacus nor the electronic calculator, but with a brief look at the slide rule. Costel Harnasz (1993) has produced a clear and illuminating account of its educational history, entitled 'Do you need to know how it works?', and relates his discussion to current concerns about the use of electronic calculators in schools. In particular, he quotes Richard Delamain (1630):

> For no one to know the use of a Mathematical Instrument, except he knows the cause of its operation, is somewhat too strict, which would keep many from affecting the Art, because they see nothing but obscure propositions, and perplex and intricated demonstrations before their eyes.
> (Harnasz, 1993, p. 142)

Harnasz contrasts Delamain's view with William Oughtred's concern that certain teachers' students were 'only doers of tricks and, as it were, jugglers'. As Delamain made technical instruments, he had a certain vested economic interest in not restricting the allowed audience. The issue is practice over understanding. Being able to 'affect the Art' is precisely at the core of the current debate over calculators: the fear of apparent sophistication of performance unrooted in understanding, and the perennial desire of teachers to be able to say that a pupil has understood when they exhibit successful practice (the latter having the advantage of being observable). Conversely, it is not clear that 'understanding' necessarily makes you a better user.

On the abacus

Historically, abacuses were widely used (and in some countries, for example Russia and Japan, still are), as were counting boards. These historical counting devices and their associated practices provide a mental image of a computation.

In an article on the Japanese abacus – the *soroban* – Catherine Hoare remarks on how, after gaining remarkable facility with the soroban in performing computations, the Japanese schoolchildren she saw (aged 8 to 11) were given mental arithmetic (six-digit) additions and subtractions:

> The pupils sat with their eyes shut or half-closed running their fingers an inch above the desk top as if the soroban were still there! At the end of each question just under half of the pupils had the correct answer, but all had attempted questions which would have been unthinkable within our conception of mental arithmetic. Their method consists of mentally visualising a soroban and working through the problem using standard techniques.
>
> (Hoare, 1990, pp. 13–14)

This account raises many questions. What range of images do pupils have when carrying out mental computations, and what support do these images offer? Are images of Dienes apparatus, for example, available to pupils who have worked intensively with it; are there physical motions in muscle memory (where the hands are doing the thinking) available to be drawn on? Hoare adds: 'Through mechanisation of operation, therefore, the soroban becomes as automatic to the Japanese as the calculator has to the younger generation of English.' Yet, as with the differences between numeration systems, the structural differences of these two devices are relevant to mathematics education.

On the calculator

Modern electronic calculators are nowhere near as 'transparent' with regard to their functioning, and therefore do not offer much imagistic support. Numbers are entered from right to left, as when written down, which acts to 'move' the digit across each 'place'. It is an interesting and open question whether this relative absence of associated imagery with a calculator is a potential weakness (the mechanisms are opaque and therefore offer very little support) or a potential strength (leaving pupils free to form their own imagery) with regard to using such devices to help gain either numerical fluency or understanding.

But what about the numerical operations? With most calculators, there is no difference between any of the four arithmetic operations and taking powers or square roots (except possibly a slight time difference in operation). All are carried out by pressing a single operation key. With the soroban, the algorithm is accessible to view, implemented by the user, and can be internalised through repetition of hand movements. With the calculator, everything is inaccessible, invisible.

The calculator has single buttons that perform an increasing variety of mathematical functions. But with a calculator, you lose the sense of an algorithm for these operations, as there is no evidence of intermediate steps. Such single buttons become *primitives*, in the sense that no further interrogation of how the calculations are being carried out is possible – they become inaccessible. What is different between a set of square-root tables and the square root button on a calculator? Written tables may not provide much clue as to their genesis, but each table is a single object open to inspection and analysis, complete with interpolation rules.

The debate about the use of calculators rages, and has done so since the 1970s. The Second International Mathematics Survey (Cresswell and Gubb, 1987) claimed to show that numeracy has declined since the first study in 1967. This coincided with a general availability of relatively cheap calculators, and an association was conjectured, understandably. However, the classroom teachers in the study claimed that they were not allowing the use of calculators.

Following the publication of the Third International Mathematics and Science Study (TIMSS) (Keys *et al.*, 1996), there was further debate about calculators. Ann Kitchen (1998) has explored the issue of teachers' reported use of calculators in different countries in TIMSS; she has shown that, in nearly every country for which data was available, children aged 9 who were encouraged to use calculators in their maths lessons performed better than those who were not. At age 14, of the four categories of frequency of calculator use, those who used calculators nearly every day performed best in only sixteen of the thirty-five countries. The issue is clearly much more complex than some commentators have suggested.

It is possible to draw the conclusion that the reduction in numeracy is due to the general reduction in the use of number skills. For example, most shops use electronic tills, and other developments in new technology have reduced the level of mental arithmetic skills required to function in everyday life. In various studies, there are reports that calculators are not being used as much as critics are assuming. (See, for example, DES, 1982, para 376.)

For much of the past twenty years, the attention of teachers has been drawn away from the very important question of how calculators can be used to best effect in the teaching of mathematics, because they have been caught up in the political argument about whether to allow pupils to use calculators. One major exception to this was the Calculator Aware Number (CAN) project, in which primary teachers were encouraged to look with open minds at what might constitute good practice in teaching with calculators.

It is worth noting here that in the sixteenth century, Johannes Kepler was rebuked by his mentor for using the latest new idea to facilitate his calculations; he used logarithms. According to Michael Mästlin, he should have done the calculations 'properly'.

The question remains, why are schools still not teaching pupils how to use calculators?

There is a general perception that calculators damage children's mathematics. In this section, we have tried to place the use of calculators in a historic and pedagogic context, to show that calculators have a role as a tool in the teaching and learning of mathematics and to suggest that their impact may have been exaggerated. The fact remains that it is possible to use calculators badly.

> I have seen one lesson in which pupils were working with Pythagoras' theorem to find the third side of a right-angled triangle, and one pupil estimated her answer out loud. She was told that it was not possible to find square roots without a calculator, despite the fact that her estimate was useful. It would have been better practice to encourage the estimation, both as a way of checking the answer and a way of reinforcing a sense of number.

Task 8.2 What are calculators good for?

The following three calculator activities are presented as examples of activities. Some of them are better than others. Consider which of them can best promote the intelligent use of calculators as tools for learning.

Calculator activity 1

Enter any three digit number less than 900 into a calculator. Now try to reduce the number to zero in at most five steps, using any of the four functions with a single digit for each step.

For example, start with 435. Then press −3 ÷ 6 ÷ 9 − 8.

From Williams and Stephens (1992)

When you have tried this first calculator activity, consider what work you did in your head. Think about how pupils might tackle this activity.

Calculators offer the possibility to produce rapid, accurate feedback for the pupil. Pupils can try many different strategies in a relatively short time, without having their progress impeded by their own difficulties with performing algorithms quickly and accurately.

Calculator activity 2

Imagine your calculator is broken.

Find the total of 738 + 872 without using the 7 or the 8 key.
How many different methods can you find for doing this?

From Haylock (1982)

When you have tried this activity, consider what problem-solving strategies you used. Again, you could consider how pupils might tackle the problem.

Calculator activity 3

Choose ten grocery items from a supermarket catalogue or a newspaper advert. Estimate their combined value. Use the calculator to calculate the actual value.

Ask some children what they use calculators for and invite them to show you how they work with one. How do they talk about what they are doing?

Try the calculator activities suggested above with pupils that you teach.

Consider what makes a good calculator activity.

Find out about your school's departmental policy on calculators.

In your journal, summarise your findings and your reflections on the role of calculators.

It is very important to be aware of the danger of inadvertently reducing pupils' mental arithmetic practice by allowing pupils, particularly slower pupils, to use the calculator as a crutch. You need consciously and explicitly to acknowledge the role of estimation and mental arithmetic when using a calculator with pupils. You can read a more comprehensive guide to the appropriate use of calculators in SCAA (1997b).

SPREADSHEETS

Mathematics in the National Curriculum explicitly mentions the role of both spreadsheets and calculators in *number* work. In number: 'pupils should be given opportunities to use calculators and computer software, *e.g. spreadsheets*' (DfE, 1995, p. 13). Although much of the power of a spreadsheet derives from using the algebraic potential of linking values in one column to those of another by means of formulae, it is, on the surface, a tool for operating on tables of numbers. Thinking of a spreadsheet as an animated table might help you to conceive of this superficially simple but mathematically sophisticated tool in a more accessible way. An initial reason for wanting to incorporate a powerful spreadsheet into the school mathematics curriculum might be that it enables teachers and students to have access on disc to large data sets, such as world record data for track and field events. Its role as an algebraic environment warrants further consideration. A spreadsheet is also a powerful tool for modelling, widely used in industry and commerce, so once you have access to this powerful resource, it is worth discovering what else it can be used for in the mathematics curriculum. It may take you some considerable time to get sufficiently acquainted with a spreadsheet package to feel confident with it, so, within reason, you will find you want to make as much use of it as possible, to make it worth the effort.

Spreadsheet activities can be thought of as being of two distinct kinds: sometimes it is appropriate to give the pupils a spreadsheet document that has already been created, and to invite them to work with this; at other times, it may be better for the pupils to create their own spreadsheet documents from scratch.

One of the big ideas about a spreadsheet is the difference between relative and absolute referencing. Task 8.3 will help you to explore this.

Researchers, publishers and others are making available sets of data that may be of interest to students of different ages. In addition, many large data sets are now accessible on the World Wide Web. For example, a website containing a database of all world records in athletics (track and field) for men can be found at: http://www.uta.fi/~csmipe/sport/eng/mwr.html A site giving equivalent data for women is at: http://www.uta.fi/~csmipe/sport/eng/wwr.html An example of the use of data from this site in a secondary mathematics lesson can be found in Hyde (1996).

The use of logical functions in a spreadsheet can provide a simple introduction to programming. One particularly useful example is 'if-then-else'. The 'if-then-else' structure is a powerful idea in its own right and it can enable you and your students to explore some interesting new ideas. Suppose, for example, you want to set up a simulation that involves a probability of 0.3. You can use a formula to enter a random number between 0 and 1 in cell A1. Then in cell B1 you can have 'IF cell

A1 is greater than 0.7, THEN make B1 take the value 1, ELSE make B1 take the value 0'. (The syntax for this in Excel would be = IF(A1>0.7, 1, 0).)

You will find more ideas of activities for pupils using spreadsheets in *Spreadsheets from SMILE* (SMILE, 1993); *Spreadsheets: Exploring their Potential in Secondary Mathematics* (Green *et al.*, 1993); and, for your own interest, *Mathematics with Excel* (Sjörstrand, 1993).

Task 8.3 Multiplication table

Using a spreadsheet, starting from cell A2, put the numbers 1 to 12 in column A. Starting from cell B1, put the numbers 1 to 12 in row 1. Now in cell B2, enter the formula A2 * B1. (In Excel, a formula will start with =; other spreadsheets do it differently.)

B2 | =A2*B1

Worksheet1

	A	B	C	D	E	F	G	H	I	J	K	L	M
1		1	2	3	4	5	6	7	8	9	10	11	12
2	1	1											
3	2												
4	3												
5	4												
6	5												
7	6												
8	7												
9	8												
10	9												
11	10												
12	11												
13	12												

Figure 8.1 Starting to build a multiplication table

Note what happens when you fill this formula down from cell B2 to B13, and then fill right from column B to column M.

Look at the formula in each of the cells.

Now do the activity again using the formula A2*B1 in the cell B2. A2 is known as an absolute reference.

Look at the resulting formulae.

Think about the effect of the absolute referencing.

You might also like to try the formula A$2*B1 in the cell B2, before you fill down and fill right as above. Again, look at the resulting formula, and think about the effect of putting in the dollar sign ($).

Now create a multiplication table, up to 12 times 12.

Task 8.4 Big data sets

Download the set of javelin data from the Web page given on page 152 into a spreadsheet. Plot the data against time. Consider why the graph takes the shape it does. Think about how you might use such an activity with pupils. Discuss your ideas with your tutor.

Task 8.5 Rolling spreadsheets

Teach your spreadsheet to emulate rolling a dice. In Figure 8.2 below, taken from an Excel worksheet, the cell B1 is highlighted and contains a formula to generate a random integer from the list 1, 2, 3, 4, 5, 6. The images of the faces of the dice are created by spreadsheet commands based on the logical function IF, THEN, ELSE.

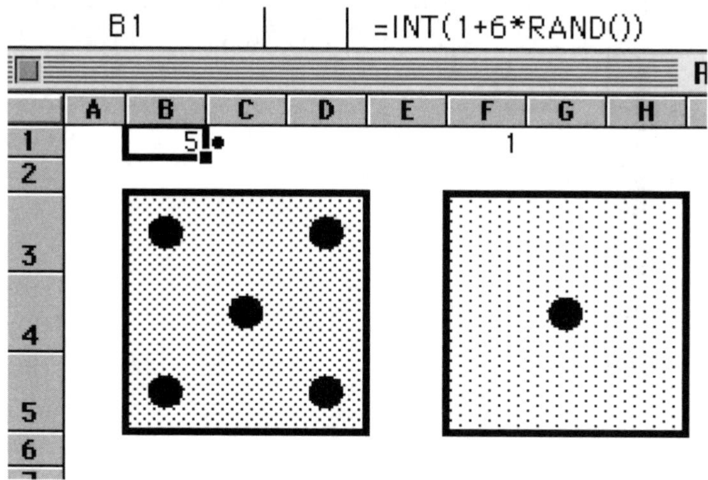

Figure 8.2 A spreadsheet to emulate two dice

You can read more about the construction of a spreadsheet like this to emulate the rolling of a dice in Neville Hunt's (1996) article.

GRAPHING DEVICES

Graphic calculators are a relatively new feature of mathematics classrooms; Kenneth Ruthven began the first major research and development project using graphic calculators in 1986 (Ruthven, 1990). However, the notion of a graphing environment, in which the user can zoom in and out and investigate intersections and local gradients, has been around longer, thanks to the insights of David Tall using the original BBC computer.

Tall developed his computer graph approach to teaching calculus in the early 1980s. The 'Graphic Calculus' software he developed for the early BBC computers was the first of its kind. The software enabled students to zoom in on a graph over a tiny range, and so to build a concept of the derivative function as the gradient of the graph. Tall's early work was published in a series of articles by the Association of Teachers of Mathematics in their journal *Mathematics Teaching*; the articles were later collected into a separate booklet (Tall, 1987). More recently, some people have applied Tall's approach to a graphing spreadsheet; these ideas have been reported in *Micromath* (see, for example, Morgan Jones and McLeay, 1996; Crawford, 1998; Morrison, 1998).

There are now a variety of graphing packages which offer such features. Some examples are:

- *Omnigraph*, a package running on PC machines and used in many secondary schools;
- *Coypu*, written by a team at the Shell Centre for Mathematics Education at Nottingham University, originally for Acorn computers, but now also available for PCs.

The most accessible tool for this approach in physical terms is the graphic calculator. Graphic calculators can be seen as the point where computers and calculators converge, an interim technology. Their most striking feature is their accessibility – owning one means that powerful technology is available as and when it is needed. They represent a major force for change in mathematics teaching and learning. Moreover, this force is generally outside the control of the educational establishment in the sense that, although there is some contact between educators and manufacturers, their development is very much market-led.

So, students can buy, and are buying, machines with the power to do much of the routine work that forms the basis for advanced level courses. There is therefore a very real need for educators to think carefully about what really needs to be learned in mathematics. Whilst this need may seem most obvious at advanced level, there is an equivalent challenge to be met in the education of younger pupils.

Some research has shown that if teachers have access to graphic calculators in their lessons, then they tend to ask more high-level questions than they would otherwise do. For example, Rich (1993) studied two teachers to investigate how the introduction of the graphic calculator affects the teachers' questioning strategies, presentation methods and beliefs about mathematics. She observed that the teacher who used graphic calculators:

- used more exploration and encouraged conjecturing;
- asked more higher-level questions, used examples differently and stressed the importance of graphs and approximation in problem solving;
- used more graphs and showed the connection between algebra and geometry in other classes.

Task 8.6 Graphic proficiency

Find a pupil or colleague who is proficient with a graphic calculator. Observe which model is being used. There are four main makes in use in the UK: Casio, Texas Instruments, Sharp, Hewlett-Packard. Try to do this activity with a Casio or a TI calculator, simply because there is more support material available for these in the UK. Invite the pupil or colleague to spend some time showing you what s/he uses the calculator for. Allow this to be a discussion between two people with different expertise.

Ask them to draw two graphs that intersect, then zoom in on the point of intersection and find the co-ordinates as accurately as possible.

In Task 8.6, you saw how to use the basic facilities of a graphic calculator to explore graphs and to find solutions of equations graphically. In order to optimise the use of the graphic calculator, you will also need to learn how to produce a table of values of a function on your calculator. Then you can begin to use in your teaching the three different representations of a function the graphic calculator offers: graphic, algebraic and numeric.

Task 8.7 offers you some open activities to try with pupils to see what mathematics is used.

Although, at the time of writing, most resources to support the use of graphic calculators have been written for post-16, this has been because of the price of the calculators, and does not imply that the technology is inappropriate for younger pupils. You can find ideas for using graphic calculators with 11–16 pupils in the *Open Calculator Challenge* available from the Open University (1993), in Graham and Galpin (1998), in Arter *et al.* (1993) and in Ruthven (1992).

New developments in calculator technology are appearing every year, so you need to keep an eye on the maths education press for news. Already, calculators are available that can be connected by a cable to a computer, and can receive data downloaded from the Internet. Remote data capture devices can collect data about motion or light or temperature, etc., and this can be loaded immediately into a calculator; devices such as this make it possible to use a calculator to control a simple robot (see Oldknow, 1998), e.g. a TI73 designed to be able to download code from the Internet.

Task 8.7 Activities to try with pupils

A) Make your calculator screen look like this.

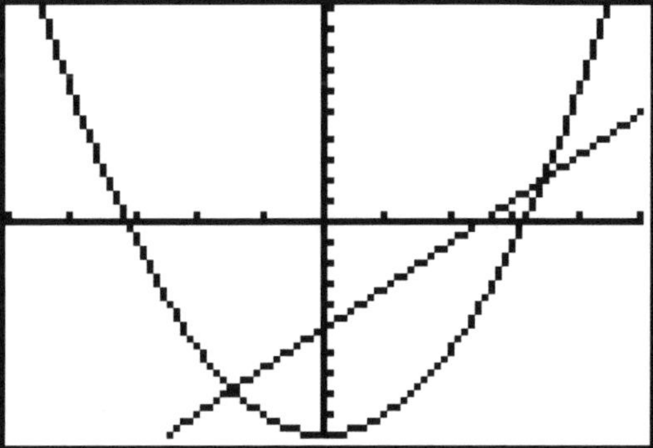

Figure 8.3 A graphic calculator screen

B) Create a picture of a face on the screen of your calculator; you should use a function, shading and lines from the draw menu, and co-ordinate plots from the statistics menu.

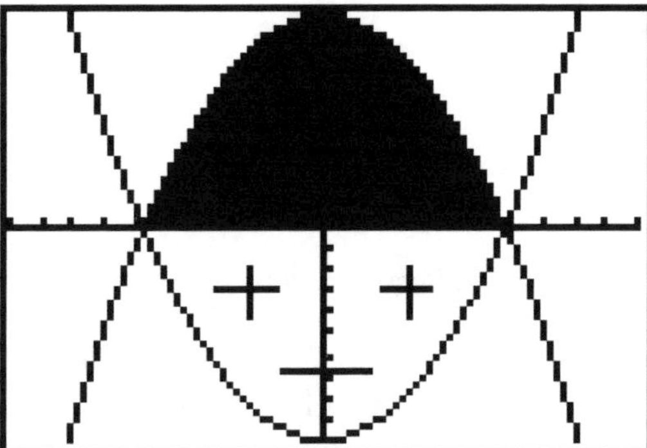

Figure 8.4 A pirate
Source: Graham, 1996, p. 15

C) Draw a line graph of $y = 3x$.
Investigate what happens if you change the number.

DYNAMIC GEOMETRY

Imagine you are trying to convince a pupil that the angle subtended by the chord BC remains the same even if the point A moves round the circle (see Figure 8.5). You trace round the circle with your finger as you speak. If only the diagram would move too.

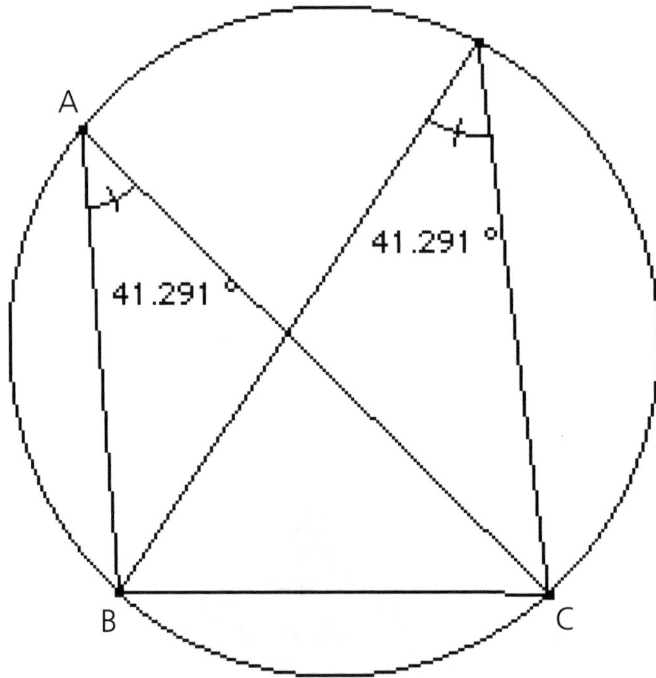

Figure 8.5 A demonstration of equal angles subtended by the same chord

There are several implementations of the idea of a dynamic diagram using Dynamic Geometry Software. Cabri and Geometer's Sketchpad are the two principal alternatives. These two software packages are fairly similar. The main difference between them that you will notice immediately is that using Cabri, you select a construction tool and then the objects to which it is to be applied, whereas using Geometer's Sketchpad, you select the objects first and then the tool that you wish to use.

Further examples of activities using dynamic geometry to recreate the geometric methods of Greek and Arab mathematicians have been discussed in a series of articles in *Micromath* (Burns, 1996; Evans, 1996, 1997). Books about geometry may give you further ideas for exploration using dynamic geometry software: some examples are Coxeter (1961) *Introduction to Geometry*; Wells (1991) *The Penguin Dictionary of Curious and Interesting Geometry*; and Bold (1982) *Famous Problems of Geometry and How to Solve Them.*

Task 8.8 Using dynamic geometry

1 Using your dynamic geometry package, create an equilateral triangle, as described in Appendix 4.
As you do this, record in your journal how your thinking develops and what problem-solving processes you use.

2 The diagram in Figure 8.6 represents a construction of a line segment x such that $x^2 = ab$.
Recreate this construction in your dynamic geometry package so that a and b can be varied. Put in the measurements of a, b and x and move the figure around to convince yourself that x is indeed $\sqrt{ab}$.

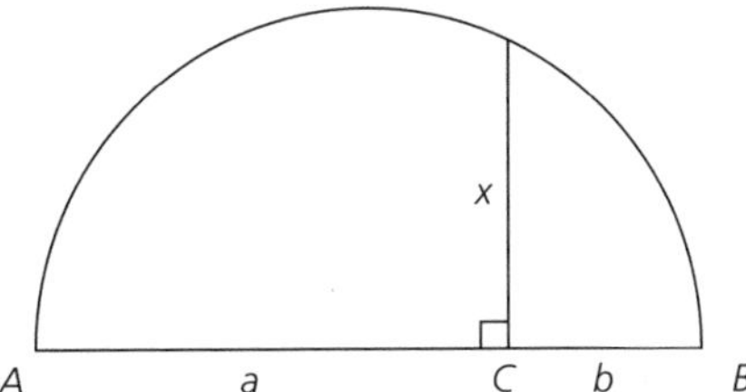

Figure 8.6 Constructing a square root

Can you explain why $x^2 = ab$? Does the dynamic geometry help you to construct a convincing explanation? These issues of the role of dynamic geometry in the mental construction of proof and explanation are explored in an article by Michael de Villiers (1995).

Issues to think about

Dynamic geometry software of this kind has clear applications in the Mathematics National Curriculum for England and Wales, as is shown in the following extracts from the Shape, Space and Measures strand of the programmes of study.

Key Stages 3 and 4:

- recognise and visualise the transformations of translation, reflection, rotation and enlargement, and their combination in 2 dimensions;
- determine the locus of an object moving according to a given rule;
- find perimeters and areas of common shapes including circles.

Key Stage 4 Further Material:

- extend their understanding of trigonometry to angles of any size;
- use angle and tangent properties of circles.

However, there are also less obvious applications. For example, recent versions of Cabri and of Geometer's Sketchpad offer far more: in addition to offering tools for transformation geometry, they provide an underlying grid and a Cartesian co-ordinate system, with which the user can explore and display equations of lines, circles and conic sections. This provides a means, starting from geometrical figures, to make the connection with algebraic representations.

Task 8.9 Solving quadratics

This activity for dynamic geometry software is based on methods used by mathematicians in ancient Greece to construct geometric solutions for quadratic problems. The activity comes from Bold (1982).

To construct the roots of the quadratic equation $x^2 - 4x + 2 = 0$, you construct the points B(0, 1) and D(4, 2). Then you create a circle with BD as the diameter. Then the points where the circle cuts the x-axis represent the roots of the equation.

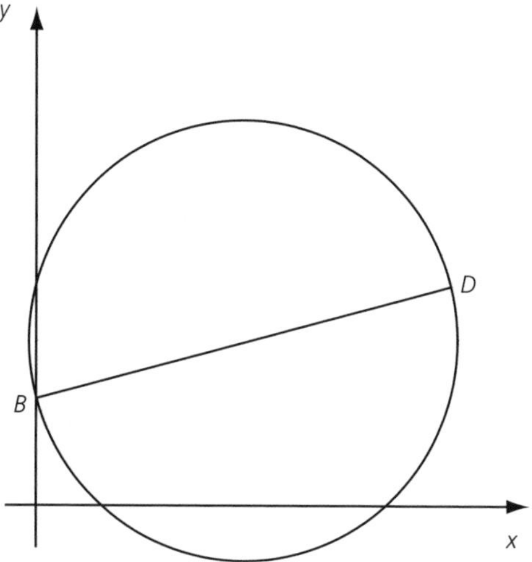

Figure 8.7 Solving quadratic equations using a circle

Keep a note of how you get on.

Consider what processes you went through, then how these activities may be made suitable for pupils and what they might learn from working on them.

What are the entry points?

Experience with other media, and other geometrical experiences, are important foundations for work with dynamic geometry software. Experiments with folding paper, or making shapes with geo-strips and elastic bands on pinboards, may all be valuable activities.

It is also possible to create stimulating images using overlaid acetates of lines and circles on an overhead projector. These can be linked together using pins to illustrate the ideas of construction, constraints and possibilities. The acetates and geo-strips can also be used to demonstrate the idea of action at a distance, which seems to be part of the fascination with playing with constructions. Plenty of time is needed for this kind of experience.

What are the big ideas in dynamic geometry?

Perhaps one of the key ideas to get hold of in dynamic geometry is the distinction between drawing and construction. The distinction appears to be a significant sticking point for teachers and pupils alike when they first use the software. Associated with the idea of construction is the idea of 'invariance': that some features of a figure will remain invariant as parts of the figure are 'dragged' around the screen. The idea of 'messing up' (Healy *et al.*, 1994) – getting students to make a drawing or design of their own choosing, and then encouraging them to try to 'mess it up' – has been used with some success to provide students with some motive for constructing their figures. The hope was that the challenge of trying to preserve their own design from the threat of being 'messed up' would encourage students to think about the construction.

The challenge of constructing particular shapes – for example, to construct a figure that will remain a rhombus whatever you drag – may also lead to some valuable ideas. Finzer and Bennett (1995) suggest that students may go through various stages in tackling such a problem:

- *drawing*:
  dragging a quadrilateral to look approximately like a rhombus;
- *under-constraint*:
  where perhaps the opposite sides are constrained to be parallel, but all sides are not constructed to be equal;
- *over-constraint*:
  where not only is the shape constrained to be a rhombus, but also the angles are constrained to be 60° and 120°;
- *appropriate constraint*:
  where the relationships used are minimal to define the figure.

Another important distinction to understand is that between dynamic coincidence and general truth. The distinction is clearly associated with the idea of construction; a general truth can be seen as being like a feature of a construction that cannot be messed up. For a deeper understanding of a general truth, it seems that the pupil needs to seek for an explanation.

Using dynamic geometry with pupils

As with spreadsheets, different teaching approaches are possible when using dynamic geometry software with pupils. One approach is to ask pupils to make a construction starting from a blank worksheet. This kind of activity may be demanding of the pupils' prior knowledge and understanding of some of the fundamental concepts behind the tools in dynamic geometry. An alternative approach that has been favoured by some teachers is to use the software to create a dynamic worksheet for the pupils to explore. You can read some teacher's accounts of using this approach in *Micromath* (Cowell, 1995 and Grayson, 1995).

Task 8.10 Creating a dynamic worksheet

Create a dynamic worksheet to teach a topic of your choice.
Try your worksheet with an appropriate group of pupils.
Observe the pupils' response to the activity and consider how you might improve your worksheet for future use.
Make notes in your journal about your ideas.

USING LOGO

Logo was originated by mathematics educator Seymour Papert; it is a programming language developed as an educational tool. Although you can think of using a spreadsheet or a dynamic geometry package as being like teaching the computer to do new tasks, the metaphor has a clearer link with reality when you are programming using Logo. In one part of Logo, turtle geometry, the screen shows an idealised turtle, which you guide around the screen using commands such as Left 45, Right 60, Forward 20. The turtle can leave a trail behind it. If you have not yet used Logo yourself, ask your tutor in school to introduce you to it.

Seymour Papert's own book, *Mindstorms – Children, Computers and Powerful Ideas* (1980), will give you some background about the origins of Logo; it also contains some interesting ideas to explore. Although Logo is seen by many as being 'only' an educational language, it is in fact a very sophisticated computer language and can be used as a vehicle for exploring deep mathematical ideas (Abelson and DiSessa, 1980).

Task 8.11 Working with Logo

1 Make the turtle draw a square, then an equilateral triangle, then a polygon. Now create a procedure to make a square of variable size. Use your procedure to make a two-by-two square the same size as your original square.

2 Explore the following procedure which is an example of a recursive procedure, that is a procedure that calls itself.

```
TO INSPI (:SIDE, :ANGLE, :INC)
FORWARD :SIDE
RIGHT :ANGLE
INSPI (:SIDE, :ANGLE + :INC, :INC)
END
```

3 A challenge

Read John Bradshaw's description of student teachers using Logo to design tessellations (Bradshaw, 1997). The article shows some interesting examples of tessellations generated using Logo procedures. Devise your own tessellation using Logo.

Entry points and big ideas

A useful introduction to using Logo in your teaching is *Making Logo Work: a Guide for Teachers* by Janet Ainley and Ronnie Goldstein (1988). There are several other books that attempt to describe the role of Logo in mathematics classrooms, but this is a good one.

One well tried and tested way of introducing Logo is to get the pupils to 'play turtle'. (See Dye, 1991 for a more complete description.) This gives them some concrete experience on which to hang their developing understanding. (For very young children, teachers have used an electronic turtle or a Pip or Roamer which moves around the floor.) Pupils need to learn to be precise and explicit in their instructions to the turtle and learn to debug procedures. Some teachers begin by asking pupils to write their name using Logo. Initially, the pupils work in direct mode, but they soon realise the need for procedures if they are to save their work. Variables can be introduced as a mechanism for altering the size of their pictures. Pupils learn to build procedures from sub-procedures, for example:

To Man	or	**To Tree**
Head		Arrowhead 50
Body		Arrowhead 30
Leg		Arrowhead 15
Leg		Arrowhead 5
Arm		End
Arm		
End		

Such procedures often need debugging, for example, when the arms appear in the wrong place. This immediate feedback, and the possibility of correction with further feedback, is an obvious benefit to the learner.

Some pupils enjoy creating and exploring patterns, such as:

To Pattern
Repeat 20 [Square Right 18]
End

Task 8.12 Using Logo with pupils

Observe a lesson using Logo, or try some Logo activities of your own with a small group of pupils. Make a note in your journal of what mathematics the pupils use.

Logo as a metaphor and as an experience brings some changes to the way in which pupils experience mathematics. One example of this is in the study of external angles of a polygon; the theorem that external angles add up to 360 degrees is replaced by the 'Total Turtle Trip' Theorem. There are many others! The spring 1991 issue of *Micromath* was dedicated to Logo, and you will find some further ideas there or in Ainley and Goldstein (1988).

TEACHING PROGRAMS

Many small teaching programs for mathematics were developed on BBC computers during the 1980s; they still have much to offer in teaching mathematics. Such programs were designed to be easy to use and to cover a small piece of syllabus. Some of them are investigative in style. Two collections of small teaching programs to look out for in your school are SMILE programs (SMILE Centre) and SLIM-WAM (Some Lessons In Mathematics With a Micro). In addition, one excellent example of a well thought-out mathematical adventure game is L – a mathemagical adventure game from ATM. If you cannot find it in school, it is worth buying a copy.

Task 8.13 Small teaching programs

Find out what small teaching programs are in your school. Spend some time exploring some of the small-scale software you find. In particular, if you have access to them, look at the SMILE programs. You can find a review of the SMILE programs for Windows in *Micromath* **12**(3), pp. 43–44.

SOME IMPLICATIONS OF CURRENT DEVELOPMENTS

Many parents who have computers at home are buying CD-ROMs for mathematics. The problem is that many of the examples available at present are not very good, either because they do not use the possibilities offered by the technology or because they do not communicate the mathematics very well. You need to be aware that some commercial organisations will loan copies of CD-ROMs to teachers for previewing.

One CD-ROM that we think is worth looking at now is based on the work of the artist M. C. Escher. *Escher Interactive CD-ROM (Exploring the Art of the Infinite)* is available from QED Books. Review carefully any CD-ROMS you find in the light of what you have learned about good practice.

Task 8.14 Mathematics and the Internet

The Internet is a rapidly growing resource. The main problem is that it can absorb a lot of time as you search from one list of sites to another. I suggest you start with Math Forum, a page from which is shown in Figure 8.8. It is a well-organised site, relatively quick to load, and includes some useful resources. The address is: http://forum.swarthmore.edu/

A second good site is St Andrews History of Mathematics site, which is a rich resource of historical material. The address is: http://www-groups.dcs.st-and.ac.uk/~history/

Try conducting a search for references to a maths topic such as Pythagoras, using a search engine such as the Yahoo Mathematics site. The address is: http://www.yahoo.com/Science/Mathematics/

Try also using Yahooligans, which is designed for pupils to use. The address is: http://www.yahooligans.com/

Visit the following Web site, follow the links and make a note of each site to which it links: http://www.westnet.com/~rickd/Kids/Math.html#-Puzzles

Further sites are to be found in Appendix 2. To save you typing in all these addresses we have created a Web site to go with the book, at http://mcs.open.ac.uk/cme/suejw

Douglas Butler (1998) (see Further Reading) has published a good overview of the mathematical resources to be found on the Web in 1998. This publication is available both on paper and as a CD-ROM, and it will save you a lot of time. It is worth noting, when you visit Internet sites in the US, that grades K (Kindergarten) to 12 are equivalent in age to our school years 1 to 13.

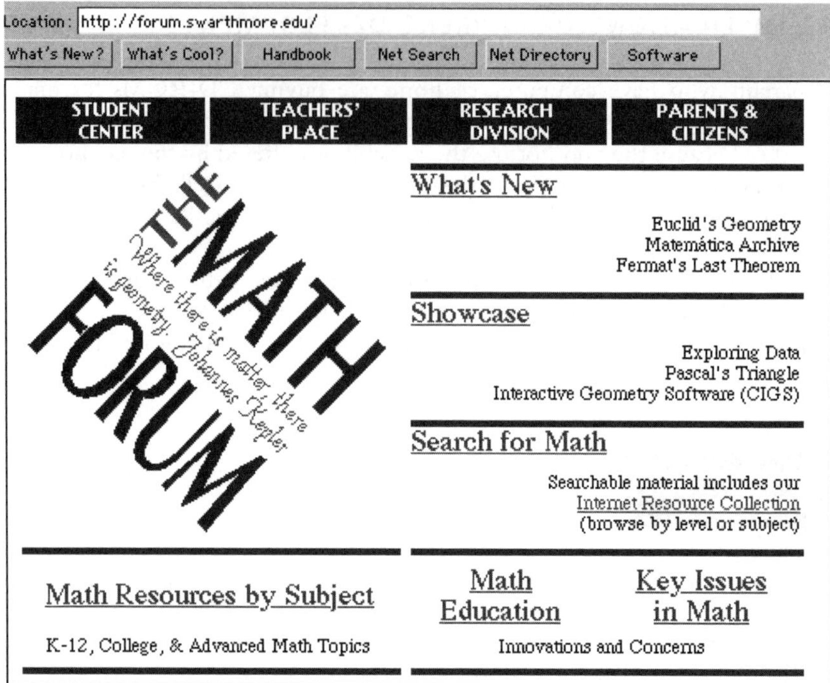

Figure 8.8 Math Forum Internet page

SUMMARY

ICT is changing rapidly. Although there is much potential for improved learning, there is also the possibility of wasting a great deal of time and resources. When using ICT in the classroom, it is worth remembering that some pupils will know more than you, and amongst the pupils there may be wide ranges of fluency and comfort with ICT, and access to machines. Be prepared to use the expertise, interest and energy that is present. One teacher of a Year 9 class discovered that one of her pupils was experienced in using a spreadsheet. Whenever members of the class working on a spreadsheet got stuck technically, she called on his expertise to help solve the problem.

Whilst you are not necessarily expert in the technology, be prepared to be confident mathematically in dealing with whatever the technology offers. For example, debugging programs is a mathematical activity, and it is possible to be helpful to a pupil by having them explain to you what they are trying to do. It is not uncommon for a pupil, half-way through their explanation of the problem, to say 'Oh, that's what's wrong, thank you', and go off, leaving you unsure precisely what you have achieved, but they are clearly forging ahead with their project. The fall-back position is 'I don't know, let's find out'.

Sometimes it is enough for you to make process observations about how your pupils are going about tackling their task, as students of this age may be immersed in technical detail and therefore not paying sufficient attention to higher-level strategic issues.

Task 8.15 Re-audit

Check back to your initial ICT audit and note how much progress you have made.

FURTHER READING

Ainley, J. and Goldstein, R. (1988) *Making Logo Work: A Guide for Teachers*, Oxford: Basil Blackwell.

This book explores the rationale of Logo and provides a number of case studies that give ideas and a clear picture of what Logo can offer.

ATM (1995) *Teaching, Learning and Mathematics with IT*, Derby: Association of Teachers of Mathematics.

This is a collection of articles from *Micromath* and other sources, which has been put together as a PGCE reader. Articles are grouped by the software to which they relate.

Butler, D. (1998) *Using the Internet – Mathematics*, Cambridge: Pearson Publishing.

This is a very valuable overview of the possibilities afforded mathematics teachers by the Internet. Available on paper or CD-ROM.

Healy, L. and Sutherland, R. (1991) *Exploring Mathematics with Spreadsheets*, Oxford: Basil Blackwell.

This is a practical book based on four years of research with pupils using spreadsheets. It includes case studies and starting points.

Micromath

This journal is designed to support and encourage the use of ICT in mathematics teaching, and has some very useful articles for beginning teachers as well as supporting use throughout your developing career. Although the journal is initially offered to members, back copies and individual articles can be obtained from the ATM office. It is also possible to order copies of individual articles from your local library.

NCET (1994) *The IT Maths Pack*, Coventry: NCET, with ATM and MA.

This pack is designed to help mathematics teachers start on the road to using technology in their classrooms. There are four booklets: *Geometry*; *Number*; *Maths in Context*; and *Graphic Calculators*. The pack includes a disc of data for use with a spreadsheet.

NCET (1996) *Dynamic Geometry*, Coventry: NCET, with ATM and MA.

A booklet written to introduce maths teachers to dynamic geometry. It includes ideas and practicalities.

SCAA (1997b) *The Use of Calculators at Key Stages 1–3*, Discussion Paper no 9.

This report pulls together in a thorough and readable document the key findings of some specially commissioned research. Calculator use in England, research into the influence of calculators and appropriate use are addressed. It is based on a report by Kenneth Ruthven, a respected researcher in the field of calculator use.

Web page http://www.argonet.co.uk/oundlesch/suppl.html
This Web page gives links to software pages mentioned in this chapter and more besides.

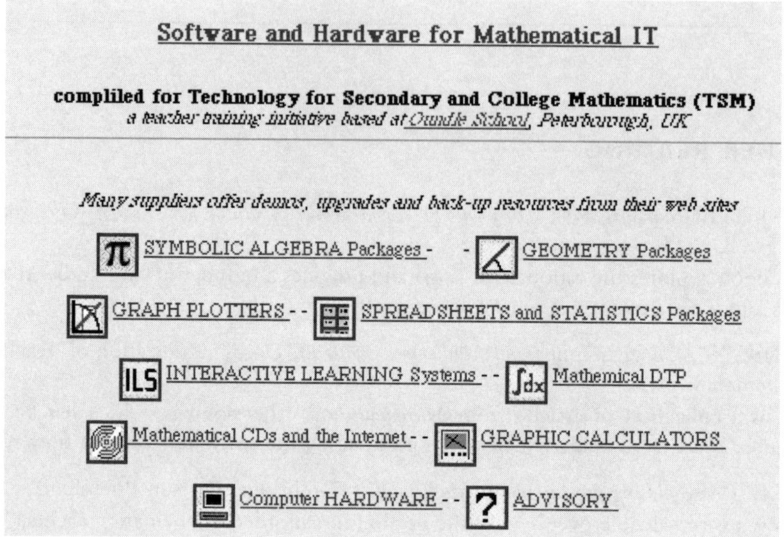

Figure 8.9 Further reading on the Internet

9 Mainstream Mathematics Teaching and Special Educational Needs

M.M. Rodd

INTRODUCTION

The aim of this chapter is to help you to become aware of pupils' special educational needs in mathematics lessons in secondary schools. Within this chapter, you are encouraged to find out about the range of special needs, and to learn about some special needs requirements in detail. You will be introduced to some useful resources and references, as well as to some of the roles you may need to take on as a mathematics teacher working with pupils with special educational needs (SEN). As well as these relatively well-defined aspects of learning about SEN, part of your preparation for teaching inclusive mainstream mathematics is to develop your empathy with the special needs children with whom you will work. The twin-track approach to inclusive mathematics teaching advocated here values both getting to know the SEN pupils and encouraging them to communicate their opinions about what would help them, whilst also finding out about these pupils' particular special needs from published resources.

In previous generations, children with limiting SEN would not have been expected to engage with and succeed at mathematics: mathematics was a 'hard' subject, intended only for the few. Times have changed. Now it is recognised that mathematics permeates our lives. To equip young people for their adult life includes helping them to understand certain mathematical ideas not only in money and measures, but also, for example, interpreting information, planning and appreciation of aesthetics. Furthermore, the technological revolution gives opportunities for meaningful problem solving for those who might otherwise get bogged down with detailed calculation. In this spirit of 'Mathematics for all', the Dearing Report showed an understanding that, for some SEN pupils, being taught the entire Mathematics National Curriculum is unrealistic. What is more, Dearing recognised the key role of the mathematics teacher:

> [a] slimmer statutory National Curriculum will, by providing time for use at the teacher's discretion, go a long way towards giving teachers the scope necessary to provide all pupils with a meaningful entitlement to a broad, balanced and relevant curriculum.
>
> (Dearing, 1996, p. 53)

OBJECTIVES

At the end of this chapter, you should:

- have an increased awareness of some of the conditions or behaviours that constitute SEN;
- be able to recognise several special needs that you may meet in your mathematics classroom;
- have some specific strategies for working with more prevalent special needs;
- know where to start looking if you want to know more about mathematical special needs;
- be aware of the frustration experienced by many children with special needs;
- have started to understand the complexities of working with other professionals concerned with a SEN pupil and the SEN pupil's family.

ORIENTING TO SPECIAL NEEDS

What are mathematical SEN? The term 'special educational needs in mathematics' often refers to children who find mathematics a struggle to learn and whose attainment is not high. But there are other important categories of 'special needs in mathematics': for example, 'Specific Learning Difficulties' like dyslexia, or pupils whose special needs arise from their extraordinary facility in general scholarship or in mathematics. Each school community has a slightly different understanding of the term, so Task 9.1 will help you to get an idea of the way in which your school uses the term.

Many children with special needs will have been diagnosed before they arrive at secondary school. These children may have a statement or substantial documentation about their requirements. The maths teacher's job is to help carry out the programme designed for that child in conjunction with the special needs team and other professionals. On other occasions, a subject teacher may be the first to recognise SEN in a pupil. Any query about a child's needs should be discussed with colleagues; your Head of Department, your tutor or the SENCO are your first ports of call. A child's eyesight may deteriorate in adolescence; information at transfer to secondary school may go astray. Temporary special needs also arise from time to time: the skiing enthusiast with a broken leg may not be able to get to your classroom on the top floor, but it is your responsibility to keep her mathematics education going! The Warnock Report (DES, 1978) suggested that 20 per cent of pupils will have some special needs during their school career.

Task 9.1 Special needs in mathematics

Arrange to speak to:

- a mathematician at your school, ideally your tutor or Head of Department;
- the school's SEN co-ordinator (henceforth referred to as 'SENCO').

Ask each of them for examples of the range of 'special needs in mathematics' in the school. You might ask each of them: 'Who are the two most different children who have special needs in maths lessons?'.

Teachers often respond more readily to an invitation to describe specific pupils than to respond to a request for a more abstract description of the 'needs' of such pupils.

The mathematics specialist and the SENCO may well give different examples. Why do you think this might occur?

'Special' and 'needs': two classroom situations

The name 'special educational needs' suggests two related questions: 'what is special?' and 'what is needed?'. Task 9.2 (overleaf) is intended to illustrate how special needs sometimes arise unexpectedly.

To assist your orientation to special needs, it could be helpful to establish a relationship with one or two special needs pupils over an extended period of time. This can be a very rewarding experience, and the regular contact can provide opportunities for the pupils to communicate their requirements gradually.

INSIGHT THROUGH ERRORS

Much information can be gleaned from studying pupils' mistakes. Kath Hart's (1981) book, *Children's Understanding of Mathematics: 11–16*, is a study of a large sample of children that offers documentation and an analysis of their errors and misconceptions including, among many others, misunderstanding language, not knowing which arithmetical operation to use in problems, and not understanding

Task 9.2 Two classroom vignettes

Read the following vignettes and answer the questions.

1 On whether a pupil has a special educational need:

> It was the beginning of the new school year. I was teaching a mixed ability Year 9 class mathematics. The pupils and I were all new to the school. I had first met the class the day before, when we did number puzzles in groups directed orally; already, I had been forming impressions of some individual pupil's capabilities by their verbal responses. No impression is fixed in one lesson, but the next day I noticed that when I gave a task explained principally on paper, one boy, Andrew, enthusiastic the previous day, was relying on his neighbour, Tim, to tell him what he had to do.

Why might Andrew seem 'different' today from the previous day? Could this involve Andrew having a SEN?

2 On classroom management and individual needs:

> Neil was in my Year 10 mathematics class (at another school). This class was set 5 out of 6; there was no classroom assistant, but there were only 17 pupils in the class. However, there were several 'personalities' who demanded attention. I had worked at the school for some years, but this class was fairly new to me. Neil never demanded attention; he smiled benignly, customarily sat on his own and usually appeared to be working. When I saw his work, he had often totally misconstrued the task. Here is a typical example.
>
> The class had been set the 'maximum volume' activity, in which they were given a rectangular piece of paper 20cm by 30cm. A square of side length x is cut from each corner of the rectangle, and the resulting shape is folded to make a lidless box. The task is to find the value of x that gives the greatest volume of box. This basic scenario can be presented in many different ways for different students.
>
> After the introduction, the pupils were free to do as much practical work as they wanted. Unlike everyone else, Neil went straight to filling in a table. He systematically set $x = 1, 2, 3, \ldots$ and worked out the volume with the formula that 'the class' had devised. By the time I got to his desk, I found that he had got to $x = 22$.
>
> Neil had documented specific learning difficulties related to autism (see below). Neil was happiest following a rule and not interacting with his peers. His peers, on the other hand, seemed to prefer interacting and not following rules. Even in a small class, Neil's education was at risk.

What classroom management strategy would you have tried at the next lesson?

Task 9.3 A longer-term relationship

1 Work regularly with one or two pupils with learning difficulties, whose attainment in mathematics is low, throughout the time you are placed at your school. As you work with the same pupils for several weeks, you will begin to understand them better and to see how profound some children's misconceptions can be. You should also find out 'ways through' to these children. It takes time!

2 If your school has any 'mathematically gifted' pupils, you may be able to contribute to their enrichment programme by providing extra resources (which will be a boon to the mathematics department) on current mathematical developments (like fractal geometry, for example) or in the form of new, challenging problems. You may also be able to engage the pupil in mathematical discussions on a more mathematical level than his or her classmates might be able to appreciate.

place value. This work can give a sense of the fundamental errors that are often made by pupils in the secondary age range.

When a pupil makes a mistake, clearly, it is important for you as a teacher to try to find out whether the error was careless, or due to a lack of understanding, or other obstacle (e.g. a reading difficulty). Sometimes, a repeated mistake may indicate a specific learning difficulty. For example, children who are good at mental arithmetic, but cannot get their 'Hundreds, Tens and Units' (HTUs) sorted out when writing, are exhibiting a behaviour associated with dyslexia. Errors can often reveal a lack of grasp of a topic that was officially 'done' ages ago – again like place value.

Here is some of Sharon's work (taken from Haylock, 1991, pp. 27–29). Sharon is working on addition of two-digit numbers in vertical form. She gets the same answer (21) to both of these additions:

$$\begin{array}{r} 25 \\ 17 \\ +\ 19 \\ \hline \end{array} \qquad \begin{array}{r} 36 \\ 18 \\ +\ 27 \\ \hline \end{array}$$

Later on, Sharon is asked to write down some numerals. She writes '10064' for 'one hundred and sixty four', and '17' for 'seventy' (which it seems she has genuinely confused, not misheard). Her lack of comprehension of place value is so immense that she avoided anything but units in her calculations (21 is the sum of the units column in both of the above additions).

Stories about children's relative competence with mental arithmetic falling apart when they are set on employing a written algorithm are legion. Derek Haylock's book also gives several examples of these (for example on pages 47–50), and there are other examples and strategies as well in *Mental Mathematics* (MA, 1992, pp. 1, 26–27).

The current resurgence of interest in 'numeracy' recognises the foundation that mental methods affords.

For further techniques on how to work in this situation, see Harry Daniels' (1988) article on 'miscue analysis', which suggests ways to find out what is going wrong in a child's understanding.

Task 9.4 Frequent errors

If you are assisting in a class and find a pupil making frequent errors in number work, use this as an opporunity to find out how she or he is reasoning:

- by asking her to explain her method to you;
- by working on some simple problems of that type mentally.

PARTICULAR SPECIAL NEEDS, STRATEGIES AND RESOURCES

In this section, you will find brief introductions to some SEN in mathematics that you might meet in your secondary mathematics teaching career. No list can be complete; new conditions are recognised as medicine and psychology progress. For example, the condition 'dyspraxia' – or clumsy child syndrome – may have particular ramifications for mathematics learning. (In a moving account, 'David's mother' relates her story and laments the lack of resources for mathematics for dyspraxic children – see issue 39 (1994) of the journal *Struggle*, details of which are in the Further Reading, and also Portwood, 1997.)

Dyspraxic children have difficulties with physical manipulation and sequencing which are important in the development of mathematical concepts. For some of the special needs listed, I shall suggest some teaching strategies, and in each case offer references to further strategies and resources.

Moderate learning difficulties (MLD)

Interviewer to Michael, aged nearly eleven: *How many years will it be until you're forty, Michael?*
Michael: *About fifty.*

(Haylock, 1991, p. 31)

These are the most prevalent conditions that you will meet in the mainstream secondary school. There is no clear dividing line between MLD pupils and other children, although some MLD pupils will have a Statement of SEN (in England, Wales and Northern Ireland) or a Record of Needs (in Scotland). Many people find mathematics difficult to learn for a host of reasons, such as poor memory, difficulty with reading or interpretation of meanings. A list of factors associated with low attainment in mathematics by a sample of teachers is also given by Haylock. The predominant categories include being perceived as 'low-achieving', having poor language skills and being immature (in terms of physical dexterity or emotion) (Haylock, 1991, p. 41).

Resources you will need to teach these pupils include patience, imagination and humour. You might have felt you had a successful lesson one day, and find the next that the mathematical point of the lesson has not been remembered. For example, I had thought that my probability lesson had 'gone well', but the next day I realised that talk of the chance of Oxford United being relegated had been considered a discussion on football. An engaging context is often a useful start; the difficulty is generalisation from the context, which is the essence of mathematics. Harry Daniels and Julia Anghileri (1995, p. 96) point out, in the context of algebra, that the capability to abstract can be a significant confidence boost for these pupils, and abstraction will often be achieved initially through verbal, rather than written symbolic, expression.

There is a fine line between recognising that we learn at different rates and in different ways, and attributing a fixed quantity of 'mathematical ability' to each child. This sort of attribution of ability has been called 'ability stereotyping' by Kenneth Ruthven. He writes how labelling people can limit expectations, which can happen frequently in school mathematics classes where those who are classified as 'low attainers' may be rewarded for incorrect answers, may not be given time to answer questions, or may not be given feedback on their work (Ruthven, 1987, p. 249).

One of the best challenges to the idea that children with weak reasoning skills, poor memories and difficult behaviour (typically members of your 'bottom set') require unstimulating mathematics came from the 'Low Attainers in Mathematics Project' (LAMP) directed by Afzal Ahmed in the 1980s. Something of their approach is captured in Statement 4 from their report *Better Mathematics*:

> Mathematics is effectively learnt only by experimenting, questioning, reflecting, discovering, inventing and discussing. Thus for children, mathematics should be a kind of learning which requires a minimum of factual knowledge and a great deal of experience in dealing with situations using particular kinds of thinking skills.
>
> (DES, 1987, p. 17)

Better Mathematics is an inspiring document that offers insight into teachers' learning as well as providing a practical resource. The Daniels and Anghileri book, mentioned above, offers general strategies for those students who find mathematics difficult, as do Larcombe (1985) and authors of various articles in the journal *Equals* (see Further Reading).

Emotional and behavioural difficulties (EBD)

This is also a very wide term, which you may feel would encompass many pupils at times in their school career. Capel *et al.* offer some 'points to consider' when working with EBD pupils that they have adapted from the DfEE's Circular 9/94:

> - appropriate school and teacher responses make a difference;
> - behaviour may improve if pupils' self-esteem is enhanced;
> - the teacher needs to be constructive and positive as well as specific about what is and is not acceptable;
> - parental involvement is to be encouraged;
> - stages 1–3 of the Code of Practice (England and Wales) describe school-based strategies which can help;
> - pupils should be given short-term goals which stretch but do not overwhelm them;
> - the curriculum should be relevant;
> - sanctions should not include educational activities as punishment.
>
> (Capel *et al.*, 1995, p. 206)

In practical terms, there are usually two alternative ways to manage a class that includes children with behavioural difficulties: harder or softer. These management styles have a strong influence on the mathematics curriculum. If you take a harder approach, you may find one unforeseen consequence of separating, quietening and reprimanding the pupils is that you deliver an individualised curriculum. This may, of necessity, have to consist primarily of short, routinisable tasks, what might be called 'junk mathematics' (DES, 1987, p. 15). On the other hand, you could opt to take a softer approach that focuses on the relationships within the class, through working with mathematical games, projects in small groups, and perhaps discussion. Be aware that this will need careful planning, especially if it is a new style of working for the pupils.

Before you change the management style, it is wise to discuss such a move with your tutor or the usual class teacher. A first step could be to take a group of, say, four pupils to try to work co-operatively round a table on a mathematical game. In this way, you should avoid a riot, as well as having a much more amenable group of people with whom to work. The children's self-esteem is likely to be raised through their achievement in mathematics, which they will be able to express in terms of words and actions rather than formal symbols.

There is a category of student whose emotional problems (as manifest in mathematics lessons) come directly from their experience of mathematics: the very thought of mathematics puts them in a mind-numbing panic. Laurie Buxton (1981), in his book *Do You Panic About Maths?*, has written about his work with 'mathophobic' adult students who make substantial strides when their confidence has been strengthened.

Hearing impairment, sight impairment and other physical disabilities

Children in wheelchairs, with hearing aids or with limited vision are integrated whenever possible into mainstream schooling. They are, however, likely to have a Statement of SEN, and so you will have professional advice to turn to for specific teaching strategies tailored to their individual needs. Children with profound physical impairments will have classroom assistants to help them in their ordinary classroom work. Working collaboratively with your pupils' classroom assistant(s) should help to offer these pupils greater opportunity of equal access to the curriculum.

Although physical disabilities vary a great deal, mathematics can be a school subject in which physically disabled pupils have far greater equality of access. In an article by Jackie Callinan (1992), you can read about a mathematics teacher who works with children with severe physical disabilities. Callinan has designed a curriculum that tries to minimise the particular problems these pupils face with spatial awareness, emotional frustration, limitations of social experience and restricted language, so that they can experience mathematical achievement like able-bodied children.

Hearing impairment puts children's mathematical attainment at risk, but is not itself a cause of their frequently being chronologically behind their hearing peers. This is the conclusion of Nunes and Moreno's (1997) research on deaf children's understanding of number. Some strategies for teaching hearing impaired children are given in Capel *et al.* (1995). Some examples of their advice include:

- give visual cues to topics being discussed;
- make sure the pupil is watching your face when you speak and sittting within three metres of you;
- repeat what classmates have said in discussion.

(Capel *et al.*, 1995, pp. 206–207)

Computers have enormous potential in helping hearing impaired children (Barham and Bishop, 1991), as their capacity to work dynamically and visually can help these pupils to develop mathematical concepts without overly relying on detailed spoken language.

For non-subject-specific advice, see John Cornwall's (1997) practical guide for mainstream teachers of pupils with physical disabilities.

Dyslexia

Dyslexia is now understood as an umbrella term (or 'syndrome') connoting certain types of brain functioning that often manifest themselves in difficulties with written symbolic material, difficulty in rote learning and short-term memory defects, even though the person may be otherwise talented in logic, art or engineering. It is conjectured that: 'the balance between the two cerebral hemispheres is different in dyslexics' (Miles and Miles, 1992, p. 2).

A dyslexic person may be good at tasks involving spatial awareness or strategy, but find it difficult to pair the symbol (either spoken or written) with the meaning. For example, a dyslexic might write sequential numbers as 11, 21, 31, 41, . . . and read these as 'eleven, twelve, thirteen, fourteen'. Miles and Miles (1992, pp. 11–12) report on dyslexics who have made substantial achievements in mathematics. Problems with the symbolic aspects of language can often mask a keen perception of structure within patterns. Logic and structures of patterns are deeply mathematical and often accessible to dyslexics, who may yet find it difficult to communicate this understanding.

Anne Henderson (1992) points out that dyslexic pupils in secondary school are often intelligent young people who are severely lacking in confidence, as they have had such problems with the symbolic and automatic recall aspects of school mathematics. Confidence building is a crucial part of their mathematics curriculum.

Dyslexics can often achieve highly on spatial or strategic tasks. Indeed, a multisensory approach to teaching dyslexics is important. Because of their short-term memory problems, geometric imagery can often help dyslexic pupils to 'plant' a concept. For example, Andrew (mentioned in Task 9.2) was not able to set out a 'long multiplication', as he could not get the columns right, even though he could calculate some TU by TU multiplications in his head. By representing multiplications as areas, he was much more successful.

Are there specific teaching strategies for dyslexics? There are some, and evaluating whether strategies designed for dyslexics may be helpful for all children is the purpose behind Task 9.5.

Task 9.5 Working with dyslexia

Read an article on an aspect of specific pedagogy for dyslexics, for example Chapters 3, 4, 6 or 7 in Miles and Miles (1992) are suitable, or a section of Chinn and Ashcroft (1993). Then try to incorporate these ideas into a lesson with one of your usual classes. Evaluate, as usual.

Dyscalculia

Some consider this condition a result of a rare neurological disorder that results in people of average or high intelligence not being able to retain knowledge or understanding of even the simplest mathematics. The mathematical attainment of pupils with this disability is very, very different from their attainment in other parts of the curriculum. However, there is disagreement among the experts (Miles and Miles, 1992, pp. 77–78; Richards, 1982, pp. 18–20) as to whether the condition can properly be distinguished from dyslexia. Miles and Miles argue that it is unlikely that a person who muddles left and right in an addition sum is always going to get the senses correct in other situations. But Richards quotes empirical evidence of pupils whose verbal and mathematical test scores are at opposite ends of the attainment spectrum: verbally competent pupils fail consistently to recall even the simplest number bonds.

Autistic spectrum and Asperger's syndrome

'Autism' is an umbrella term for a disability arising from an impaired capacity for social interaction. This disability leads to problems with language and communication, and therefore learning in a school classroom is especially difficult for pupils with autism who may exhibit 'challenging behaviour'. People with autism vary: 'from withdrawn individuals to those who are "active but odd"' (Jordan and Powell, 1995, p. 4).

The term 'Asperger's syndrome' is often used for 'high functioning' autistic individuals. Some people with Asperger's syndrome may well be exceptionally gifted in some particular like mathematics, yet still be socially inept (like the main character in the film 'Rain Man').

For these children, 'relevant' mathematics can be even more of a mystery than pure mathematics. An emphasis on 'real-life' mathematics can obscure the logic of the subject, because of the confusing social and linguistic details, rather than motivating it by placing it in a relevant context. For example, money is often used to help a child understand decimals, whereas for a relatively 'high functioning' autistic child, decimals, once understood, can be used to help explain how the currency functions. These children may be able to suceed in mathematics if language and social interaction are recognised as a significant hurdle and if they are taught the mathematics first.

Jane Inglese has written an excellent, short introductory article on children with 'autistic spectrum disorders', whose prevalence is becoming increasingly recognised. Inglese points out that:

> many of our stock-in-trade approaches – presentation, questions and problem-solving tasks mediated by language are likely to give rise to confusion. [But because of the] ordered patterns, predictable outcomes and neat, memorable patterns which numbers offer [autistic or Asperger's children are often comfortable with numbers].
>
> (Inglese, 1997, p. 18)

These children are also often good at the geometric aspects of the curriculum, which does not demand so much productive language. Inglese remarks that these children: 'challenge the teacher to conceive of a kind of mathematical thinking which does not use internalised language but visual representations' (Inglese, 1997, p. 18).

A more thorough, but general, reference is Jordan and Powell's (1995) book, which gives a cognitive perspective on the way in which people with autism think and also offers some strategies to assist teachers to help their pupils with autistic spectrum disorders to learn.

Frequently absent children

It is difficult to plan a curriculum for a child who attends school sporadically. There are various categories of such children, for example:

Sick children and pregnant schoolgirls

The social services and health services have a role here, but there is a real need to get subject specialists involved with older children who are unable to attend their school. One visit to the home of such a child (probably to be organised through the head of year) can give a tremendous boost to the pupil's interest, the parents' confidence and a sense of the pupil still being part of the school community. (See Carol Orton's (1995) piece, 'A parent's search for a question' for a personal story.)

Truants or school refusers

There are all sorts of reasons that children truant. When they return, it is often only for a day or so, after which you may not see them for another month. Tasks based on their interests are most likely to help their self-esteem and sense of belonging in the school. For example, Perry was a frequent truant, but he could, and would, access mathematics through art activities, which he would continue even when not at school. (There are many excellent books available linking art and mathematics; for a teaching approach see, for example, Jones, 1991.)

'Exceptionally able' children

Every comprehensive school, statistically, should have the occasional pupil who is different by virtue of their exceptional understanding of mathematics. As Krutetskii's seminal work on able mathematical children reported, these exceptional children exhibit a range of different abilities: some are more logic-based, others more verbal. Some are very quick and others 'just' deep:

> In obtaining information, these children grasp the formal structure of a problem. In processing mathematical information, they think in mathematical symbols; generalise broadly; curtail mathematical processes; are flexible in mathematical activity; strive for elegant, concise solutions. They have a memory for mathematical relationships, concepts and proofs.
>
> (Krutetskii, 1976, pp. 350–351)

It may be threatening, especially as a new teacher, to be asked to teach a pupil who may be a more promising mathematician than oneself. As with other special needs, you can contribute to such a child's education most effectively when you understand their particular need and work towards satisfying their requirements.

Exceptionally capable pupils do not need to do twice as many exercises as most pupils just because they are able to work faster – they may, in fact, need only half as many, because they catch on more quickly. Requiring such a pupil to do 'lots' may cause the pupil to become bored, and the lack of a challenge may lead to carelessness. The strategy often taken for these pupils is that of 'enrichment', which usually has two forms (both of which have strengths).

- Additional material is given to the able child to work through either alone or with some help from the teacher. For example, some aspects of group theory might be a suitable topic for an exceptional 11–16 student.
- Problems that differentiate by outcome. These are open-ended tasks given to the class of pupils, which give the opportunity for group discussion.

There are many resources that can be used to enrich the experience of these pupils. For example, the Mathematical Association has a 'Society for Young Mathematicians', which can provide support. Any book on mathematical puzzles, such as those by Martin Gardner (1978) or David Wells (1992 and 1994), could also be useful. There are several Web sites that provide both mathematical challenges and communication with other mathematicians, for example the 'on-line maths club', NRICH, at http://www.nrich.maths.org.uk

A very talented pupil, Sian, drew my attention to another requirement of these pupils: they need to be taught to struggle with difficulties! Sian told me about a problem, which she did not see how to do immediately, and in response to which she had found herself panicking. When you understand very easily, you may, nevertheless, need guidance on how to approach deep and challenging problems for which understanding is not immediate.

English as a second (or third or . . .) language

In Chapter 7, Communicating Mathematically, you read about some of the ways in which language affects learning, specifically in mathematics. Children who are not completely fluent in English (E2L) have special needs in trying to speak school mathematical English. Their linguistic difficulties can sometimes mask their mathematical competence. Alan Bishop has a salutary story about such a child, Mohammed, who was: 'bored and listless by being in a low set because his mathematical aptitude was obscured by his English language weakness' (Bishop, 1991, p. 30). This Year 9 pupil showed that he understood some level 7/8 mathematics but was not being given the chance to develop his mathematics as he was placed in a 'bottom' set.

The question about how much English the E2L pupils need to be taught to enable the development of new mathematical concepts within the British school system is very subtle and clearly depends on the pupils and context. At nursery level, I have observed language support teachers encourage bilingual development of concepts like number, shape and measure. This bilingual (or multilingual) approach seems ideal where it can be well resourced and supported. It encourages mental flexibility as well as developing the pupil's self-confidence within the increasingly melding cultures of home and school.

Task 9.6 Foreign mental arithmetic

If you are essentially monolingual, this task will help you to appreciate the difficulties experienced by many E2L students in mathematics.

When you were at school, you may have studied a modern foreign language. Find someone else who studied this language to the same standard as you, and give each other a mental arithmetic test in the foreign language.

This activity can be fun, but it can also help you to feel how brilliant your mathematical understanding is compared with your ability to respond to the questions. ESL students feel this cognitive–linguistic gap in every class.

There are some further activities of this sort in *Talking Maths, Talking Languages* (ATM, 1993a, pp. 17–19).

In the secondary classroom, skilled multilingual mathematical support is not often available for E2L pupils, and so classroom materials become more important. However, as Bishop (1991) reports from his work:

> The language aspect of the materials was a continual cause for comment among teachers and pupils, largely because most available texts seem to make little concession to the E2L beginner. Consequently, much time was spent by both mathematics and E2L support teachers in explaining what many of the words meant and what one was supposed to do in any particular exercise.
>
> (Bishop, 1991, p. 36)

Appropriate classroom materials need not just be text-based: practical work, visual representations and technological advances can both cut through the language barrier and become media for inducting the E2L pupil into using school mathematical English, which is vital for his or her future.

MORE GENERAL ASPECTS OF SPECIAL NEEDS

Frustration: a special needs common denominator

If there is anything common to all special needs pupils, it is the greater probability of their being frustrated within the mainstream class. Imagine simply not quite being able to see or hear. Imagine being always given unchallenging work because it was felt that something 'straightforward' would keep you quiet. Imagine having to do exercise after exercise of some mathematics that is obvious to you and that you understood immediately years ago. Imagine never understanding any teacher's explanation, and having to hope for a task and a helper to guide you through it.

Task 9.7 Frustration

Consider some other special needs and imagine the type of frustration that might arise. Do this in two ways: first, by focusing on the special need (e.g. dyslexia), and second, by trying to empathise with one of the special needs pupils with whom you have worked. Are there any different insights available from the two approaches?

What can a class teacher do to minimise frustration due to the special need? This does *not* mean the teacher should minimise the pupil's struggle or effort. On the contrary, those of us who have studied mathematics have experienced the 'frustration' of working on a problem that refuses to yield as well as the satisfaction when it does. Learning to apply mental effort to solve mathematical problems is a major achievement for children of all capabilities; part of a secondary mathematics teacher's job is to help children develop their mental 'muscles'. The frustration arising from a special need is essentially different from 'mathematical struggle' or mental effort.

Complementary to pupil 'frustration' is pupil 'satisfaction'. Haylock (1991, p. 2) reports how he found, in his research, that low-attaining pupils rarely had the opportunity to experience the satisfaction that mathematical achievement can give. Indeed, for every special need mentioned above, the teacher's challenge is to turn 'frustration' into 'satisfaction' caused by that pupil's own mathematical achievement.

As a mathematics teacher, you could aim to maximise struggle or effort while minimising frustration. In so doing, you have to work within the constraint of the special need and the mathematics curriculum. For some children, you cannot push the challenge too far before the frustration becomes overwhelming. For others, lack of a challenge may exacerbate their frustration.

One of the team: managing SEN in a mainstream school

Schools have certain statutory responsibilities for pupils with SEN (see Daniels and Anghileri, 1995, pp. 130–132). These are translated into school policy by the SENCO and other staff. Most teachers will have some SEN pupils and so become, *de facto*, part of the special needs team. The following features have been identified as contributing to successful teaching of pupils with SEN within the mainstream classroom:

- clear specification of roles and responsibilities;
- detailed record keeping;
- careful organisation of resources;
- regular meetings to plan and evaluate;
- flexibility.

(Daniels and Anghileri, 1995, pp. 134–135)

One of the roles of the SENCO is to ensure that everyone who should know about a particular pupil's special need is (a) aware of the need; (b) set to help with that need. For example, everyone who teaches a child who is prone to epilepsy should be aware of the possibility that s/he may have a fit, and be able to cope while someone else goes for more specialist help.

Task 9.8 SEN channels of communication

The aim of this task is for you to find out about what sort of information about pupils' SEN is communicated from whom, to whom, and in what manner. Because much of this kind of information is confidential, it may not be possible to talk with your SENCO about particular individuals. Indeed, it might be as well to do this task as part of a 'whole-school professional programme' seminar with other students or NQTs.

To get a sense of the variety of information, types of expertise and forms of communication, please ask your SENCO:

- to describe some of the different sources from which information about children with special needs, in particular SEN, comes (e.g. medical services, psychological services, parents, social services, other LEA sources);
- to outline, typically, which staff s/he sends information to about a specific child's SEN, and what s/he anticipates that member of staff will do with the information (e.g. file it, induct another member of staff, design/acquire new curriculum materials);
- to explain how information about a child's special needs is disseminated (e.g. case conference, staff meeting, written communication to subject teachers, confidential conversation).

Managing your special needs auxiliary

Various terms are used to describe the 'classroom assistants' employed to help children with special needs. What term is used in your school?

A difficult job for a new teacher is the management of the 'special needs helpers' who are attached to pupils with special needs statements to provide them with in-class support in your lessons. It is a task requiring tact and vision. The pointers to good practice listed above may help you in this important task. The variety of these 'classroom assistants' is as wide as the special needs of the children they are employed to help. A few are trained teachers, many are wise and wonderful people, but some classroom assistants are not at ease with mathematics. They may need your guidance and help in providing appropriate support for the pupils.

For example, my Year 9 were working on multiplication by ten. The classroom assistant was working with Conrad and had told him to multiply by 10 by 'adding a nought'. When I found out that this had been the instruction to Conrad, I understood why all his answers the next day (when the assistant was not there) were but a tenth of my expectation. The assistant genuinely thought that she was helping Conrad get the answers efficiently by telling him what to do. But she was working on an instrumental level (Skemp, 1976). Conrad had no substantial multiplication schema, and this was needed before he was able to incorporate symbolic manipulation (appropriate positioning of the zero) in his multiplication calculations.

Working in a classroom with a classroom assistant can be a tremendous opportunity, but you need to plan carefully to take full advantage of it. In some ways, it is like team-teaching a lesson, where you take the lead and the classroom assistant provides support. Your lesson is more likely to be successful if you are able to involve the assistant in your planning before the lesson, and to plan not only what you will do, but also how the assistant is to assist.

For a young, student or newly qualified teacher, working with someone of a different generation can sometimes be socially awkward, but a collaborative model of teaching can provide a positive approach that respects the contributions of both teacher and assistant for SEN pupils. As an example, in the earlier section on emotional and behavioural difficulties, I reported that pupils who find mathematics difficult usually generalise initially by verbalising their findings, rather than writing them symbolically. A useful collaborative role that the assistant could play would be to help pupils verbalise their findings, prior to encouraging them to write.

SUMMARY

As this chapter is being written, substantial changes have been proposed to special needs provision. In particular, more and more SEN children are now being educated within mainstream schools. This increasing inclusion has been going on since since the Warnock Report (DES, 1978) raised awareness about the prevalence of SEN. Inclusion will feature in subsequent legislation for two reasons:

- the moral stance that society should respect all its members;
- the economic pressure that separate special education is expensive and variable in its quality.

In the next century, a greater proportion of pupils who have SEN will be welcomed into mainstream classrooms. The challenges will be substantial. Teachers will be expected to know about a given pupil's condition, so that they can plan for their learning, communicate with their parents or carers, and manage their learning support. And the rewards of teaching pupils with SEN as part of a whole school community will be enormous. What is more, as you enlarge your teaching repertoire to deal with SEN requirements, your increased flexibility and skill will be of benefit to all the people you teach.

FURTHER READING

Buxton, L. (1981) *Do You Panic about Maths?: Coping with Maths Anxiety*, London: Heinemann Educational.

The message of this book is salutary for any mathematics teacher: intelligent people can leave school having a real fear of mathematics. Buxton's case studies make compelling reading and give insight into how our affective side affects learning; this awareness should be particularly relevant when teaching pupils with SEN.

Chinn, S. J. and Ashcroft, J. R. (1993) *Mathematics for Dyslexics*, London: Whurr Publishing.

Whilst this book is targeted for dyslexics, its practical advice on a multi-sensory teaching approach can be helpful for many pupils (including those without SEN).

Daniels, H. and Anghileri, J. (1995) *Secondary Mathematics and Special Educational Needs*, London: Cassell.

This recent publication contains substantial background to mathematics teaching and SEN. In several places, the authors have taken a historical perspective towards developments in the cultural acceptance of SEN, educational legislation and specific SEN provision, which gives a helpful picture of this important part of teaching practice, particularly in England and Wales. Detailed references are given to others' research, making this also a useful reference book.

DES (1987) *Better Mathematics: A Curriculum Development Study*, London: HMSO.

This book is a report on a long-term project, which initially focused on low attainers in mathematics, then widened its brief to consider teaching methods for pupils of all attainment levels. Part of the report shows that good teaching, which helps raise low attainment, can help improve any given current attainment. Another part of the report communicates the importance of teachers' involvement in curriculum development.

DfE (1994) *The Code of Practice on the Identification and Assessment of SEN*, London: DFE.

This code applies in England and Wales; it is covered in an accessible way in the companion volume (Capel *et al.*, 1995, section 4.6). Further information may be obtained from the informative, sometimes critical, historical outline given in the first chapter of Daniels and Anghileri's comprehensive book on special needs and secondary mathematics (1995, pp. 1–16). In Scotland, advice about pupils' special needs is communicated through the Parents' Guide, the Curricular Assessment and the HMI document on Effective Provision. In Northern Ireland, a Code of Practice is due in September 1998.

Equals (formerly called *Struggle*)

This is a termly magazine, dedicated to mathematics and special needs, and is published by the Mathematical Association. The majority of the articles are by teachers and others working directly with people with special needs; the articles are short and practical.

Haylock, D. (1991) *Teaching Mathematics to Low Attainers 8–12*, London: Paul Chapman.

This practical book focuses on the 'middle school' age range, but many of the children's difficulties are also to be met in older pupils. Haylock gives plenty of suggestions for engaging activities, many of which are suitable for the entire low-attaining secondary cohort. A particularly useful feature of this book is the detail with which a conceptual problem is analysed; this is then followed by specific activities offered as a potential remedy.

10 Getting the Whole Picture

John Westwell

INTRODUCTION

As a mathematics teacher, it is natural that you will want to give much of your attention to teaching mathematics in mathematics lessons. However, it is also important that you consider your broader responsibilities as a teacher. Section 1 of the Education Reform Act 1988 places a statutory responsibility upon schools to provide a broad and balanced curriculum that:

- promotes the spiritual, moral, cultural, mental and physical development of pupils at the school and of society;
- prepares pupils for the opportunities, responsibilities and experiences of adult life.

It is clear from these requirements that your role as a teacher is much broader than solely assisting the mental development of pupils within the field of mathematics. One way to consider your role is to examine what contribution you can make to the whole curriculum experience of your pupils. A second approach is to consider your part in developing a pupil as a whole person. Both are addressed in this chapter.

You may, however, initially consider that it is quite enough for you to concentrate on developing pupils' mathematical knowledge, skills and understanding. To take this view, though, is to miss opportunities that arise from taking whole-curriculum and whole-person perspectives. Instead, if you do address the broader aspects of your role, then the personal qualities and attitudes that support pupils' learning of mathematics will be fostered at the same time.

OBJECTIVES

By the end of this chapter, you should be able to:

- understand better your role as a maths teacher in contributing to a whole-curriculum perspective;
- appreciate the opportunities and difficulties presented by developing cross-curricular links;
- be more aware of your responsibility to contribute to the personal development of your pupils;
- plan more effectively for teaching that addresses the development of the whole person.

THE WHOLE CURRICULUM

Although the secondary school curriculum has traditionally been organised into subjects with their own slots on the timetable, there has long been recognition that the curriculum is much more than a series of discrete learning experiences. Consequently, there have been attempts over the years to describe the *whole curriculum*. When the England and Wales National Curriculum was introduced, the National Curriculum Council (1990) published guidance in a series of papers linked to this issue. Elements that were seen to contribute to the total curriculum experience of pupils were:

- National Curriculum subjects;
- religious education;
- additional subjects;
- cross-curricular dimensions, skills and themes;
- extra-curricular activities.

Some of these elements are of more relevance to you than others, and will be addressed in the sections that follow, but first it is important to consider the impact of the whole curriculum on pupils' attitudes towards mathematics.

Attitudes towards mathematics

One of your aims as a maths teacher is likely to be that your pupils develop positive attitudes towards mathematics. Not only can this support more effective learning, but it is also a valid objective in its own right. There have been various official descriptions of attitudes to be fostered and encouraged, including this list produced by HMI (DES, 1985) and used again in the National Curriculum non-statutory guidance (DES/WO, 1989b, p. B11):

- fascination with the subject;
- interest and motivation;
- pleasure and enjoyment from mathematical activities;
- appreciation of the power, purpose and relevance of mathematics;
- satisfaction derived from a sense of achievement;
- confidence in an ability to do mathematics at an appropriate level.

(DES, 1985, p. 25)

These are challenging objectives, all the more so when you consider that every experience that pupils have of learning or using mathematics will shape their attitudes:

> During every mathematics lesson a child is not only learning, or failing to learn, mathematics as a result of the work he is doing but is also developing his attitude towards mathematics. In every mathematics lesson his teacher is conveying, even if unconsciously, a message about mathematics which will influence his attitude. Once attitudes have been formed, they can be very persistent and difficult to change. Positive attitudes assist the learning of mathematics; negative attitudes not only inhibit learning but [. . .] very often persist into adult life and affect choice of job.
>
> (DES, 1982, para. 345)

It is essential, therefore, that you pay attention to your pupils' mathematical experience, not only in maths lessons but right across the curriculum. Pupils will be forming their attitudes towards mathematics as they use it in other subjects, so it is important that this be a positive experience.

Links with other subjects

A good way to start developing a whole-curriculum perspective is to establish a working partnership with a colleague who teaches another subject. You can help each other develop an understanding of the links between your respective subjects at different levels. You need to establish how and when mathematics is needed and used in the other subject. As a result, your colleague will understand more about the mathematics, how it is taught and the difficulties that pupils may have with it. You, in turn, will understand more about how mathematics is used in different contexts and when it might be helpful to introduce pupils to particular topics.

Having developed this greater understanding of the links between the subjects (a worthwhile objective in its own right), it is possible to go further and plan some lessons collaboratively. This could lead to:

- some lessons in the other subject that build on the links with maths;
- some lessons in mathematics that build on the links with the other subject;
- some co-ordinated lessons in both subjects that have a related focus.

It is also important to establish how maths lessons can contribute to learning in the other subject as well. The benefit for pupils of such collaboration is that they have greater opportunity to practise using their knowledge, skills and understanding and to develop greater appreciation of the 'power, purpose and relevance of mathematics'.

If you are to establish good links with other subjects, then there are some significant barriers to overcome. The most serious hindrance to progress is 'lack of time'. Most maths teachers recognise the potential for links, but find it difficult to organise enough time for establishing them effectively with their colleagues. Cross-curricular work rarely takes top priority. This is linked to the strong subject matter culture that exists in many secondary schools. Leadership within schools needs to challenge this culture if any meaningful cross-subject links are to be established. At the same time, investing in resources for any cross-subject initiatives will support this change. However, having said this, much can still be accomplished by two teachers who are enthusiastic to develop links and are prepared to grapple with the problems.

Task 10.1 Measure audit

The purpose of the task is to investigate pupils' experience of measuring across the curriculum and to produce a report making recommendations to the mathematics department. By talking to as many different subject teachers as is feasible, investigate the following questions.

- What sort of measures do pupils use within the subject, e.g. time, capacity, weight, etc.?
- What units are normally used for the different measures?
- How much practical measuring do pupils do?
- What measuring instruments do they use?
- Are they required to estimate measurements at all?
- At what stages do the pupils first use the different measures?

Also, find out how the mathematics department currently addresses the 'measures' strand through their schemes of work. Write a summary of the results of your investigations. Also make written recommendations to the department regarding:

- the stage at which certain measures should be addressed;
- the balance of time spent on different sorts of measures;
- the kind of practical measuring experiences pupils should have.

Cross-curricular skills

There are many skills that have relevance across the curriculum, such as communication skills (oracy, literacy), numeracy, problem solving and study skills. All teachers have a shared responsibility in these areas, and this is emphasised by the requirement in Ofsted inspections to report on how pupils' numeracy, literacy and IT skills are developed across the curriculum. However, for this to be successful, there needs to be some co-ordinated planning. In their original guidance in this field, the NCC stated: 'The National Curriculum Council considers it absolutely essential that these skills are fostered across the whole curriculum in a measured and planned way' (NCC, 1990, p. 5). This means that schools need to have policies for how they address these different cross-curricular skills. Just as there are difficulties with cross-subject links, establishing whole-school policies presents even more complex problems. Different schools can consequently be at quite different stages of development in this area.

Task 10.2 Towards a whole-school numeracy policy

Given the greater attention currently being placed on standards of numeracy, schools are going to become more and more accountable for the way in which numeracy is addressed across the curriculum. In this task, you are to explore how your school is addressing this issue. Investigate whether your school has a policy for numeracy. If it does, read it and investigate:

- how it was developed and who was involved;
- how successfully it is being implemented;
- its impact upon the maths department.

If the school does *not* have a policy, investigate:

- whether there are plans to develop one;
- what barriers there have been to developing a policy already;
- what role the maths department expects to play in the development of a future policy.

Record in your journal key lessons that emerge from your investigation.

Even when school policies on cross-curricular skills are not that coherent, you still have a responsibility to help your pupils develop the full range of skills. This includes considering how you structure lessons to help pupils develop their communication skills, planning activities to give pupils experience of extended problem-solving situations, and helping pupils to reflect upon the ways in which they learn most effectively. The other area in which you should meet the need to address core skills is in post-16 courses. Vocational qualifications already require pupils to demonstrate skills of communication, application of number and information technology; other post-16 courses may also have a core skill element (see Chapter 11).

Cross-curricular themes

Whilst the curriculum continues to be framed by tight subject boundaries, there will always be areas of study that do not fit neatly into the domain of single subjects. For example, it is generally accepted that health education is of value to all pupils, but there is no single subject where this can be adequately addressed. This is one example of what the NCC called a *cross-curricular theme*. In 1990, five such themes were identified, which although 'by no means a comprehensive list, seem to most people to be pre-eminent. It is reasonable to assume that they are essential parts of the whole curriculum' (NCC, 1990, p. 4). The themes were economic and industrial understanding; careers education and guidance; health education; education for citizenship; and environmental education. Which themes are considered essential will change over time, and their relative prominence depends upon how effectively they are promoted. In the late 1990s, for example, there is a growing interest in citizenship becoming the key cross-curricular theme.

Some maths teachers have long recognised the value of addressing some of these themes within their teaching. They have devised resources and activities that have both enriched pupils' mathematical experience and developed their knowledge and understanding in the field being considered. Some of this work has been written up and can act as a stimulus for other teachers. Organisations that have an interest in promoting the place of certain themes within the curriculum can also be good sources for ideas and resources. For example, the World-Wide Fund for Nature (WWF, 1990) has published a book on mathematics and environmental education. However, resources are not always available for some of the themes. For example, if the careers education and guidance theme is to be addressed successfully, then some research work needs to be undertaken.

Finally, the case for the maths teacher taking whole-curriculum issues seriously is put strongly by the mathematics educator Brian Hudson:

> I would argue for a whole school approach to environmental education and regard my role as a teacher as involving the education of the whole child. In adopting such an approach, I would expect that I would be more likely to achieve my objectives as a mathematics teacher given the greater level of interest, motivation and understanding on the part of the pupils. At the same time, I would be contributing to their personal development and helping prepare them for their future role as citizens in an increasingly complex and interdependent world.
>
> (Hudson, 1994, p. 124)

Task 10.3 What use is mathematics?

For many pupils, there seems to be little connection between the mathematics they study at school and their future working life. In this task, you are asked to plan and teach a lesson or a series of lessons that draws upon the experience of someone who uses mathematics in their work. Preparation will need to begin some time in advance of the lesson.

Begin by establishing contact with someone whom you consider to use mathematics in their work. Discuss together how mathematics is used and consider together how this could be presented to pupils. Plan a lesson that involves:

- a description of your contact's work;
- opportunity for pupils to find out more about your contact's career;
- explanation of the way in which mathematics is used within the work;
- a task that simulates the kind of mathematical work done by your contact.

This sort of lesson is significantly enhanced by having your contact person play a full part, but there is still value in the approach if this proves not to be possible.

After the lesson, find out how both your contact and your pupils found the lesson, and consider what would improve similar lessons in the future.

THE WHOLE PERSON

As pupils move from primary to secondary school, they experience a major shift in the way their learning is organised. From having had essentially just one teacher, who was responsible for their all-round education, they now have many teachers for many different subjects: the unit of structural organisation is the subject as much as the class. Schools try to support pupils through this transition by assigning them a tutor, who is intended to offer the pupils the pastoral care that they need. However, pupils spend the large majority of their time with the subject teachers. What is their role in seeing the pupil develop as a whole person? This section examines this question from the point of view of the maths teacher.

Personal qualities

There has been a long tradition within mathematics education that recognises the contribution that it can make in developing the pupils' personal qualities. The HMI made explicit the qualities they believed should be encouraged through mathematics education (DES, 1985, p. 24), including: being imaginative, creative, flexible; systematic; independent in thought and action; co-operative and persistent. There is a similar list in the National Curriculum non-statutory guidance (DES/WO, 1989b, p. B10). Plainly, though, these qualities do not develop as a matter of course: 'To achieve success in each aspect, it is essential that the classroom approaches are designed so as to foster its development' (DES, 1985, p. 25). It is important that, in evaluating the effectiveness of lessons, you consider the impact of your teaching approaches on the development of the pupils' personal qualities.

Task 10.4 Observing qualities and attitudes

For this task, observe a mathematics lesson and consider the impact on the pupils' attitudes towards mathematics and the development of their personal qualities. Prepare an observation sheet that lists positive attitudes (see earlier section) and the personal qualities described in this section.

During the lesson, record examples of:

- pupils displaying positive attitudes;
- pupils displaying negative attitudes;
- pupils exhibiting positive personal qualities;
- the teacher actively encouraging positive personal qualities.

After the lesson, write up your observations in your journal and reflect upon the impact on the lesson. In particular, consider how the teacher might have done things differently in order to have had a greater impact on the development of the pupils' qualities and attitudes. Finally, record in your journal the attitudes and qualities that you will aim to foster within your teaching.

Personal development

There is general acceptance that schools must address the personal development of their pupils. This is shown by schools acknowledging the importance of establishing a supportive ethos, and by the provision of Personal and Social Education (or variations) courses. However, since the 1988 Education Reform Act, schools and curriculum bodies have given much more attention to how all teachers can contribute to the personal development of their pupils. This has been addressed by considering the categories of spiritual, moral, social and cultural (SMSC) development. Although the 1944 Education Act had also referred to these aspects of education, schools had not been held to account for their general curricular provision in this area. This changed significantly with the 1992 Education (Schools)

Act, which saw the birth of Ofsted and required Registered Inspectors to report on the SMSC development of pupils within the schools they inspected.

Beyond these curricular and inspection requirements, the standards for QTS in England and Wales require teachers to engage pupils by 'exploiting opportunities to contribute to the quality of pupils' wider educational development, including their personal, spiritual, moral, social and cultural development' (DfEE, 1998, p. 13). There is, therefore, a responsibility for you as a mathematics teacher, as with other issues addressed in this chapter, to consider the implications for your curriculum planning and classroom practice. Rather than trying to develop tight definitions of these different aspects of personal development, it is easiest to approach the area by considering some examples of mathematics teaching that demonstrate the wide range of opportunities open to the teacher.

Spiritual development

For some mathematics teachers, the area of spiritual development is the most problematic of the aspects of personal development. They associate it with religion, and believe it to have no place within mathematics lessons. However, this perspective suggests both a restricted view of spiritual development and a limited understanding of the nature and history of mathematics. One aspect of spiritual development that is widely accepted as being important is the experience of awe and wonder.

Greg Morris, a mathematics adviser, suggests that:

> In mathematics lessons students have the chance to meet something so large they can not easily comprehend it, to be struck by something of such beauty or elegance they cannot fail to appreciate it, to appreciate something of such power that they are humbled by it.
>
> (Morris, 1995, p. 36)

An area in which he suggests there is opportunity for this type of experience is when pupils encounter the idea of infinity.

There have been very few resources developed to support this sort of work in mathematics education. However, a recent initiative, the Charis Project, deliberately set out to develop resources that would promote pupils' spiritual and moral development across the curriculum. In the introduction to the mathematics resources (Charis Project, 1997), the editors highlight three approaches that the writers used in producing the materials. The first approach takes advantage of the wide range of human situations in which mathematics has been developed and applied. Consequently, it is possible to choose contexts that allow pupils both to work mathematically and to reflect on spiritual issues that emerge from the context. For example, one unit uses a range of mortality statistics to develop pupils' skills in applying probability theory whilst, at the same time, allowing them to consider their own mortality and their attitudes to life and death.

The second approach recognises within the history of mathematics examples of people who through exploring ideas within mathematics have also gained insight into broader areas. Indeed, biographies of mathematicians will sometimes illustrate how they often had quite diverse motivations for studying the subject. An example of a field that crosses over from mathematics to other domains is our understanding of truth. One Charis unit explores the truth of a series of statements about prime numbers. Pupils investigate the validity of different statements and consider how they might prove or disprove them. They are then encouraged to reflect on how, in general, they come to accept statements as true and how much they value seeking the truth.

The third approach used by the writers was to recognise how mathematics has been used to model and understand the universe. By working on such models, the pupils will also have the opportunity to develop a sense of wonder at the world around them. For example, the field of fractals, whilst inspiring in its own right, still offers only a limited model of an even more wonderful world. However, for any of these approaches to work, you also need to consider the implications for your teaching methods. In particular, pupils need to be given the opportunity both for personal reflection and group discussion.

Moral development

There are two principal ways in which you can promote the moral development of your pupils within mathematics lessons. The first is through considering your classroom as a community of people who inevitably encounter ethical issues as you work together. As a maths teacher, it is your responsibility to establish a culture in your classroom that promotes effective learning. A fundamental aspect of this is how people relate to each other. This includes teacher–pupil relationships and pupil–pupil relationships. You will no doubt have clear values and beliefs about the way in which you want people to work together and to treat each other in your classroom. In communicating your values and your expectations to pupils, you are contributing to their moral development by presenting a particular set of coherent ethical principles.

You will soon realise, however, if you did not already know, that the simple presentation of moral or ethical values does not mean that your pupils will automatically come to share these values. Even if they do, they will not necessarily behave in accordance with them. Consequently, you will have to handle situations where pupils behave in a way that you believe is ethically unacceptable. Such situations are key opportunities for moral development because they provide the opportunity to encourage pupils, either as individuals or as a group, to reflect. Sometimes this is difficult to do in the heat of the moment, and so a more extended reflection might be kept back until the end of the lesson. The other side of the coin in this area is being realistic about your own actions. Sometimes you will behave in ways that are not consistent with your values, and so it may be appropriate to acknowledge this to the class. Pupils often have a very keen sense of fairness, and so will most probably pick up your inconsistencies if you do not get there before them.

The second way in which you can promote moral development in mathematics lessons is more closely related to the subject. Moral issues can be raised through your choice of contexts. For example, a resource produced by the Development Education Centre in Dorset contains a unit built around the issue of refugees (DEED, 1993). Students use statistics to explore the position of refugees and address the way in which they are treated by our society. One of the Charis Project units explores the issues linked to educational opportunity for children around the world (Charis Project, 1997). Both of these topics encourage pupils to use their mathematics to engage with issues of justice in society.

This use of mathematics is part of an important tradition within mathematics, and can be seen particularly in the history of statistics. For example, Florence Nightingale developed and used statistical techniques to campaign politically for better medical conditions. As with work on spiritual development, there are implications for your teaching methods. Giving pupils an opportunity to debate the issues they encounter is essential if any significant development is to occur. They should also be given the opportunity to respond meaningfully to the issue if they feel strongly about it. All of this means that there is the need for sensitivity on your part, as you begin to open up what can be quite controversial issues.

Social development

In the same way as a classroom is inevitably a moral domain, it is also a place full of social interaction. This means that maths lessons have the potential for supporting pupils' social development. For example, the maths classroom can be a place where pupils learn to:

- work collaboratively in teams;
- both present and listen to ideas and arguments;
- tolerate and appreciate differences in people.

However, it can also be a place where none of this happens. It is your responsibility to make it happen. You may hear maths teachers say 'I can't do all that collaborative, interactive stuff; the pupils just haven't got the social skills'. This is an attitude that is essentially about abdicating responsibility. It is as though the teacher is saying 'Let somebody else develop them socially and then, perhaps, I might attempt more ambitious teaching approaches'. However, as with many of the issues raised in this chapter, by abdicating responsibility, teachers are also missing out on an opportunity to enhance their pupils' mathematical development. The more that we come to understand about the importance of social interaction in the process of learning, the more important it becomes for the maths teacher to pay attention to the social domain.

Assuming, then, that you accept and indeed value your role in promoting the social development of your pupils, what implications does this have for your planning, teaching and assessment? One issue that you should reflect upon when planning is the extent to which you are providing pupils with the opportunity to use and develop their social skills. For example, if in your lessons there is little opportunity for your pupils to interact, then obviously there will be less scope for social development. Instead, over a period of time, you need to plan your lessons so that you make increasing demands upon the pupils' social skills. Indeed, it can be helpful to view this as a structured training or induction programme for your pupils.

Within the lessons, you need to make explicit what you expect of the pupils. Sometimes this may require you to indicate the type of social interaction that you are looking for from the pupils. For example, you might show how different pupils can take on different roles within groups, or you might offer phrases that pupils can use when they disagree with each others' ideas. As the lesson progresses, as well as monitoring your pupils' mathematical progress, you can also be assessing and offering feedback on the extent to which they are meeting your stated expectations. The end of the lesson provides an opportunity both for reflection and for further feedback on how well the pupils have demonstrated the social interaction that you are wanting to develop. You may also use this time to suggest targets to pupils for future development.

Cultural development

In considering your role in the cultural development of your pupils, it can be helpful to consider two aspects of this development. One is helping pupils to become more aware and appreciative of their own culture and the culture of the society within which they live. The second is helping pupils to understand more about the diversity of cultures that exist both in their own nation and around the world, whilst encouraging them to show respect towards people of these different cultures.

In order to engage with your responsibility in this area, it is important to recognise mathematics as part of culture. Ernest suggests:

> Mathematics is part of human culture, and the mathematics of each culture serves its own unique purposes, and is equally valuable. Consequently, school mathematics should acknowledge the diverse cultural and historical origins and purposes of mathematics, and the real contributions of all, including women and non-European countries.
>
> (Ernest, 1991, p. 265)

For some maths teachers, this may mean that they must learn a new history of mathematics, which offers more than the traditional Eurocentric perspective, so that they can acknowledge the key role of many cultures in the shaping of today's mathematics. George Joseph's (1994) valuable work tracing some non-European roots of mathematics provides a helpful and thorough introduction to this field.

For many pupils, however, mathematics may seem to be almost *a*cultural – a body of knowledge with no historical or cultural roots. Sadly, this can also be the case for many mathematics graduates. Indeed, you may need to start to build up your own knowledge in this area. It is worth investigating the cultural roots of some aspect of the current mathematics curriculum, and considering how your research might enrich the teaching of that topic. By introducing pupils to the social and cultural roots of mathematics, their beliefs about the nature of the subject will begin to change. However, maths educator Derek Woodrow warns against a tokenistic approach in this area: 'Care must [. . .] be taken not to introduce such topics as marginal and trivial activities since this can imply a dismissive view of other societies and values. The same problem relates to the inclusion of historical information' (Woodrow, 1989, p. 231). As well as doing your own research in the field, there are many resources available that you will find helpful. Shan and Bailey's book (1991) and Dodd's resource book (1991) offer good examples.

A further aspect of cultural research that you need to do as a maths teacher is to learn more about the cultures of the pupils in your lessons. This will help you to be more alert to opportunities to acknowledge pupils' cultures within your teaching. Indeed, the knowledge that pupils bring from their cultures can act as starting points for a range of mathematical topics. For example, different traditions of geometric design or different ways of calculating may emerge in a culturally rich classroom.

Task 10.5 Reading resources critically

It should be clear from this chapter that if you are to take seriously your responsibility for the personal development of your pupils, then there are implications both for the resources you use and the teaching methods you employ.

For this task, you need to choose one of the key resources used by the teachers in your school. You should then critically analyse it by bringing the following questions to it.

- What images, if any, are presented by the resource of the different cultures that exist in British society and particularly among the pupils in your school?
- How much opportunity does the resource provide for pupils to engage with the cultural and historical roots of the mathematics they are studying?
- What contexts are used within the resource to provide an opportunity for discussion and reflection about moral and spiritual issues?
- How much does the resource suggest tasks that require pupils to work collaboratively and learn through social interaction?

Write a short report in your reflective journal highlighting the strengths and weaknesses of the resource in these four areas, and identify what supplementary resources might be needed if the personal development of pupils is to be fostered effectively in their mathematics lessons.

In talking about pupils' culture, it is, however, important to realise that this is not just at the level of ethnic identity. It is also about your pupils' everyday experiences of life. For example, the pupil who works on the market stall, the pupil whose hobby is flying model aeroplanes and the pupil who attends a dance class outside school each brings experiences to the classroom that can contribute to a whole group's mathematical development. However, as well as trying to acknowledge your pupils' cultures in this way, you also need to check that the everyday resources you use do not give a hidden message about the real value placed upon the pupils' cultures.

SUMMARY

You have a responsibility as a mathematics teacher that extends beyond just developing your pupils in mathematics. You have a part to play in supporting their development in a range of cross-curricular skills as well as supporting your colleagues as they use mathematics in teaching their subjects. You are also responsible for supporting pupils in their personal development, which includes spiritual, moral, social and cultural elements. If you are to teach mathematics in a way that effectively addresses both the whole person and the whole curriculum, you will need to examine the resources and methods you use critically. However, one of the benefits from adopting such an approach is that your pupils will be likely to develop more positive attitudes to learning mathematics.

FURTHER READING

Charis Project (1997) *Charis Mathematics, Units 1–9 and Units 10–19*, Nottingham: Stapleford Centre.

These two sets of resources produced by the Charis Project mathematics team offer a helpful introduction to approaches for promoting spiritual and moral development within mathematics lessons. The units cover a wide range of contexts and KS4 mathematical content. The approaches illustrated by the materials should help you to develop your own activities for this aspect of your teaching.

Hudson, B. (1994) 'Environmental issues in the mathematics classroom', in M. Selinger (ed.), *Teaching Mathematics*, London: Routledge, pp. 113–125.

Brian Hudson's chapter provides a helpful introduction to the importance of having a whole-curriculum perspective in teaching mathematics. He illustrates, through using the example of environmental issues, how pupils can be encouraged to appreciate the importance of mathematics for society.

Shan, S. and Bailey, P. (1991) *Multiple Factors: Classroom Mathematics for Equality and Justice*, Stoke: Trentham Books.

Sharan-Jeet Shan and Peter Bailey's book offers an excellent introduction to the role mathematics teaching can play in both moral and cultural development of pupils. The authors illustrate how certain groups in society can be disadvantaged by certain teaching methods and resources. They go on to offer a whole range of ideas and sources that will help you both to challenge injustice and to increase cultural understanding within your lessons.

11 Teaching Mathematics Post-16

Ann Kitchen

INTRODUCTION

Teaching mathematics post-16 will set you a whole new range of challenges and delights. First of all, the goals of those you teach will be much more diverse than those of pupils up to age 16. Second, the structures of further education (FE) colleges, sixth-form colleges and 11–18 schools are very different from each other. Not only will you need to make sure that you are fully familiar with the mathematics syllabus that your students need to cover so that nothing gets omitted, but you must also gear your style of teaching to students who are more mature.

The difference between teaching pupils and students, some of whom may be older than you, needs to be appreciated. In addition, your role as a mathematics teacher may not be as clearly defined in FE as elsewhere. Part of your teaching may be in workshops or as a provider of service teaching for other subjects. A further challenge for the immediate future is that post-16 qualifications, and hence the teaching you will be required to do, are likely to continue to change dramatically.

What about the delights? On the whole, all your students are there because they want or need to do some mathematics. Many, having gained a good grade at GCSE, will have chosen to do A-level mathematics. Some will have struggled with mathematics in the secondary school and will be looking for a fresh start, trying to improve their GCSE grade. Then there will be the mature students who have come back for help with specific areas of maths that they feel will be of use to them. Mathematics is important to them. In addition, in many cases you will have the opportunity to do mathematics that is interesting and challenging to you. It may be in an A-level investigation or it may be through an unfamiliar context in a GNVQ syllabus.

OBJECTIVES

By the end of this chapter, you should:

- be able to look for and evaluate different modes of teaching used post-16;
- be aware of how to prepare to teach a new topic for students post-16;
- understand the strengths and weaknesses of calculators and computers in teaching and assessing mathematics post-16;
- understand the suitability of each of the different qualifications available for your students' abilities and aspirations;
- realise the importance of syllabuses, past papers and published texts in producing a balanced teaching programme;
- be aware of how the different pressure groups have influenced the shape of mathematics post-16.

POST-16 INSTITUTIONS

There are three types of institution offering mathematics courses. These are:

- 11–18 schools, either under direct local authority control, grant-maintained institutions or independent schools;
- sixth-form colleges, originally under local authority control as part of their 11–18 provision;
- colleges of further education.

The first two cater mainly for students wishing to take academic qualifications, whilst the last offers a wide range of academic and vocational qualifications. Most students at 11–18 schools and sixth-form colleges will be attending full time. They may have part-time jobs but these will usually not be related to their study.

Students at colleges of further education are often attending part time. They may have jobs that relate to the course they are taking, or they may be trying to gain new qualifications to allow them to change their careers.

Whilst the choice of institution will be a matter for each student, as a teacher you should be able to offer advice to your pupils. Therefore, you should be aware of the breadth of courses available in mathematics post-16.

Task 11.1 The diversity of provision

Call in at your local college of further education and ask for details of the mathematics courses they are offering and their general brochure. Do the same for a sixth-form college and a school that offers post-16 mathematics.

- At whom does the information appear to be targeted?
- What do institutions see as their specific strengths?
- Compare the teaching provision at each for A-level mathematics.
- How do they differ in entry requirements, teaching time, style of teaching?
- Make a table showing the variety of courses available at each of these institutions.
- What advice could you give to a student trying to decide where to study for A levels, GNVQs?
- Look at the profile of the mathematics department in each institution.
- Does this tell you anything about working within these institutions?

Discuss your findings with other student teachers and your tutor.

STUDENTS POST-16

Your students may range in age from 17 to 77+ and will expect to be treated as adults. Many of the strategies you use with younger students will be inappropriate. One of the most difficult tasks in teaching in this sector is to encourage your students to take responsibility for their own learning. They will probably be used to having their learning planned for them, and many will want to continue in this way. It is vital that your students are helped to set up goals and timetables for their own learning. The dividing line between this and leaving them to drift along is a very fine one.

Modular syllabuses help to overcome this by allowing the external assessment to provide motivation. The student who has failed to plan successfully for the first module can learn from his or her mistakes and improve before too much harm is done. However, modular syllabuses also have the drawback that some students rely on the fact that tests can be repeated and hence fall further and further behind. This can distort your teaching programme, as they will expect to receive help on earlier modules that others have passed, instead of concentrating on the current module.

The first few weeks in a sixth-form college or a college of further education can be extremely demanding on both you and your students. Your students are likely to have come from a wide range of backgrounds, and your first task will be to make sure that you do not start at a totally inappropriate level. You may find that the level of algebraic mastery of your students is very variable. It may be tempting to start with a few weeks of solid algebraic techniques, but you should think very carefully before embarking on such a course.

Mathematics has traditionally been seen as a hard subject and, until recently, the drop-out rate from post-16 mathematics courses in the first few weeks has been very high. Your A-level students will probably range from those with a grade C at Intermediate level GCSE to those with a grade A* at Higher level. The difference in content covered between the two is large, and you must be familiar with it. Your task is to merge the learning of new and interesting mathematics with the revision of the skills that your students should have already mastered, so that they do not lose all confidence in their ability to do mathematics.

Many A-level syllabuses allow you to do this by running two modules at the same time, one pure and one application. Equally, you must not allow those students who have already covered much of the early work to become bored. One way to overcome this is to encourage such students to study for an AS level in Further Mathematics.

Looking at teaching styles

Teaching students rather than younger pupils will not reduce the need for careful lesson planning. College timetables often dictate that your teaching will occur in large chunks. It is quite common to find a session of two-and-a-half hours for a mathematics class. This means that you may see your group only once or twice a week, so a badly planned lesson can mean that a week's teaching has vanished unprofitably. Especially at the start of their post-16 career, students may rebel at what seem, to them, petty rules such as having to arrive on time for lessons. This must be handled sensitively but effectively. Watch the strategies that other teachers use to prevent such problems recurring, and discuss them with your fellow students. Which strategies are appropriate and why?

Whilst whole-class teaching is often appropriate post-16, it must not be taken to mean a diet of lecturing from the front. Such lecturing may enable you to get through the syllabus but it will be at your students' expense. The principles discussed in Chapter 4 are still relevant here, and it is desirable to use a variety of teaching styles: teaching from the front; teacher-led discussion; group work; example and practice; practical work; and investigations. However, you need to integrate these techniques together carefully if they are to be effective. Plan ahead, and let students know what the deadlines are for the coming term.

A study for the GCE Boards on teaching styles looked at how often students in different subjects experience each of twenty-two different ways of interacting in the classroom. The twenty-two different forms of interaction are listed in Table 11.1. A graph showing a comparison between their frequency of use in English and mathematics lessons is given in Figure 11.1.

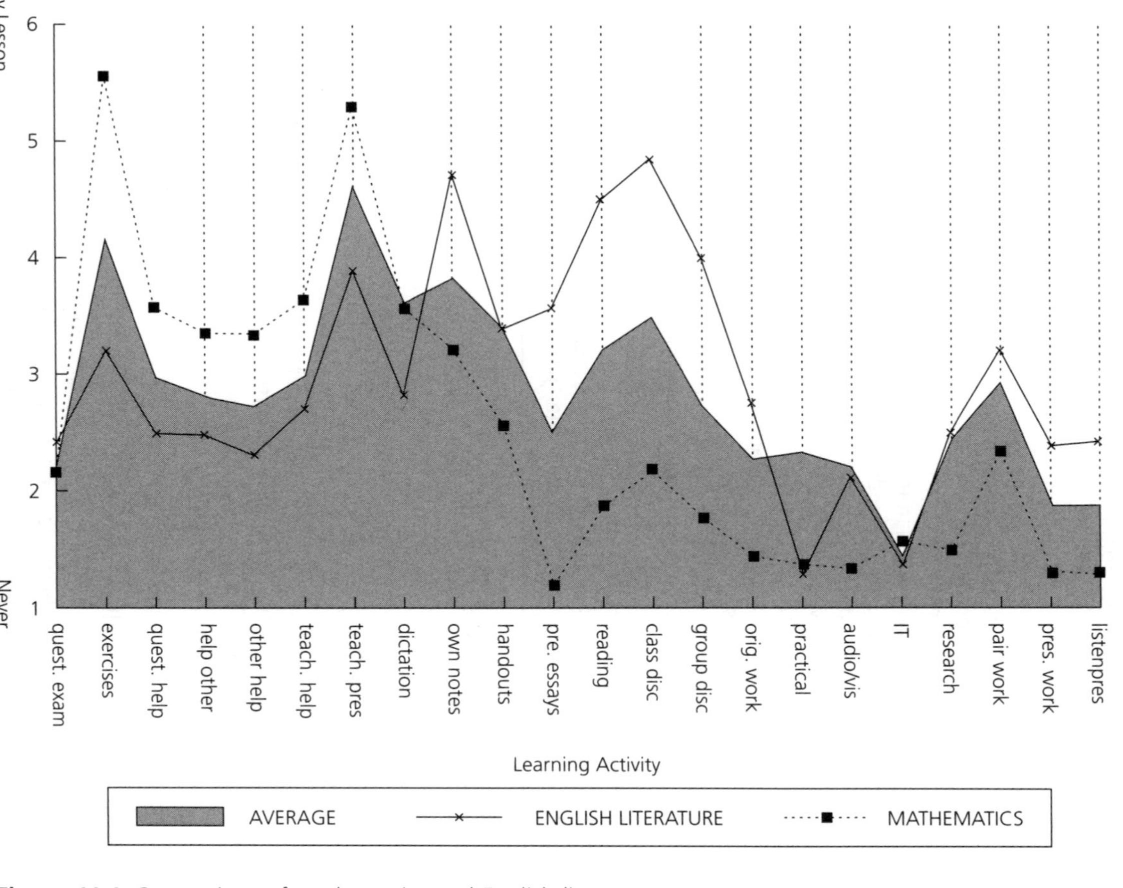

Figure 11.1 Comparison of mathematics and English literature
Source: NICCEA, 1994, p. 14

Table 11.1 Twenty-two ways of interacting in the classroom

1	Presentations of a topic by the teacher (chalk and talk)
2	Exercises (working examples)
3	Working questions from previous exam papers with help
4	Working questions from previous exam papers under exam conditions (fixed time, no help)
5	Preparing essays
6	Reading
7	Class discussions led by the teacher
8	Discussions in groups
9	Having notes dictated to you
10	Making your own notes from lessons
11	Using duplicated notes (handouts)
12	Practical work (using apparatus or making things)
13	Using audio or visual material
14	Making use of IT
15	Researching a topic (using a variety of reference material)
16	Working in pairs
17	Presenting your work to the class
18	Listening to another student present their work to the class
19	Giving help to another student
20	Receiving help from another student
21	Receiving individual help from your teacher
22	Producing original work (experiments, poetry, designing, composing, criticism)

Commenting on the results shown in Figure 11.1, the report says:

> Some of the most dramatic differences can be seen between Mathematics and English Literature in the chart . . . where Mathematics A-level teaching appears to have been dominated by 'exercises' and 'teacher presentation'. 'Dictated notes' were also common, as was 'Working questions from previous exam papers with help', and 'helping' in various forms. By contrast, English Literature A-level teaching appeared to be more varied. The more common activities were 'Classroom discussion', 'making own notes' and 'reading'.
>
> (NICCEA, 1994, p. 13)

There is a place for all of these teaching styles in effective mathematics teaching. Keep them in mind when you plan and teach your own lessons.

Sometimes you will be faced with a question to which you do not immediately know the answer. How you choose to respond might depend on your preferred teaching style. In Task 11.2, you will consider some possible responses.

Preparing to teach a topic

Whilst it is likely that you will be following a scheme of work, this does not mean that you can afford to wait to read the next chapter until the night before you teach

Task 11.2 Responding to hard questions

Despite all your preparation for an A-level lesson, a student has asked a question to which you do not immediately know the answer. How will you respond?

There are several possible strategies. Look at the following suggestions and decide which could be used positively and which should be avoided. Think through the reasons for your choices carefully. Add any other responses that you think might be effective.

- Ask the group if anyone can help.
- Admit that you need longer to think about it and will come back next lesson with the answer.
- Ignore the question and hurry on.
- Suggest they ask someone else.

a topic. You are almost certain to come to grief if you try. Before you start to teach a course, look through the syllabus and highlight any areas where you are unsure of the mathematics. Take the recommended text and work through the examples. Highlight those areas you think are not well explained. Get help from a fellow teacher if you need to, but remember to make notes on what problems you had and how the answers were explained to you. Once you have dealt with the areas of mathematics that you are unsure of, you can start to prepare to teach it effectively.

Write down the content that you need to cover in the lesson. Look for links with content that students have already mastered. Binding your students' mathematical knowledge into a coherent whole rather than learning it as a series of unrelated topics will enable them to become more confident. Check that you can do all the examples you are going to ask them to do. (Remember that textbooks are notorious for mistakes in their answers, and there can be nothing more dispiriting than getting a different answer from that in the back of the book, whether you are a student or a teacher.)

Asking students to conduct practical experiments can be a rewarding way of teaching mathematics. You may feel more confident the first time if you work as a class with a single set of apparatus in the front. Although practical work is often thought to be best used in mechanics, it can be used to reinforce ideas of algebra, graph plotting, calculus and statistics.

Many more ideas on teaching through practical work can be found in materials from the Mechanics in Action project at Manchester University (Williams and Kitchen, 1989; Savage and Williams, 1990) and in *Practical Statistics* (Rouncefield and Holmes, 1989).

You will probably find it useful to recap the previous lesson at the beginning of the next. At the end of each lesson, check your progress against your teaching plan. If you are behind schedule, decide how you can make up time without losing the quality of your teaching.

Task 11.3 Using a practical

Look at the task sheet in Appendix 5. Work with a group of fellow students to find the velocity and acceleration of a ball rolling horizontally or up and down a slope.

Hints on the mathematics used are also given in the appendix. Work through the mathematics given, replacing the data with your own. Notice how many topics are reinforced as you go through the modelling process shown in Figure 11.2.

As you work with your colleagues, note how many of the teaching activities are used.

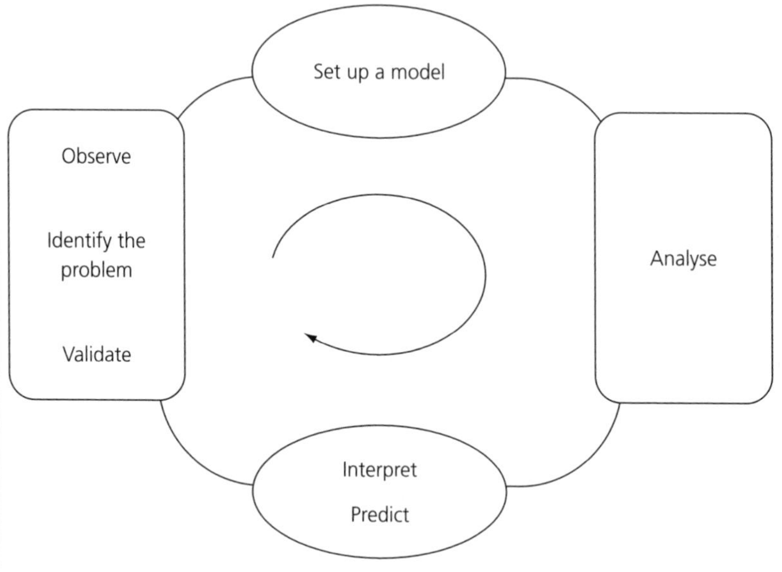

Figure 11.2 The modelling process
Source: Burns, 1994, p. 209

THE USE OF TECHNOLOGY IN POST-16 MATHEMATICS

One question that has aroused a great deal of controversy over the past few years is the place of calculators and computers in mathematics. In many courses, your students will be expected to be able to use technology effectively, whether it is a graphic calculator or a spreadsheet or a computer algebra system (CAS) such as *Derive*. In addition, however, they will need to know when its use is inappropriate and be able to use strategies when it is not available.

Many people in higher education feel that such technology has no place in the true study of mathematics. This view was given an added impetus by the decision of SCAA that at least 25 per cent of the examination of A-level mathematics must be taken without the use of a calculator. The decision that, at the same time, between 3 per cent and 10 per cent of the marks should be awarded on their understanding and use of technology did not redress the balance (SCAA, 1997d).

In an article for the *Mathematics Gazette*, Tony Gardiner discusses many of the pitfalls that may occur if technology is improperly used as a replacement for meaningful algebra (Gardiner, 1995, p. 532). Much of what he says can be true if calculators and CAS are not handled properly. Most current teachers trained before such technology became widely available, and there has been little time or money for meaningful In-Service Training (INSET) in their use.

Some A-level syllabuses, such as NEAB's 16–19 Mathematics, expect students to become fluent in the use of a graphic calculator. However, none of the Examination Boards at present allows the use of CAS other than as a tool in coursework. There has been much discussion on whether this will change with the new proposals for 2002. Many of the issues for calculator use that were discussed in Chapter 8 are important here too:

- the importance of using the new Direct Algebraic Logic calculators;
- the problems in algebraic understanding caused by the old-style calculators;
- the importance of estimation to check that calculator calculations are correct;
- the importance of reinforcing number bonds by use of mental arithmetic where appropriate rather than reaching blindly for the calculator;
- the strengths of the graphic calculator in allowing the whole of a calculation or set of calculations to be displayed on a screen.

Many strategies, however, will relate to the more complex work done post-16.

It may be that your first encounter with a graphic calculator will be with a post-16 class. The variety of different types of calculator that your students bring to your class may cause problems when you want to make use of this technology in your teaching. You need to be familiar with the kinds of facilities available on a graphic calculator and to think about their role in teaching.

Task 11.4 Using a graphic calculator for advanced topics

The aim of this task is to ensure that you are confident in using a graphic calculator and understand its place in teaching a mathematical topic at A level.

You will need a graphic calculator and a copy of either SMP (1992) *Calculus Methods*, Chapter 1, or Neill (1994a) *Nuffield Advanced Mathematics*, Book 1, Chapter 2.

Work through one of these chapters, making sure that you understand the teaching points that the authors feel are strengthened by the use of a graphic calculator.

Maths educator Ros Sutherland and her colleagues have written a book to support the use of spreadsheets with GNVQ students (Sutherland *et al.*, 1996). The developments of computer algebra systems and powerful new calculator technology have significant implications for the teaching and learning of algebra. The discussion booklet *Algebra at A level* (ATM/MA/NCET, 1995) explores a number of questions that arise for the A-level curriculum when computer algebra systems are widely available. There is discussion of what should be in the mathematics curriculum and how it should be assessed. If you cannot obtain a copy from your library, you can write to ATM or MA (see Appendix 2 for the addresses).

QUALIFICATIONS POST-16 IN ENGLAND AND WALES

The past thirty years

Post-16 qualifications have evolved from three very different bases. The first was the General Certificate of Education (GCE), an academic qualification whose purpose was to provide a hurdle for entry into university. The second was the craft and guild qualifications, which were gained after a five- or seven-year apprenticeship and which were the forerunner of our vocational qualifications. The third basis was qualifications in specific skills such as typing or shorthand that could be awarded after study at a technical college.

The first GCE A-level providers were university organisations. Some, such as London, were based on a single university, and others were based on a group of universities. The Joint Matriculation Board (JMB) was initially founded by the four universities of Manchester, Liverpool, Leeds and Sheffield, joined shortly afterwards by Birmingham, to ensure candidates for entry had suitable qualifications. They offered three levels of mathematics qualifications: GCE ordinary (O) level, additional ordinary (AO) level and advanced (A) level. The syllabus content was largely decided by the lecturers at these institutions, and so there could be large differences among the syllabuses of each of the providers.

These qualifications were designed for no other purpose than preparation for university entrance, and many students left school without them. However, GCEs soon became used as a school-leaving qualification for those going on to apprenticeships and the world of work. To ensure that more students left with a recognised set of qualifications, the government set up regional providers of the Certificate of Secondary Education (CSE) to provide a lower level of qualification at age 16.

The government then decided that all qualifications should be brought under their control, and the Schools Examination Council was set up to approve all academic examination syllabuses for students up to the age of 16. This evolved via the Schools Examination and Assessment Council (SEAC) into the School Curriculum and Assessment Authority (SCAA). The vocational qualifications were put under the remit of the National Council for Vocational Qualifications (NCVQ). These two bodies merged in October 1997 to form the Qualifications and Curriculum Agency (QCA), which is currently responsible for the validation of all general, vocational and academic qualifications offered to students up to the age of 18.

Following the recommendations of the Dearing Report (Dearing, 1996), the various Examinations Boards and Vocational Awarding bodies have now amalgamated (some more formally than others) to form three large examinations groupings, details of which are given in Chapter 6. These are now responsible for producing syllabuses and administering the examinations that satisfy QCA guidelines for both vocational and academic qualifications.

Advanced and Advanced Supplementary (soon to become Advanced Subsidiary) levels (A and AS levels)

At present, in 1998, there is great flexibility about type of examination and content of A and AS levels. Some awards are examined through modules that can be retaken as often as required, with the best marks counting towards the final award; some have just two terminal papers; and some have a core, examined at the end of the award, plus options and/or coursework. They all have to contain the common core of 30 per cent pure mathematics, 10 per cent statistics and 10 per cent applications. Some awarding bodies offer module examinations three times a year, some twice.

Task 11.5 The A-level common core

The mathematics core has changed dramatically over the past fifteen years. In this task, you are asked to look at the A-level mathematics core. If you are unable to find a copy of this in your school, you can obtain a copy from the maths team at QCA at the address given in Appendix 2.

Arrange to interview a small group of three or four A-level mathematics students. Ask them about their career aspirations, and what mathematics in the A-level syllabus they think will be most useful to them in their future careers.

Afterwards, study the content of the A-level core. Try to see the content through the eyes of a university mathematician, an engineer, a business manager and an accountant.

Should vectors appear in the core? How much?

Should probability appear in the core? How much?

Remember that the core does not define the whole of an A level. Does this matter? Could you devise a Mathematics A-level syllabus that you think would satisfy all of these users?

When you have worked at the issues raised in the questions above, you should read the paper by Kitchen and Lord (1996) listed in the Further Reading for this chapter.

The whole system has grown unmanageable and has been reviewed. The new proposals, which are due to take effect for students starting in 2000, will simplify this considerably. There will be a maximum of seven different syllabuses, all of which will be modular. They will have six modules for an A level and three modules for an AS. Half of these modules must cover the prescribed pure mathematics core. The module examinations will be available twice a year. No module examination can be taken more than twice, and the last pure modules in an award can be taken only at the end of the course (all the module examinations can be taken together at the end of the course if required). One of the more controversial decisions is that at least 25 per cent of the examination must be taken without a calculator or with only a single-line-display calculator.

A levels are designed to lead on to academic study at university. Whilst some syllabuses may have up to 20 per cent coursework, many will have none at all. A levels are graded from A to E and U: A being the highest grade and E being the lowest pass grade. Most students will be asked to offer three A levels for university entrance.

General National Vocational Qualifications (GNVQ)

At the moment, GNVQs are also going through a period of evolution. They were designed as a suitable qualification for students who did not want to choose to study A levels, with their emphasis on specific subjects and assessment through external examinations. They enable students to choose a broad area of study, such as engineering or leisure and tourism, which they will study through project work. Whilst there may be some external testing, the majority of the assessment is through a portfolio of student work. Students can be awarded a GNVQ at one of three levels: Foundation, Intermediate and Advanced. Each level is awarded either at Pass, Merit or Distinction. A student gaining a GNVQ at Advanced level is judged to have done the equivalent of two GCE A-level awards.

Each GNVQ has a minimum of twelve units. Some, like engineering, have specific mathematics units that are assessed by a multiple-choice test, set and marked by one of the vocational qualification providers – RSA, C and G, BTEC – and a portfolio of tasks, set and assessed by the college. Others have a set of numeracy skills that must be mastered somewhere within the GNVQ as a whole, and which are assessed internally. The difficulty with the numeracy skills is that it is very hard to get any consistency of teaching and assessment.

In addition, all GNVQ students must pass the core skills units of Communication, Application of Number and Information Technology. Again, the assessment for the 'core skills' units is based within each college. Thus, Application of Number may be taught within the specific GNVQ or may be taught as a separate unit by the Mathematics Department of the college. There is currently much discussion about whether these core skills should be required as part of an overarching qualification for students taking A levels. You can obtain full details of the content and assessment for the core skills from the QCA.

A new set of GNVQ free-standing units in mathematics is being developed. The most distinctive feature of the free-standing GNVQ mathematics units is the way in which they combine mathematical principles with applications to allow students to learn to use and apply mathematics to support their other studies, work and interests. A full rationale of these units can be found in the document 'Free-standing GNVQ Mathematics units: what do they demand of students?' (Wake, 1997).

National Vocational Qualifications (NVQ)

These qualifications may be gained partly at college but are mainly taught and assessed within the world of work. They are based on a series of competences that students can show that they have mastered. So, for example, courses in bricklaying, secretarial skills, hairdressing, catering and other qualifications could either be awarded through study at colleges or credited through achievement shown at work.

General Certificate of Secondary Education (GCSE)

Whilst this is essentially a qualification for the end of Key Stage 4, some students will not have achieved a high enough grade and will be looking to improve their performance. This is not easy. Many students will come to your classes feeling that they have failed at mathematics. You will find that you need many different strategies when teaching GCSE resit classes. Many colleges use a combination of an individual learning plan and workshop provision. Each student is assessed at the start of the course, and a series of exercises and worksheets tailored to the student's needs are provided. Staff are available throughout the day in the mathematics workshop where students can seek help.

Task 11.6 Diagnosing where help is needed

You are starting with a new group of GCSE resit students. They are taking a one-year course to improve their grades to a C or above.

Choose a suitable GCSE syllabus and study the content and some sample papers. Devise a questionnaire and/or test that will help you diagnose the weaknesses of your students at the beginning of the course. How can you discover where students need help without reinforcing their feelings of inadequacy?

Try your questionnaire or test on some of your fellow student teachers. Use the responses to devise a programme of study for one of the students.

During your school or college experience, study the structure of the resit provision. Ask the teacher responsible for his or her evaluation of its strengths and weaknesses.

If possible, talk to some students on the resit course to get their perspective.

Such a system can succeed well, but some students are unwilling to seek help in the workshop. They dislike not having a single member of staff. In addition, different members of staff find it difficult to oversee the learning in its totality. This is especially true if the learning plan is not well structured.

A more usual plan, especially in 11–18 schools, is for the students to be class taught in the same way as they were at Key Stage 4. This can succeed where students just needed more practice to improve their examination technique, but often all it does is to reinforce the students' sense of alienation. Whatever the teaching strategy, it is important for students to see improvement in their learning as the course progresses. Try to build on their strengths.

TEACHING IN POST-16 INSTITUTIONS

The different structures of post-16 institutions mean that you have to master a wide range of teaching styles. These include whole-class teaching, using lectures and workshops and helping students with supported self-study. Within each of these, however, the prime requirement is to be able to allow the student to cover and master all the content within his or her specific syllabus. It is your responsibility to ensure that you keep up to date with any changes.

Task 11.7 Using examination board materials

The purpose of this task is to understand the relationship between an A-level syllabus, the examinations and any published teaching materials.

You will need a syllabus for one of the mathematics A-level awards, a series of past papers and mark schemes, examiners' comments for the papers and some A-level textbooks. If you are in a school or college where there is A-level mathematics, this will be straightforward. If not, you will need to obtain a syllabus and some sets of past papers from one of the examination boards.

Look through one of the papers and write down the topics you think each question is assessing. Match these with the content in the syllabus. Is there a close match? Find a suitable chapter in the A-level textbook. Does it enable you to cover the topic in sufficient depth to answer the question?

Does the syllabus give enough detail to work from?

Look at the comments in the examiner's report. Can you understand why students might make the mistakes discussed? Find some ways of helping students to avoid them.

Discuss your findings with other student teachers and your tutors.

STANDARDS AND PARTICIPATION AT A LEVEL

Falling standards in mathematics A level?

There has been a great deal of controversy on whether standards have fallen over the past twenty years. Much of this discussion has come from the higher education institutions, who were alarmed at the growing weaknesses they perceived in their entrants. Whilst it is true that the universities are finding that the mathematical knowledge of their student intake is falling, it cannot be said to be due to any great lowering of standards at A level, certainly not at the grade A boundary. You can read a discussion of this issue in an article in the newsletter of the London Mathematical Society (Burns, 1995).

The government enquiry into standards at A level between 1975 and 1995 found evidence for a slight lowering of standards at the E grade boundary, whilst, apart from a lowering of demand in algebraic techniques, the standards of most of the content mastery at the grade A boundary remained unchanged (SCAA, 1996a). The main reason for the increasing mathematical weakness of new undergraduates is that most mathematics and engineering departments are now admitting students with a much wider range of mathematical attainment (Sutherland and Pozzi, 1995; Kitchen, 1996). In 1995, only 41 per cent of students accepted to read engineering had an A-level mathematics qualification, and in the same year over 30 per cent of students accepted to read for a degree in mathematics had a grade C or less in A-level mathematics, something that would have been unheard of ten years ago. Mathematics is still perceived as one of the hard A levels, along with physics.

The gender divide

When teaching A-level mathematics, it will soon become apparent that there is not an equal gender balance. The national ratio of male to female students at A level is around 3:2. The youth cohort study, 'Science and mathematics in full-time education after 16' (Cheng *et al.*, 1995), found no obvious statistical reason for such a gender imbalance in the take-up of mathematics at A level, even after controlling for GCSE results in mathematics. There was, however, a wide variation in the gender mix, with some schools and colleges having a much more equal balance than others. Your aim should be to encourage all able students to continue with their mathematics post-16.

SUMMARY

The role of the mathematics teacher in a post-16 institution is complex:

- you will have to be confident with a wide variety of mathematical content from application of number to advanced mathematical concepts;
- the management structure is often unclear, with a single department having a large number of part-time staff;
- the content of courses is changing all the time;
- the students come from very diverse backgrounds and past experiences;
- new technology in graphic calculators and computers will provide a challenge;
- timetabling may often put constraints on the lesson structure that are not ideal.

Whilst you will have to work within all these constraints, you will also find that you must have a complete mastery of the mathematics needed.

FURTHER READING

ATM/MA/NCET (1994) *The IT Maths Pack*, Coventry: National Council for Educational Technology.
This pack contains books, activity sheets and software. Whilst it is also useful for pre-16 teaching, using the materials yourself will allow you to gain familiarity with the workings of a graphic calculator and to look at other software.

ATM/MA/NCET (1995) *Algebra at A level*, Derby: Association of Teachers of Mathematics.
This book explores a number of questions that will arise when computer algebra systems are widely available. There are sections on mathematical skills, modelling and conceptual understanding. In addition, the book looks at possible ways in which the curriculum and assessment may change.

Dearing, R. (1996) *The Dearing Report: A Review of Qualifications for 16-to-19-Year-Olds*, London: School Curriculum and Assessment Authority.
This report comes in the form of a number of booklets, comprising a summary, the full report and a number of appendices. There are two sections that are particularly relevant to mathematics: 'Mathematics and the Sciences' and 'The Full Report'. Whilst it appears unlikely that all the recommendations will be followed, they give a good picture of the establishment view of mathematics post-16 in 1996.

Kitchen, A. and Lord, K. (1996) 'The interface between mathematics post-16 and higher education', in Haines, C. and Dunthorne, S. (eds), *Mathematics Learning and Assessment: Sharing Innovative Practices*, London: Arnold, pp. 1.12–1.26.
This chapter gives a comprehensive account of the various mathematics qualifications available post-16 from A-level syllabuses, GNVQ to Scottish Highers. It compares the 1993 and 1984 A-level mathematics cores, and discusses the various approaches to teaching and assessment post-16.

12 Professional Development

Christine Shiu

INTRODUCTION

Initial training for teaching is the beginning of a process of life-long learning. Successful teachers of secondary mathematics develop and adapt their practice both to the framework within which they operate and to their own growing knowledge and awareness of what mathematics can most usefully be taught and of how pupils learn mathematics.

Classroom teaching is often quite an isolated activity, but much professional development comes about through contact with other teachers and their experiences: sometimes by direct contact, at other times indirectly through reading their writings or through video and audio tapes of practice. As well as gaining new ideas and insights from such contact, it is possible to gain personal support and sympathetic yet constructively critical feedback on one's own ideas.

The purpose of this chapter is to help you to find effective sources for support at the beginning of your career and to identify your individual needs for further professional development and how you might meet these as your career progresses.

OBJECTIVES

By the end of this chapter, you should:

- be aware of the particular strengths that you can offer to a school and a department, and of your priorities for early professional development;
- be able to make use of this awareness in identifying and applying for suitable posts;
- be ready to take advantage of the induction opportunities in your first post;
- be aware of a range of sources for continuing professional development.

FINDING THE RIGHT POST

Your development as a mathematics teacher will get off to the best start if you become part of a supportive department, in a post whose demands are well matched to your own existing qualities as a teacher, but which nevertheless offers opportunities for gaining new competence.

Think first about what you bring to the profession of teaching mathematics. The Career Entry Profile pack (TTA, 1997) that you will receive from the TTA when you become an NQT provides an assessment of your strengths as a teacher on completion of initial training as agreed between you and your mentor. These are probably under discussion as you read this chapter and should inform your thinking as you apply for teaching posts. The first step is to think about what sorts of schools and mathematics departments you might wish to teach in and be suited for. The booklet *Starting as a Secondary Mathematics Teacher,* published by the Mathematical Association (see Further Reading) is worth consulting at this point.

Schools that cater for secondary pupils vary in many ways, some obvious, some less so. You will have got to know quite a lot about the particular school in which you have trained, but how much do you know about other secondary schools in the neighbourhood and in other parts of the country? What features are you looking for in your first teaching post? Would you like it to be similar to your training school or are you looking for different challenges and opportunities?

It is easy to find out factual information about schools, such as the number on the roll, the age-range catered for, whether the school has a sixth form, whether it is mixed or single-sex, comprehensive or selective, religious or secular, rural, suburban or inner city. Some of these aspects may be important to you, others may be immaterial, and you will need to think about whether there is a practical characteristic that appeals to you strongly or one that you wish to avoid.

Possibly even more important than any of the above, however, is the ethos of the school and, in particular, of the mathematics department. Whilst you may get clues about ethos from hearsay reports or reading the school prospectus, you can only really find out about it by spending time there, talking with and observing teachers and pupils, separately and together. It is important to discover school policy on interpersonal issues, for example equal opportunities, bullying, partnership with parents and how these policies are implemented in practice. How do members of the mathematics department view their aims, what approaches are used in teaching mathematics and what resources are available? What sort of atmosphere prevails in the classes and how do pupils respond to what is on offer? What are the policy and provision for the professional development of members of staff?

Task 12.1 Characteristics of teaching posts

Make a list of the characteristics that a mathematics teaching post might have. You might do this in three columns, according to characteristics you regard as essential in the post you hope for, those characteristics that are desirable, and those that would be counter-indications for you.

Compare your list with your own strengths as a teacher, and see if you want to modify your aspirations and hence your lists.

Your application is what makes the first impression on a school and its staff and governors. A well-presented letter, which reflects careful consideration of the post as described and appropriate responses, accompanied by a clear, well-laid out curriculum vitae (CV), will merit further consideration. Equally, a scruffy letter with an out-of-date CV will create a bad impression and may well filter you out of the shortlist. Letters can be hand-written but CVs must always be word-processed (and keeping the computer file allows you to up-date it whenever necessary). Even if there is an application form, it should be accompanied by a covering letter, and you could also include your CV.

As you compose your application, it is worth considering what a school is likely to want to know about you. Just as you want to know about school ethos, they will want to know how well you will fit into their community. They will be interested in your personal qualities and your attitudes and approaches to mathematics teaching. At an interview, you may be asked questions to elicit these. For example, a popular interview question is to invite you to describe two mathematics lessons you have given, one of which went well and one that didn't work out as you had planned, and to give an account of what you learned from *each* of these situations. It pays to think ahead and to have anticipated how you would answer such a question.

They will also, of course, have many questions about your specific background and experience, and how it relates to the post they are advertising. Would you, for example, be able to undertake A-level teaching or to work with children with special educational needs? Are you familiar with a particular software package? Any such matters should be indicated on your CV, and it is reasonable to refer to this, but also to take the opportunity to elaborate on your experience and interests.

Task 12.2 Prepare your CV

Draft and prepare your CV now. If you have already written a CV, check to see that what it contains is relevant, up-to-date and clearly structured. Amend any aspects that can be improved.

The usual pattern for a CV is as follows.

Name

Contact address

Date of birth

Secondary and higher education and qualifications, including your teaching qualifications.
It is a good idea to set this out as a table with columns for educational institution, dates attended and qualifications gained (also with dates).

Employment history, in reverse chronological order.

Other relevant information, such as additional qualifications, voluntary work, publications, musical or sporting achievements, etc.

Names and addresses of two or three referees.

Now you are ready to begin your search for a suitable post. The major source of advertisements for teaching posts is the national press, notably *The Times Educational Supplement*, but also the weekly education sections in *The Guardian* and *The Independent*. If you are limited to specific geographical areas for some reason, it is also worth looking in the local press. You may be able to obtain a list of local vacancies through your training school, or directly from the Local Education Authority (LEA).

Once you have found an advertisement for a post that seems to be suitable for you, and submitted an application that has gained you a place on the shortlist, the next stage is the actual interview. As well as the mental preparation advised as you compiled your application, it can be very helpful to try out your interview skills on a critical friend. Consider who might help you to rehearse likely scenarios and who will give you honest criticism and constructive advice. If you find a friend who is willing to help, arrange a time and place where you can have your practice interview undisturbed, and let your mock interviewer be the first to know the outcome of the real thing, especially if it is a cause for celebration.

THE FIRST YEAR OF TEACHING

Some of the main influences on the way you teach mathematics, especially at the beginning of your career, are the people you have seen teaching. This includes teachers who have taught you mathematics in the past as well as people you have worked with recently. You may be unaware of the most positive influences, perhaps because when you witnessed them your attention was on the mathematics not the person, whereas you may have very vivid recollections of practice you definitely do not wish to emulate.

Task 12.3 Significant memories

Try to recall salient moments from your experience of mathematics teaching – as learner, observer or teacher.

Recall a teacher who has made a vivid impression on you. Try to describe an incident that captures what you remember.

Picture yourself witnessing someone working on some mathematics and recall a moment when you were acting as a teacher for them. Perhaps this went as you anticipated, or perhaps you were surprised, even unpleasantly so, but nevertheless you are likely to have learned something from the incident.

This is a good moment to reflect on the kind of mathematics teacher you want to be and to begin to work on this right from the start. Look back to your journal entry for Chapter 1 (Task 1.2) and consider whether the experience you have gained since you wrote it makes you wish to modify it or add some new points.

As a full-time teacher, you will probably have relatively few chances to watch your colleagues teaching, so it worth planning to make the most of it when you do. You may also want to think about how you can interact with other teachers, directly and indirectly, in ways that help your teaching to develop.

You will have had a mentor in the school where you did your teaching practice. In your first year as an NQT, there are opportunities for the mentoring process to continue as you work together on your *Career Entry Profile* (TTA, 1997). Once again, time is precious so it is best for both you and your mentor to plan ahead and agree what you want to work on and how you are going to do that. The MA (1995b) booklet *Starting as a Secondary Mathematics Teacher* (available from the Mathematical Association at the address given at the end of the chapter) is a useful source of ideas and advice.

Your LEA will have a policy and framework for supporting NQTs, and this often includes a series of meetings for all such teachers in your area. If your first post is in an LEA school, you will have automatic access to this programme and will receive information about it. Even if you teach in a grant-maintained school, you may find that there is an arrangement for you to participate in the programme, or the school itself may be large enough to provide its own programme.

Task 12.4 Supporting NQTs

Find out what support your school or LEA offers to NQTs.

DEVELOPING AS A TEACHER

Teaching can be a stressful occupation. Some aspects of stress reduce with experience; others may come about because of the need to cope with continual change. The sub-title of Guy Claxton's (1989) book *Being a Teacher* is 'Coping with change and stress'. In it, he argues that finding one's own scope for controlling change and working on being the kind of teacher one aspires to be is an essential component of coping with stress. Although his book is addressed to all teachers, secondary teachers of mathematics will find much in it that helps them to plan and control their own professional development.

Even when you no longer have the formal support of a mentor, colleagues can be a key source of support and professional development. You may be able to arrange to spend occasional time observing a willing colleague teach. It is important to agree beforehand how you will do this. Will you be simply an observer, or will you be a more active participant in some parts of the lesson? Is there something particular you want to look out for? (For example: will you be focusing on what the teacher does or what the pupils do; are you particularly interested in the factors that get a lesson off to a good start, or how to draw together what has happened at the end of the lesson?) Which of you will decide what this is to be? Will you take notes during the lesson, and can you both afford some time for discussing the lesson afterwards?

Having a critical friend is beneficial in many walks of life, and teaching is no exception. Even when no formal mentoring arrangement is on offer, you can seek out a colleague who would be willing to be your critical friend, perhaps on a mutual basis. Such a mutual arrangement is sometimes referred to as co-mentoring (Jaworski and Watson, 1994). In the long term, you will probably also seek to develop what Jaworski and Watson call an 'inner mentor'.

In-service courses and events

All schools set aside some time for 'in-house' professional development. In your first post, you will find out the programme for this in your school. Some of the time is likely to be spent on whole-school issues; at other times, the mathematics department will work together on issues they have identified for themselves. At first, you may wish to listen to your colleagues and discover the way in which the department works together, but be ready for the opportunity to take a more pro-active role, perhaps by preparing and leading some aspect of a planned INSET session.

There will also be local courses and INSET sessions available to teachers from a range of schools, perhaps organised by the LEA or through meetings arranged by some other agency or group.

The Association of Teachers of Mathematics (ATM) and the Mathematical Association (MA) were both mentioned in Chapter 1, and various publications of theirs have been referred to throughout this book. Is there perhaps a local branch

Task 12.5 Meeting other maths teachers

Find out what local opportunities, both formal and informal, there are for associating with other teachers of mathematics and working together on issues of mutual need and interest.

of one or the other? Going to local branch meetings can be a useful way of finding out about the services these organisations offer and seeing some of their publications before deciding whether to become a member of the national organisation. Both offer reduced subscriptions to students and NQTs, so it is worthwhile investigating them as early as possible so as to take advantage of any special offers.

Both the ATM and the MA hold their annual conferences during the Easter holidays, and both have occasional day conferences, usually on Saturdays, focused on particular issues of current concern. Again, it is worth finding out at an early stage whether there is any local funding that could offer financial support for attending such a conference.

Other organisations that hold one-day conferences in various parts of the country may also offer agendas that appeal to you. Three such are the Gender and Mathematics Association (GAMMA), the British Society for the History of Mathematics (BSHM) and the British Society for Research into Learning Mathematics (BSRLM). Contact details of these are given in Appendix 2.

Journals and books

The professional associations are an excellent source of publications for teachers of mathematics. ATM publishes two journals.

- *Mathematics Teaching*, which appears quarterly, has articles and reviews on a wide range of issues relevant to all mathematics classrooms.
- *Micromath*, which, as its name suggests, focuses on the roles and uses of computers and calculators in mathematics teaching and learning, has one issue a term.

Two journals of the Mathematical Association are of particular interest to the secondary teacher.

- *Mathematics in Schools*, which is classroom focused, is published five times a year.
- *Mathematical Gazette* is a quarterly journal in which most articles deal directly with mathematics rather than its teaching, but these can be a rich resource for sixth-form teaching.

Both associations have a range of other publications for teachers, and these include physical materials, software and posters for classrooms, as well as books and pamphlets.

Reading what others, including classroom teachers, have written, trying out some of the ideas and perhaps contributing a letter of feedback to a journal, are all ways of working on your own ideas about teaching. After a while, this can lead to writing up your reflections on some teaching ideas or experiences of your own and submitting them to a journal.

There are a number of books about mathematics teaching available from bookshops and through libraries, some single-authored, others edited collections of readings. Among those you may find useful as a beginning teacher are: Backhouse *et al.* (1992); Costello (1991); Pimm (1988); Pimm and Love (1991); and Selinger (1994). Two other books, which have been around a little longer but which have attained almost classical status as sources of teaching ideas, are *Notes on Mathematics for Children* by ATM (reissued 1985) and *Starting Points* (Banwell *et al.*, 1986).

Up-to-date information about mathematics education can often be found through the World Wide Web. Some useful sites are to be found in Appendix 2 and on the Web site http://mcs.open.ac.uk/cme/suejw

DEVELOPING AS A MATHEMATICIAN

An important way of creating a classroom atmosphere conducive to the learning of mathematics is for the pupils to be taught by teachers who themselves are engaged, and seen to be engaged, in the process of doing mathematics. An example of someone 'being a mathematician' helps learners to form a picture of what that means and gives them some strategies to emulate.

Some teachers choose to undertake personal study of mathematics as direct professional development. The quotation below is from the writing of a teacher who chose to do just that.

> Reflections on my own learning gradually moved away from describing the personal significance of particular incidents and started to address the question of how these events informed my understanding of the processes of learning mathematics. Although demanding, the process of trying to put mathematical ideas into words had been crucial to forming insights into ways of thinking. By listening to others, I became aware of the differences in representation and language which supported or obscured our individual understandings. I realised how much I had assumed and how little I really knew about the children I taught.
>
> (Hatch and Shiu, 1997, p. 167)

School-based in-service sessions devoted to doing mathematics together as a department can also be invigorating, as well as casting light on how pupils learn. A publication that is suitable for initiating mathematical activity either by an individual or a department is *Learning and Doing Mathematics* (Mason, 1999; see Further Reading).

A frequent (and motivating) starting point for personal mathematical activity is the need to teach a topic for the first time or even to teach a topic that you have not previously studied. Sometimes the first stage is to find a textbook to develop your own understanding of the topic; at other times, finding a fruitful teaching approach to traditionally awkward topics is more pressing. The Open University Centre for Mathematics Education pack '*Preparing to teach* . . . ' (mentioned in Chapter 4) offers a general way of analysing a mathematical topic before teaching it, as well as specific ideas on teaching angle, ratio and probability. The companion pack, '*Developing own thinking*', deals with some very general ideas underpinning large areas of mathematics.

Another aspect of developing as a mathematician is finding out about the different media through which a topic can be introduced – especially, perhaps, through use of calculators and computers. So doing some personal work on, for example, graphic calculators (see Galpin and Graham, 1997a and 1997b) or exploring specific software packages such as Cabri can be doubly beneficial.

Task 12.6 Unsure about an area of maths?

Identify a particular area of mathematics you feel apprehensive about teaching. This might be a particular topic, or it might be an approach using some unfamiliar technology. List possible sources of help and information such as colleagues, resources within school, material from books or journals or via the Internet. Draft a brief plan for working on this that includes an assessment of the time you might spend on it.

CAREER DEVELOPMENT

To end this chapter, spend a few minutes looking ahead and envisaging how you would like your career as a mathematics teacher to develop. What do you hope to be doing in five years' time, and what formal qualifications are there that might help you to achieve your ambitions?

At the time of writing, the notion of an 'expert teacher' who works in classrooms with children and colleagues in key curriculum areas is being discussed. Such a role is seen as a way of rewarding good teachers for 'staying in the classroom', and maximising the use of their expertise within a school. It may be that dedicated qualifications will soon be designed for 'expert teachers', so if it is a potential role that appeals to you, it is worth looking out for opportunities to gain such a qualification.

A more conventional role is that of head of department. The holder of this post is still very involved in classroom work, but also takes on developmental and administrative responsibility for co-ordinating mathematics teaching within a school. Here again, it is worth looking out for the mooted subject-leader qualification.

Another school-based role that appeals to many teachers is that of mentor for student teachers. Training is often available when a mentor is appointed, and is normally provided by the partnership that places student teachers in the school.

If you would like to take a more theoretical or research-oriented exploration within mathematics education, then a master's course might suit you. You may find a local institution that offers part-time or full-time higher degrees, or a distance-taught course (such as those offered by the Open University) might have practical advantages according to your situation. Eventually, you might choose to go on to a doctorate. As well as being of intrinsic interest, a higher degree will enhance your eligibility for a variety of senior posts, and you can choose the topics you work on according to your longer-term ambitions.

SUMMARY

Now you are ready to start on your career as a secondary mathematics teacher. What you learn about teaching and learning mathematics over the next few years, and what your pupils learn about mathematics, will depend on what you have already learned, the new experiences you have and the use you make of them. As a mature professional, you have the opportunity and the responsibility to make choices about those experiences. The more interested you become in how you operate as a teacher, the more interesting and rewarding teaching will be. Good luck!

FURTHER READING

Claxton, G. (1989) *Being a Teacher*, London: Cassell.
This book is about how to be a successful schoolteacher at a time of uncertainty, change, increased pressure and conflicting demands. It explores the scope that individuals have for staying positive and how they can deal with the pressures in the most effective way.

Mason, J. (1999) *Learning and Doing Mathematics*, York: QED.
This book focuses attention on fundamental processes of mathematical thinking. It turns out that these are neither new (you already know how to employ them but you may not always do so when appropriate) nor are they restricted to doing mathematical problems. The same processes are involved in both *doing* and *learning* mathematics.

MA (1995b) *Starting as a Secondary Mathematics Teacher*, Leicester: Mathematical Association.
Whatever your route into mathematics teaching, this booklet offers advice from making the first application through to the interview and your first year as that all-important NQT. As the authors acknowledge, at the time of writing the rules and regulations were constantly changing, and indeed they are still changing, but do not worry – the goal posts keep moving for all teachers.

TTA (1997) *Career Entry Profile Pack*, London: Teacher Training Agency.
From June 1998, all providers of initial teacher training are required to provide NQTs with a TTA Career Entry Profile. The purpose of the Profile is to convey a summary of information about new teachers' strengths and priorities for their further professional development. It includes a *pro forma* guide for recording the targets and action plan for the induction period, as agreed between the school and the NQT.

Appendix 1
Glossary of Terms

All items with * appear in the list of useful addresses in Appendix 2.

APU	The Assessment of Performance Unit was established in 1975, within the DES, to provide information about general levels of performance of pupils in schools, and how these change over time. In 1989, this function became part of the Schools Examination and Assessment Council (SEAC).
AT	Attainment Target
ATM*	Association of Teachers of Mathematics
Basic skills	Literacy, numeracy and ICT for all pupils
BECTa*	The British Educational Communications and Technology Agency
BSHM*	The British Society for the History of Mathematics
BSRLM*	The British Society for Research into Learning Mathematics
BTEC	Business and Technician Education Council
CARN*	The Collaborative Action Research Network
Core skills	Application of Number, Communication, Information Technology, Improving Own Learning and Performance, Working with Others, Problem Solving, also known as Key Skills
DES	Department of Education and Science, became DfE
DfE	Department for Education, became DfEE
DfEE*	Department for Education and Employment
GAIM	Graded Assessment in Mathematics
GAMMA*	The Gender and Mathematics Association
GCSE	General Certificate of Secondary Education
GNVQ	General National Vocational Qualification
HIMED*	History in Mathematics Education

HMI	Her Majesty's Inspector(ate)
ICT	Information and Communication Technology
IMA*	Institute of Mathematics and its Applications
IT	Information Technology
ITT	Initial Teacher Training
Key skills	Application of Number, Communication, Information Technology, Improving Own Learning and Performance, Working with Others, Problem Solving, also known as Core Skills
KS	Key Stage
LEA	Local Education Authority
LMS*	London Mathematical Society
LMS	Local Management of Schools
MA*	Mathematical Association
NC	National Curriculum
NCC	National Curriculum Council, merged with SEAC in 1993 to form SCAA
NCET	National Council for Educational Technology, now BECTa
NCTM*	National Council for Teachers of Mathematics, an association for teachers of mathematics, based in the United States, with members across North America
NCVQ	National Council for Vocational Qualifications (now part of QCA)
NFER*	National Foundation for Educational Research
NQT	Newly Qualified Teacher, a teacher in their first year of teaching
Ofsted	Office for Standards in Education
OU*	Open University
PGCE	Postgraduate Certificate in Education
PoS	Programme of Study
QCA*	Qualifications and Curriculum Authority, 1997–present, brought together the work of NCVQ and SCAA, with additional powers, to provide overview of curriculum, assessment and qualifications from pre-school to higher vocational levels.
QTS	Qualified Teacher Status
RSS*	Royal Statistical Society
SATs	Standard Assessment Tests
SoAs	Statements of Attainment
SCAA	Schools Curriculum and Assessment Authority, 1993–1997
SCITT	School-Centred Initial Teacher Training
SEAC	School Examination and Assessment Authority, 1988–1993, merged with NCC to form SCAA
SEN	Special Educational Needs
SENCO	Special Needs Co-ordinator
SMP	School Mathematics Project
TGAT	Task Group on Assessment and Testing
TTA	Teacher Training Agency
WO	Welsh Office

Appendix 2
Sources and Resources

USEFUL ADDRESSES

ATM

The Association of Teachers of Mathematics is one of the two mathematics teacher organisations in England (the other is the Mathematical Association). ATM was originally founded in 1952 as the Association for Teaching Aids in Mathematics; it became the ATM in 1962. It publishes two journals, *Mathematics Teaching* and *Micromath,* as well as many other materials concerned with the teaching and learning of mathematics. It also organises an Easter conference and local groups which meet from time to time. Write or phone for a catalogue and details of student membership.

Contact address: ATM, 7 Shaftesbury Street, Derby, DE23 8YB
Tel: 01332 346599
Web site: http://acorn.educ.nottingham.ac.uk/SchEd/pages/atm

BECTa

Following recent initiatives from the UK government on ICT, the National Council for Educational Technology (NCET) has been renamed the British Educational Communications and Technology Agency (BECTa). The new agency is undergoing substantial reorganisation, and its responsibilities include running and developing the National Grid for Learning. Write or phone for a catalogue.

Contact address: BECTa, Milburn High Road, Science Park, Coventry, CV4 7JJ
Tel: 01203 416669
Web site: http://www.becta.org.uk/

BSHM

The British Society for the History of Mathematics is an organisation of those interested in the history of mathematics at all levels, whether as practising teachers wanting to make use of history in their teaching, or academic historians. Further information about meetings (including the HIMED conferences) and other activities can be obtained from:

Contact: June Barrow-Green, Faculty of Mathematics and Computing, The Open University, Walton Hall, Milton Keynes, MK7 6AA

BSRLM

The British Society for Research into Learning Mathematics has been active since 1978, and provides a central forum for UK mathematics educators interested in research. The group is open to anyone involved or interested in mathematics education and organises some day meetings (on Saturdays) and one weekend meeting each year. Members receive information about meetings, a newsletter and the proceedings of past conferences.

Contact: Tim Rowland, Institute of Education, University of London, 20 Bedford Way, London, WC1H 0AL
Tel: 0171 612 6231
Web site: http://www.scism.sbu.ac.uk/~lermans/BSRLM

CARN

The Collaborative Action Research Network was originally known as 'The Classroom Action Research Network'. It is an international network of practitioners who are interested in using research as an integral part of their working practice. The journal *Educational Action Research* has close links with CARN. It is a fully referenced international journal that is published three times a year and is a useful source of research papers on action research.

Contact: Claire Burge, 23 Warrington Road, Ipswich, IP1 3OU

Chartwell-Yorke

Specialises in Derive, Cabri, TI-92 and support material.

Contact: Philip Yorke, Chartwell-Yorke, 114 High Street, Belmont, Bolton, BL7 8AL
Tel: 01204 811001

DfEE

Publishes, amongst other things, the requirements for courses of initial teacher training, Circular 4/98. Copies are available from the DfEE publications line or from the Web site.

Contact address: DfEE, Sanctuary Buildings, Great Smith Street, London, SW1P 3BT
Tel: 0845 60 222 60
Web site: http://www.open.gov.uk/dfee/dfeehome.htm

GAMMA
The Gender and Mathematics Association is a network of teachers who share a common interest in girls' achievements and involvement in mathematics. They publish a newsletter twice a year, run an annual day conference, and organise a residential three-day conference for schoolgirls studying A-level mathematics (called MAYF – Mathematics and Your Future). Further information can be obtained from:

Contact address: GAMMA, c/o ATM, 7 Shaftesbury Street, Derby, DE23 9YB

Government Statistical Service
A standing committee co-ordinated by ONS (Office for National Statistics). The Web site includes a guide to official statistics.

Tel:
public enquiry unit 0171 233 9233
library 0171 533 6256 (free publications e.g. UK in figures)
sales desk 0171 533 5678 (priced publications)
Web site: http://www.ons.gov.uk

HIMED (History in Mathematics Education) is an annual conference of BSHM; further details from:

Contact: John Earle, 20 Dunvegan Close, Exeter, EX4 4AF

Institute of Mathematics and Its Applications (IMA)
Web site: http://www.ima.org.uk

London Mathematical Society (LMS)
Society of pure mathematicians

Contact address: De Morgan House, 57–58 Russell Square, London, WC1B 4HP
Tel: 0171 323 3686
Web site: http://www.lms.ac.uk/

MA
The Mathematical Association is one of the two mathematics teacher organisations in England (the other is the Association of Teachers of Mathematics). The MA was originally founded as the Association for the Improvement of Geometrical Teaching (AIGT) in 1871, and changed its name in 1897. It publishes several journals, including *Mathematics in School*, *The Mathematical Gazette* and *Struggle*, as well as other materials concerned with the teaching and learning of mathematics. It also runs an Easter conference and has local branches that meet regularly. Write or phone for a catalogue and details of student membership.

Contact address: Mathematical Association, 259 London Road, Leicester, LE2 3BF
Tel: 0116 2703877
Web site: http://members.aol.com/mathsassoc/MAhomepage.html

NCTM
The American Maths Teachers organisation. Publishes *Mathematics Teacher.* Also publishes yearbooks on a different topic each year. Publications may be bought direct or through QED (see below).

Web site: http://www.nctm.org

National Foundation for Educational Research (NFER)
The Mere, Upton Park, Slough, Berkshire, SL1 2DQ
Tel: 01753 574123

NRich Online Maths Club
http://nrich.maths.org.uk

Open University, Centre for Mathematics Education
In addition to the well-known undergraduate mathematics materials, the OU also produces in-service materials for mathematics education, all of which are of a very high standard. Ask for a catalogue.

Centre for Mathematics Education, The Open University, Walton Hall, Milton Keynes, MK7 6AA
Tel: 01908 653550

Oxford Educational Supplies
Suppliers of calculators, graphic calculators, Derive, Cabri II and supporting materials. Offer a sale or return scheme to enable evaluation of new products. This enables you to try any of the graphic calculators, OHP versions, PC links, and support material, for 30 days. Ask for a catalogue.

Contact: Oxford Educational Supplies Ltd, Unit 19, Weston Business Park, Weston on the Green, Bicester, Oxon, OX6 8SY
Tel: 01869 343369

Pearson Publishing
Publishes books and CD-ROMS about the Internet

Chesterton Mill, French's Road, Cambridge, CB4 3NP
Tel: 01223 350555

QCA
If you ring the order line for a copy of the QCA catalogue, they will send it free of charge. You will then see the full range of materials you can obtain from QCA; these include discussion papers (e.g. about the role of calculators), copies of statutory tests, and reports on tests and standards.

Contact address: QCA, Newcombe House, 45 Notting Hill Gate, London, W11 3JB
Tel: (customer services) 0171 229 1234
Tel: (publication order line) 0181 867 3333
Web site: http://www.crownbc.com/qca/menu.htm

QED
Largely a distributor rather than an originator of books and materials, they keep large stocks, so things can be obtained quickly.

Contact address: QED, Room 1, Stonehills House, Stonehills, Welwyn Garden City, AL8 6NH
Tel: 0345 402275
Fax: 01707 334233
Email: QEDBooks1@aol.com

John Bibby, QED Books, is a useful source of historical books. His catalogue is available from:

Contact address: QED Books, 1 Straylands Grove, York YO3 0EB
Tel: 01904 424381

The Royal Statistical Society (RSS)
12 Errol Street, London, EC1Y 8LX
Tel: 0171 638 8998
Web site: www.maths.ntu.ac.uk/rss/index.html

SMILE Centre
The SMILE Centre, 108a Lancaster Rd, London, W11 1QS
Tel: 0171 221 8966
Web site: www.rmplc.co.uk/orgs/smile/index.html

Tarquin Publications
Excellent selection of books, posters, software, gridsheets, wooden puzzles, etc. They are also distributors for DIME and Leapfrogs. Ask for a catalogue.

Contact address: Tarquin Publications, Stradbroke, Diss, Norfolk, IP21 5JP
Tel: 01379 384 218

Texas Instruments
Loans class sets of calculators for teachers. Also has information about INSET.

Tel: 01234 213394
Helpline: 0181 230 3184
Web site: http://www.ti.com/calc/

JOURNALS

Mathematics in Schools (MiS)
Produced by the Mathematical Association (MA) for members five times a year, this professional journal publishes articles on a wide range of topics connected with teaching and learning the mathematics curriculum. It is aimed at teachers of mathematics, especially those who teach the 7–16 age range. Contact is via the MA office, listed on p. 232.

Mathematics Teaching (MT)
This is one of two professional journals about the teaching and learning of mathematics produced by the Association of Teachers of Mathematics (ATM), the other being *Micromath*. Launched in 1955, *MT* is now a well established and widely-read quarterly. The journal covers a broad range of topics that relate to the practice of teaching mathematics at all levels. Contact is via the ATM office, listed on p. 230.

Micromath (MM)
This is the second (and more recent) of two ATM professional journals, which first appeared in 1985 and is published three times a year. It is a journal about learning and teaching mathematics with new technology, with articles and overviews by specialists and classroom practitioners (who are at times the same). Contact is via the ATM office, listed on p. 230.

Teaching Statistics
This is a journal for teachers who use statistical ideas, whether in mathematics or in other subjects such as biology or economics. The purpose is to show how statistical ideas can illuminate work in these areas and to help teachers teach statistics with understanding. Articles emphasise teaching and classroom activities. The journal is published by the Teaching Statistics Trust; further details can be obtained from Teaching Statistics, RSS Centre for Statistical Education, University of Nottingham, NG7 2RD.

WEB SITES

There is a great range and variety of Web sites in mathematics education.
We have given some sites throughout the book. Up-to-date versions can be found at the site we have made to go with the book: see http://mcs.open.ac.uk/cme/suejw

Appendix 3
Making Closed Tasks Open

Some examples of the ways in which closed tasks can be modified to make them 'open' are shown in Table A3.1. These are taken from page D7 of the *Mathematics National Curriculum Non-Statutory Guidance* (NCC, 1989).

Table A3.1

<table>
<tr><th>Closed task</th><th>Modified task</th></tr>
<tr><td>2 + 6 − 3 =</td><td>What numbers can you make from 2, 3 and 6?</td></tr>
<tr><td>3 × 5 =</td><td>Make up some questions whose answer is 15</td></tr>
<tr><td> 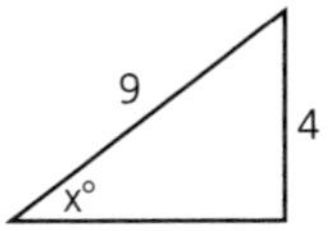9
4
x°
Find the value of x</td><td>Investigate what the sine button on a calculator does</td></tr>
<tr><td>Continue this sequence:
1, 2, 4 . . . .</td><td>Discuss how the sequence
1, 2, 4 . . . might continue</td></tr>
<tr><td> 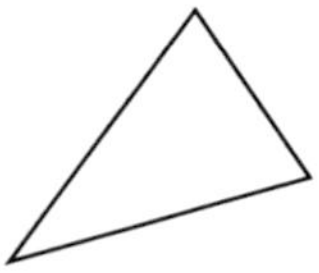Find the area of this triangle</td><td> 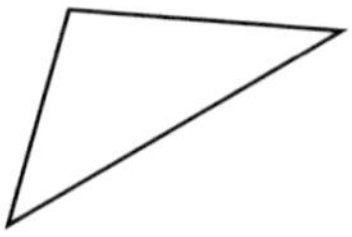Construct some triangles with the same areas as this one</td></tr>
<tr><td>What do we call a five-sided shape?</td><td>What shapes/configurations can you make with five lines?</td></tr>
<tr><td>Play a particular board game</td><td>Design a board game for four people using a dice and counters</td></tr>
<tr><td>Draw the graphs of
1) $y = 3x + 5$
2) $y = 2x - 5$
3) $y = 6 - x$</td><td>Investigate the graphs of $y = ax + b$ for different values of a and b</td></tr>
<tr><td>Copy and complete this addition table:
<table><tr><td>+</td><td>4</td><td>7</td></tr><tr><td>2</td><td></td><td></td></tr><tr><td>6</td><td></td><td></td></tr></table></td><td>Investigate the possible ways of completing this table:
<table><tr><td></td><td></td><td></td></tr><tr><td></td><td>3</td><td>4</td></tr><tr><td></td><td>7</td><td></td></tr></table></td></tr>
</table>

Appendix 4
Starting with ICT: Practicalities for Beginners

In this appendix, an introductory description is offered for six of the tools discussed in Chapter 8: graphic calculator, spreadsheet, dynamic geometry, Logo, CD-ROMs, Internet. The first level, 'Acquainted', represents having met and used the tool enough to know what it is. This appendix will tell you what the tool is and how to get started.

You will make most progress if you have personal access to the technology with which you need to teach. If, in addition, you see technology as a logico-mathematical environment, new to you, in which you are operating as a mathematician, those many frustrations you encounter will be tackled in a way that will enhance your teaching.

0 GENERAL

Contact BECTa Bookshop and ask for a copy of 'Software for Mathematics', a list of major applications and suppliers' addresses. Ask also for their current catalogue and take a look through the maths section.

1 GRAPHIC CALCULATORS

A graphic calculator is a calculator with a big screen that enables the user to draw graphs, zoom in and out, and experiment. Many come with options of function, polar, or parametric graphs. It is also possible to tabulate functions and to explore sequences. Once you get started, much more becomes possible.

The Casio 7000g was one of the earliest graphic calculators. Then Texas Instruments brought out the TI-81, which many people found easier to use because it

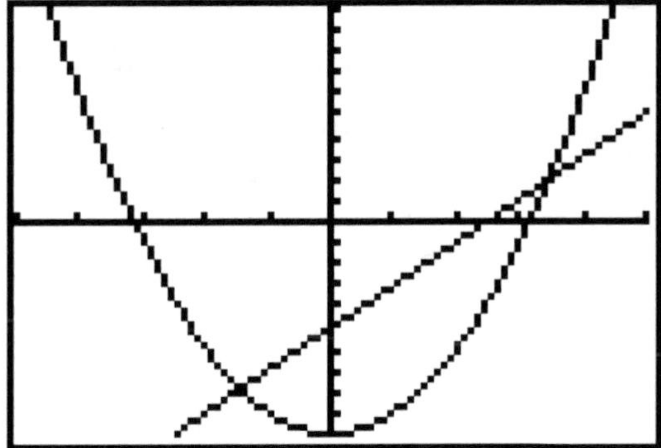

Figure A4.1 A graphic calculator screen

employed a system of menus. The Casio equivalent was the 7700g. Both of these had a friendly starting section in the manual.

Now there is a wide range to choose from. You will be able to borrow a graphic calculator if you do not want to buy one yet. Either your school may be able to loan you one, or Texas Instruments run a loan programme. Contact TI or Oxford Educational Supplies (see Appendix 2). If you are an absolute beginner, we recommend the new series of books by Graham and Galpin (1998) that go with the TI-83, available from Oxford Educational Supplies.

If you decide to buy your own, it is cheaper to buy from an educational supplier such as Oxford Educational Supplies than from a high street shop.

Work through the 'Getting started' section of the manual.

2 SPREADSHEETS

A spreadsheet is an electronic table that offers an algebraic environment in an accessible format. Cells are labelled by their row and column. Figure A4.2 shows cell B1 highlighted; from B1, the formula = A1 times three has been 'filled down' to all the cells below. The result is part of the three times table.

Most computers these days come with a spreadsheet built in. The spreadsheet Excel is widely available in schools and colleges in Britain, both on Mac and PC computers, and it is an industry standard. However, any equivalent spreadsheet with a graphing facility, such as ClarisWorks on a PC or Eureka on an Archimedes computer, will do similar things, very often in much the same way.

For absolute beginners, there are very good starter books for commercial use, such as O'Hara, S. (1993) *Easy Excel*, Que Corporation, ISBN 0 88022 820 2.

You should find that there is a spreadsheet somewhere in the school; usually, but not always, this will be Excel, which is published by Microsoft, or it might be Eureka if the department uses Archimedes computers.

A spreadsheet can be a tool for generating and exploring simulated data. The random number generator can be used to set up simulations of random processes.

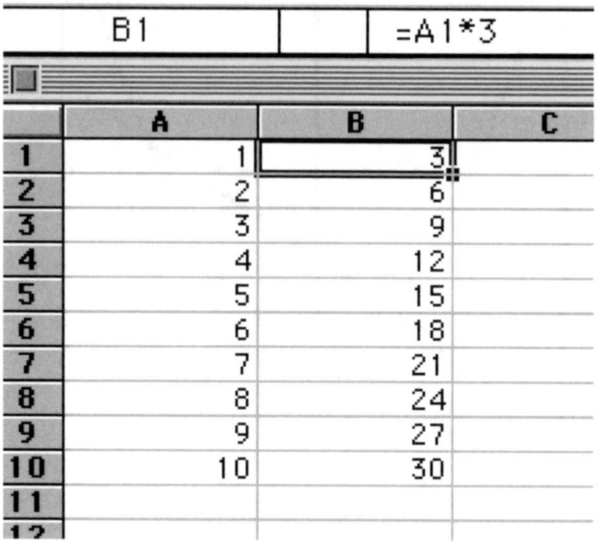

B1 =A1*3

	A	B	C
1	1	3	
2	2	6	
3	3	9	
4	4	12	
5	5	15	
6	6	18	
7	7	21	
8	8	24	
9	9	27	
10	10	30	
11			

Figure A4.2 A spreadsheet

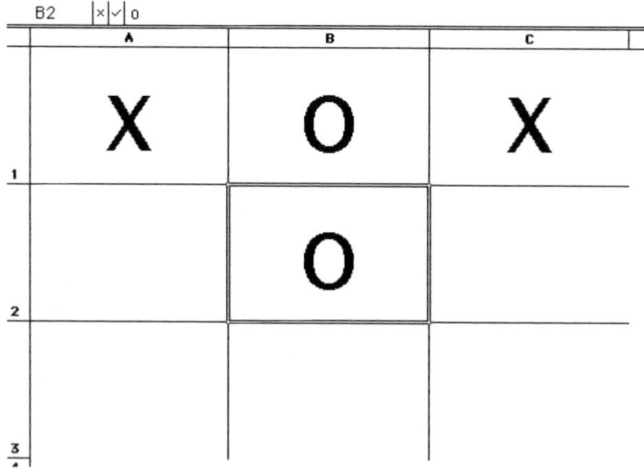

Figure A4.3 Altering the presentation of a spreadsheet

The simulated data is easily formatted and, after manipulation in Excel, it can easily be exported to other packages. Use the spreadsheet to generate lottery numbers. The random number generator is one of a wide range of functions that can be pasted into a sheet from a built-in library.

If you start working with macros, a form of programming with a spreadsheet, you will be able to set up sheets to explore families of functions, and to use animated graphs to explore what happens when you change the values of the parameters.

On a lighter note, pupils enjoy changing the presentation of the spreadsheet, for example the font size, the column width and the row height, as in the Figure A4.3.

3 DYNAMIC GEOMETRY

Dynamic geometry software has points, lines and circles as basic objects, and allows constructions such as the mid-point between two points. So, for example, in Figure A4.4, two points are made, then a line segment is drawn between them; two circles are then constructed using the original points as centre and radius point for one, and vice versa for the second. Finally, a third point is identified as a point of intersection. A triangle is constructed using the three points. As either of the two original points are moved around, the diagram changes, but the triangle stays equilateral.

There are three main versions available for PCs and Macs and one for Archimedes computers at the time of writing. You can obtain a trial copy of

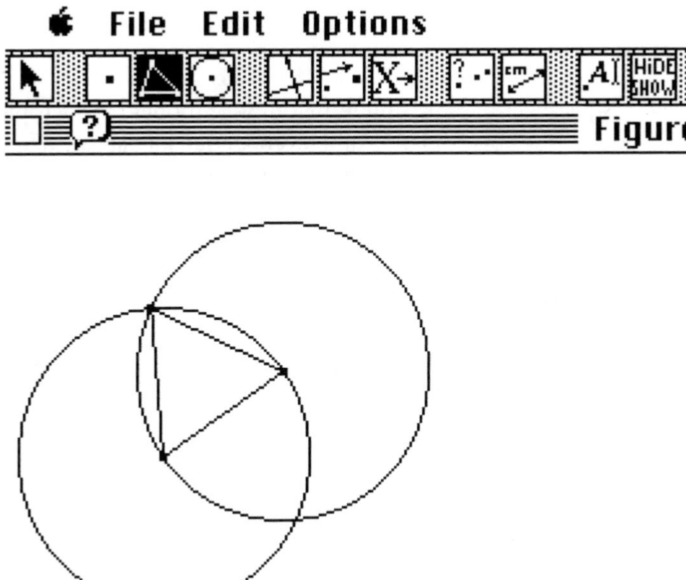

Figure A4.4 Dynamic geometry

your chosen dynamic geometry package either by contacting the suppliers or by downloading from the Internet. In addition, there is a 'calculator' implementation of Cabri on a TI-92 from Texas Instruments, so if you want to try ideas with a class you can borrow a class set.

Write to QED for a demonstration copy of Geometer's Sketchpad and Cabri – this should come with a 48-page booklet of starter activities for about £5. Oxford Educational Supplies will supply a demonstration disc of Cabri 2 free of charge. See Appendix 2 for addresses.

4 LOGO

Logo is 'the name for a philosophy of education and for a continuously evolving family of computer languages that aid its realization' (Abelson and diSessa, 1980, p. 412). Papert (1980) has written an inspiring account of the thinking behind Logo. As there are various implementations available, you will need to be aware of variations.

The fundamental idea is that the pupil is instructing a turtle to move and construct geometric objects, or trajectories. So, for example, if the turtle were told:

Forward 40
Right 90
Forward 40
Right 90
Forward 40
Right 90
Forward 40

it would draw a square. From this simple beginning, modelling of topics such as Newtonian motion, 3D co-ordinates, and even general relativity (Abelson and diSessa, 1980) are possible, but there are many steps in between! Perhaps the most interesting feature of the Logo languages is that they support recursion.

A copy of MSW Logo can be downloaded from the Internet. For example, there is a Windows version at http://www.softronix.com/logo.html or you can use the ATM page http://acorn.educ.nottingham.ac.uk//SchEd/pages/atm/newsletter/mswlogo.htm

Your school will almost certainly have a copy. Experiment a little before you start Chapter 8.

5 CD-ROMS

Contact a CD supplier such as AVP and Cambridge CD-ROM. Ask for a copy of their catalogue. Choose a CD-ROM and ask for an inspection or loan copy.

6 THE INTERNET

If you do not yet know anything at all about the Internet, one very useful resource will be *The Internet* published by Dorling Kindersley. Local libraries will often be able to guide you into getting started.

Start by typing in http://mcs.open.ac.uk/cme/suejw and then point and click to follow the links from there. The links are represented by underlined text, as you can see in Figure A4.5.

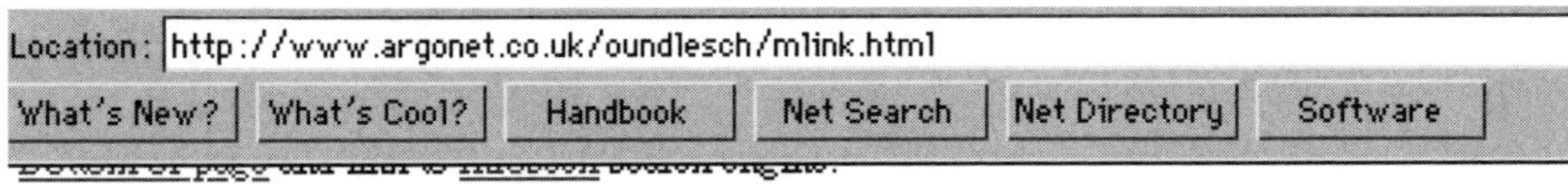

CONTENTS OF THIS PAGE:

1. Mathematical Associations and Magazines
2. Mathematical Resources
3. Mathematical Entertainment

4. Statistical Resources
5. Other Lists of Useful Links

6. Software and hardware for mathematical IT *(separate page)*
7. General Reference and Academic Sites *(separate page)*

- **1. Mathematical Associations and Magazines** - Back to contents - Search

UK
The Mechanics in Action home page
MicroMath
M.A.: home page
ATM: home page

MEI (Mathematics in Education and Industry)

Figure A4.5 Mathematics sources on the Internet

Appendix 5
Practical Task – Rolling Balls

ROLLING ALONG

You have to investigate the motion of a ball as it rolls along a horizontal track.

You will need: A large table, a hard, smooth ball, a short ramp, some track and a tape measure or a couple of metre rules, three wooden blocks, some stopwatches and some Blu Tack

Set up the apparatus as shown:

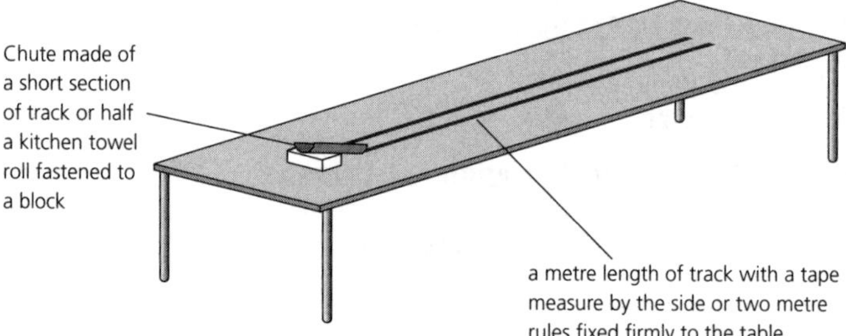

Figure A5.1 Apparatus needed for ball-rolling task

Release the ball near the top of the ramp so that it rolls nearly to the end of the track before stopping. (Release it from lower down the slope if it goes straight off the end of the track.) Mark your release point by fixing a small block above the ball. Release the ball several times. How fast is it going? Make some predictions.

Now start your measurements. Place a small block on the track 40 cm from the bottom of the chute. Release the ball from the marker on the chute and measure the time taken from the bottom of the chute to the block. Repeat this several times and take an average. What sort of average should you take?

Move the block to 70 cm and repeat, then go to 90 cm and finally allow the ball to come to rest. Fill in the table:

Average time taken from bottom of chute (sec)	....	....	....	....	....
Distance travelled from bottom of chute (m)	0.4	0.5	0.7	0.9	....

Enter the data in your graphic calculator and try to fit a function to it. (It should go through (0,0). Why?)

Differentiate your function to get the velocity of the ball. What does this tell you about the motion? You may need to change your function if what it tells you about the motion is patently wrong.

You should now be able to calculate the acceleration of the ball and hence the force acting on it. Placing blocks under the table legs nearest the end of the track will enable you to investigate the motion of a ball rolling up and down a slope.

GENERAL NOTES ON ANY PRACTICAL INVESTIGATION

Practicals can be used in two ways. The first is as a means of validating theory you have already learnt. The second is to build up a picture of a real-life situation. This can be explained by subsequent learnt theory. You must learn how to record and analyse data and interpret your results.

Experimental technique

Experimental technique is important in any practical. The following notes may help you when investigating motion.

Accuracy

What sources of inaccuracy are there? For instance, in measuring time, do the errors due to your reaction time at the beginning and end of the run cancel each other out? Stopwatches are difficult to use for times less than 0.6 sec. Consider the use of a mean or median in choosing which measurement to use in your analysis.

Repeatability and consistency

The data collected *must* be obtainable by other experimenters at other times. It is also important that the experiment is consistent, especially if you are using different runs to collect a set of measurements. Assume that the same thing happens each time you start the experiment, so you can interrupt the run at different points.

When rolling a ball down a slope, for example, it must be released from exactly the same point each time, and also it must roll smoothly down the track without bouncing from side to side. The following points may help with timing.

1 Have a few dummy runs to get yourself familiar with the stopwatch.
2 Call out 3, 2, 1, Go! as you start.
3 An audible signal at the end of a run will mean your reaction time errors are minimised.

Make sure you measure the distance travelled carefully. You will be modelling the ball as a point source. In reality, you must allow for its radius.

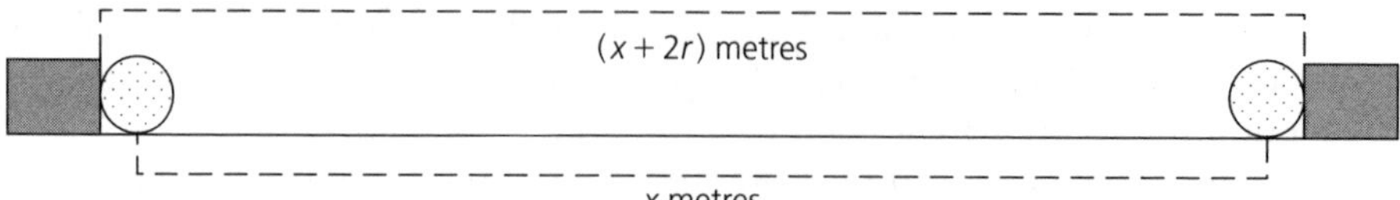

Figure A5.2 Allowing for radius when measuring distance

A student carried out the practical and recorded her results and calculations. Read them carefully and then follow them using your own data.

1 I set up the practical and collected some data. I repeated each measurement 5 times and took the median value.
I got the following data points (0,0), (0.4,0.4), (0.61,0.5), (1.01,0.7), (1.19,0.8), (2.06,0.98) and plotted them on my graphic calculator.

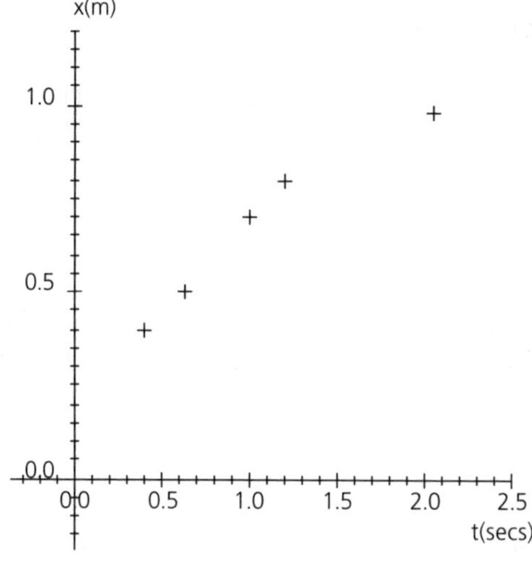

Figure A5.3 Plotted points on a graphic calculator

(I plotted time on the horizontal so I could differentiate to get the velocity.)
The ball stopped at 98 cm.

continued . . .

2 I tried to fit a function to the data. As the graph must pass through the point (0,0), a straight line was not appropriate*. There seemed to be two possibilities. These were:

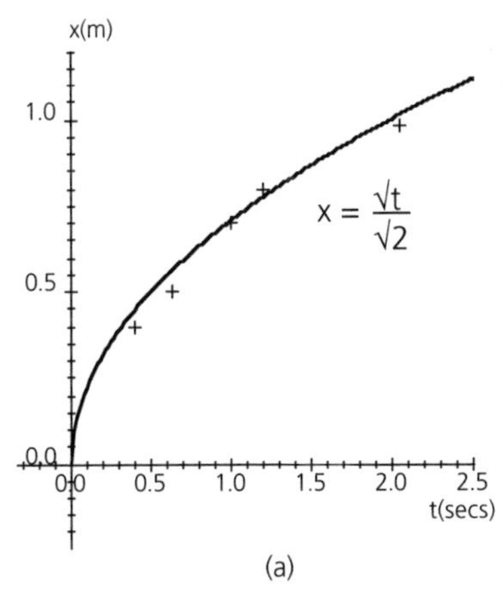

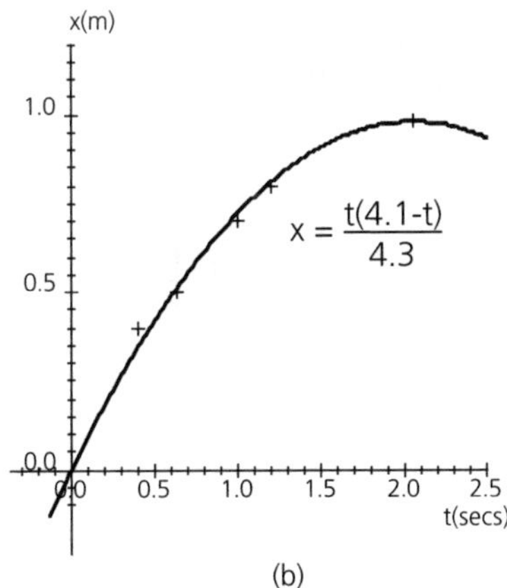

Figure A5.4a and b Two possible curved graph lines

3 The velocity of the ball is given by the slope of the curve. I differentiated both functions to get the slope.

For $x = \frac{\sqrt{t}}{\sqrt{2}} = \frac{\sqrt{2}}{2} t^{0.5}$

$v = \frac{\sqrt{2}}{4} t^{-0.5}$

The slope when t = 0 is infinitely great, i.e. the velocity is greater than the speed of light. Hardly likely.
Also the slope is never zero, so the ball never stops moving. Again this was not what happened, so the graph is not a good model of the motion.

For $x = \frac{t(4.1 - t)}{4.3}$

This differentiates to give v = 0.953 − 0.465t

The slope when t = 0 is about 0.9, i.e. the speed is around 1 m s^{-1}.
Also when t = 2.05 the speed is zero. Admittedly, after this the ball appears to go backwards, but this only showed me that the model only holds between t = 0 and t = 2.05.
On the whole this seems to fit what actually happened rather well.

4 To find the acceleration and the force I used the model x = t(4.1 − t)/4.3, v = 0.953 − 0.465t.

The acceleration of the ball is $^{dv}/_{dt}$ or -0.465 ms^{-2}.

continued . . .

The mass of the ball is 40 grams.

Thus the force acting on the rolling ball would appear to be around is 0.02 Newtons.

* I didn't join the points up with straight lines because that would mean the ball appears to speed up and slow down in jerks.

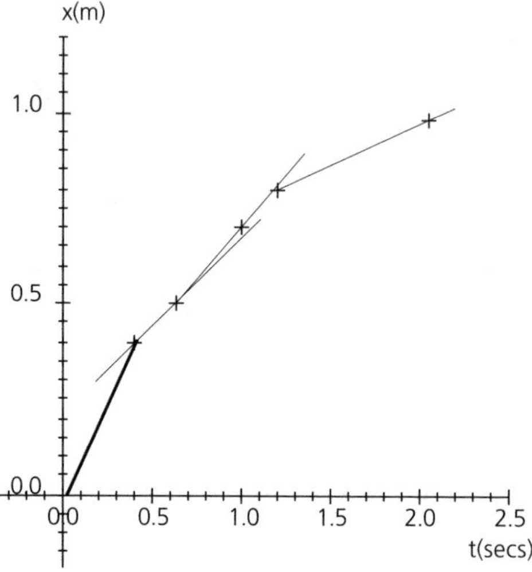

Figure A5.5 The rejected straight-line graph

References

Abelson, H. and diSessa, A. (1980) *Turtle Geometry*, Cambridge, MA: MIT Press.

Ainley, J. (1987) 'Telling questions', *Mathematics Teaching* **118**, 24–26.

Ainley, J. and Goldstein, R. (1988) *Making Logo Work: a Guide for Teachers*, Oxford: Basil Blackwell.

Albers, D. J. (1986) 'Paul Halmos', in Albers, D. J. and Alexanderson, G. L. (eds), *Mathematical People – Profiles and Interviews*, Cambridge, MA: Birkhäuser-Boston, pp. 119–132.

APU (1986) *Decimals Assessment at Age 11 and 15*, Berkshire: NFER–Nelson.

APU (1988) *Attitudes and Gender Differences*, Berkshire: NFER–Nelson.

Arter, P. *et al.* (1993) *Graphic Calculators in the Mathematics Classroom*, Leicester: Mathematical Association.

Askew, M. and Wiliam, D. (1995) *Recent Research in Mathematics Education 5–16*, London: HMSO.

Askew, M., Bliss, J. and Macrae, S. (1995) 'Scaffolding in mathematics, science and technology', in Murphy, P., Selinger, M., Bourne, J. and Briggs, M. (eds), *Subject Learning in the Primary Curriculum: Issues in English, Science and Mathematics*, London: Routledge, pp. 209–217.

ATM (1985, reissue) *Notes on Mathematics for Children*, Derby: Association of Teachers of Mathematics.

ATM (1989) *Exploring Assessment, an ATM Discussion Book*, Derby: Association of Teachers of Mathematics.

ATM (1993a) *Talking Maths, Talking Languages*, Derby: Association of Teachers of Mathematics.

ATM (1993b) *Using and Applying Mathematics*, Derby: Association of Teachers of Mathematics.

ATM (1993c) *In Our Classrooms: Strategies for the Teaching of Mathematics*, Derby: Association of Teachers of Mathematics.

ATM (1994) *Teaching, Learning and Mathematics*, Derby: Association of Teachers of Mathematics.

ATM (1995) *Teaching, Learning and Mathematics with IT*, Derby: Association of Teachers of Mathematics.

ATM (1998) *Teaching, Learning and Mathematics: Challenging Beliefs*, Derby: Association of Teachers of Mathematics.

ATM/MA/NCET (1994) *The IT Maths Pack*, Coventry: National Council for Educational Technology.

ATM/MA/NCET (1995) *Algebra at A level*, Derby: Association of Teachers of Mathematics.

Backhouse, J., Haggarty, L., Pirie, S. and Stratton, J. (1992) *Improving the Learning of Mathematics*, London: Cassell.

Banwell, C. S., Saunders K. D. and Tahta, D. G. (1986) *Starting Points*, Diss, Norfolk: Tarquin Publications.

Barham, J. and Bishop, A. (1991) 'Mathematics and the deaf child', in Durkin, K. and Shire, B. (eds), *Language in Mathematical Education,* Buckingham: Open University Press, pp. 179–187.

BERA (1992) *Dialogue: Policy Issues in National Assessment*, Policy Task Group on Assessment, Avon: Multilingual Matters Ltd.

Bishop, A. (1991) 'Teaching mathematics to ethnic minority pupils in secondary schools', in Pimm, D. and Love, E. (eds), *Teaching and Learning School Mathematics*, Sevenoaks: Hodder and Stoughton, pp. 26–43.

Blair, H., Dimbleby, B., Loughran, B., Taylor, I. and Vallance, J. (1983) 'A Birmingham maths trail', *Mathematics in School* **12**(4), 14–15.

Boaler, J. (1997) *Experiencing School Mathematics: Teaching Styles, Sex and Setting*, Buckingham: Open University Press.

Bold, B. (1982) *Famous Problems of Geometry and How to Solve Them*, New York, NY: Dover.

Borasi, R. (1992) *Learning Mathematics Through Inquiry*, Portsmouth, NH: Heinemann.

Boyd, W. (1973) *Emile for Today*, London: Heinemann.

Bradshaw, J. (1997) 'Tessellating with Logo' *Micromath* **13**(3), 24–26.

Brown, L., Hewitt, D. and Mason, J. (1994) 'Ways of seeing', in Selinger, M. (ed.), *Teaching Mathematics*, London: Routledge, pp. 85–94.

Brown, M. (1981) 'Place value and decimals', in Hart, K. (ed.), *Children's Understanding of Mathematics: 11–16*, London: John Murray, pp. 48–65.

Budge, D. (1997) 'Boost to morale on maths and science', *The Times Educational Supplement* **4239**, September 26th, p. 1a.

Burns, S. (1994) 'Changing A level Mathematics', in Selinger, M. (ed.), *Teaching Mathematics*, London: Routledge, pp. 204–211.

Burns, S. (1995) 'Mathematical abilities of students entering higher education', *London Mathematical Society Newsletter* **225**, March.

Burns, S. (1996) 'Omar Khayyam and dynamic geometry', *Micromath* **12**(2), 28–30.

Butler, D. (1998) *Using the Internet – Mathematics*, Cambridge: Pearson Publishing.

Buxton, L. (1981) *Do You Panic about Maths?: Coping with Maths Anxiety*, London: Heinemann Educational.

Callinan, J. (1992) 'Mathematics and physical disabilities', *Struggle* **34**, 17–19.

Capel, S., Leask, M. and Turner, T. (1995) *Learning to Teach in the Secondary School*, London: Routledge.

Charis Project (1997) *Charis Mathematics, Units 1–9 and Units 10–19*, Nottingham: Stapleford Centre.

Cheng, Y., Payne, J. and Witherspoon, S. (1995) *Science and Mathematics in Full-time Education after 16*, London: DfEE.

Chinn, S. J. and Ashcroft, J. R. (1993) *Mathematics for Dyslexics*, London: Whurr Publishing.

Claxton, G. (1989) *Being a Teacher: Coping with Change and Stress*, London: Cassell.

Cocker, M., Critcher, H., Stevens, W. and Rigby, J. (1996) 'Starting a secondary school maths club', *Mathematics in School* **25**(5), 33–36.

Connolly, P. and Vilardi, T. (eds) (1989) *Writing to Learn Mathematics and Science*, New York, NY: Teachers College Press.

Cooper, B. (1985) *Renegotiating Secondary School Mathematics*, Barcombe, Sussex: Falmer Press.

Cooper, B. (1994) 'Secondary mathematics education in England: recent changes and their historical context', in Selinger, M. (ed.), *Teaching Mathematics*, London: Routledge, pp. 5–26.

Cornwall, J. (1997) *Access to Learning for Pupils with Disabilities*, London: David Fulton.

Costello, J. (1991) *Teaching and Learning Mathematics 11–16*, London: Routledge.

Cowell, K. (1995) 'Geometer's Sketchpad', *Micromath* **11**(2), 13–15.

Coxeter, H. S. M. (1961) *Introduction to Geometry*, New York, NY: John Wiley.

Crawford, D. (1998) 'Introducing gradient functions and differentiation with a spreadsheet', *Micromath* **14**(1), 34–39.

Cresswell, M. and Gubb, J. (1987) *The Second International Mathematics Study in England and Wales* (International Studies in Pupils Performance Series), Windsor: NFER-Nelson.

Dadd, T. (1998) 'Mathematics eNRICHment activities', *Micromath* **14**(2), 35–40.

Daniels, H. (1988) 'Misunderstandings, miscues and mathematics', *British Journal of Special Education* **15**(1), 11–13.

Daniels, H. and Anghileri, J. (1995) *Secondary Mathematics and Special Educational Needs*, London: Cassell.

Davis, P. J. and Hersh, R. (1986) *The Mathematical Experience*, Harmondsworth, Middlesex: Penguin.

de Villiers, M. (1994) 'The role and function of a hierarchical classification of quadrilaterals', *For the Learning of Mathematics* **14**(1), 11–18.

de Villiers, M. (1995) 'An alternative introduction to proof in dynamic geometry', *Micromath* **11**(1), 14–19.

Dearing, R. (1996) *The Dearing Report: A Review of Qualifications for 16-to-19-Year-Olds*, London: School Curriculum and Assessment Authority.

DEED (1993) *Summing up the World*, available from DEED, Kingsleigh School, Hadow Road, Bournemouth, BH10 5HS.

DES (1978) *Special Educational Needs* (the Warnock Report), London: HMSO.

DES (1982) *Mathematics Counts*. Report of the Committee of Inquiry into the Teaching of Mathematics in Schools, chaired by W. H. Cockcroft (the Cockcroft Report), London: HMSO.

DES (1985) *Mathematics from 5 to 16*, Curriculum Matters 3, London: HMSO.

DES (1987) *Better Mathematics: a Curriculum Development Study*, London: HMSO.

DES/HMI (1979) *Mathematics 5–11: A Handbook of Suggestions*, London: HMSO.

DES/WO (1987) *National Curriculum Task Group on Assessment and Testing* (TGAT), London: HMSO.

DES/WO (1988) *Mathematics for Ages 5 to 16* (Proposals of the Secretary of State for Education and Science and the Secretary of State for Wales), London: HMSO.

DES/WO (1989a) *Mathematics in the National Curriculum*, London: HMSO.

DES/WO (1989b) *Mathematics in the National Curriculum. Non-Statutory Guidance*, London: HMSO.

DES/WO (1991) *Mathematics in the National Curriculum (1991)*, London: HMSO.

DfE (1994) *The Code of Practice on the Identification and Assessment of Special Educational Needs*, London: Department for Education.

DfE (1995) *Mathematics in the National Curriculum*, London: HMSO.

DfEE (Department for Education and Employment) (1998) *Teaching: High Status, High Standards*, Circular 4/98.

Dickinson, C. and Wright, J. (1993) *Differentiation: A Practical Handbook of Classroom Strategies*, Coventry: National Council for Educational Technology.

Dickson, L., Brown, M. and Gibson, O. (1984) *Children Learning Mathematics*, London: Cassell.

Dodd, P. (1991) *Mathematics from Around the World: A Multicultural Resource Book*, available from 73 Beech Grove, Whitley Bay, Tyne and Wear, NE26 3PL (Tel: 01912 525892).

Dörfler, W. and McLone, R. R. (1986) 'Mathematics as a school subject', in Christiansen, B., Howson, A. G. and Otte, M. (eds), *Perspectives on Mathematics Education*, Dordrecht, Holland: D. Reidel, pp. 49–97.

Dye, B. (1991) 'Introducing Logo', *Micromath* **7**(1), 18–19.

Eagle, R. (1995) *Exploring Mathematics through History*, Cambridge: Cambridge University Press.

Ernest, P. (1991) *The Philosophy of Mathematics Education*, Basingstoke: Falmer Press.

Evans, W. (1996) 'René Descartes and dynamic geometry', *Micromath* **12**(1), 30–31.

Evans, W. (1997) 'Omar Khayyam's insight into the cubic equation', *Micromath* **12**(3), 28–29.

Fauvel, J. and Gray, J. (1987) *The History of Mathematics: A Reader*, London: Macmillan.

Finzer, W. F. and Bennett, D. S. (1995) 'From drawing to construction with Geometer's Sketchpad', *Mathematics Teacher* **88**(5), 428–431.

Galloway, D., Leo, E., Rogers, C. and Armstrong, D. (1996) 'Maladaptive motivational style: the role of domain specific task demand in English and mathematics', *British Journal of Educational Psychology* **66**, 197–207.

Galpin, B. and Graham, A. (1997a) *Tapping into Mathematics with the TI-80 Graphics Calculator*, Harlow, Essex: Addison-Wesley.

Galpin, B. and Graham, A. (1997b) *Tapping into Mathematics with the TI-83 Graphics Calculator*, Harlow, Essex: Addison-Wesley.

Gardiner, A. D. (1995) 'Back to the future', *The Mathematical Gazette* **79** (November), 526–532.

Gardner, M. (1978) *Mathematical Carnival*, Harmondsworth, Middlesex: Penguin.

Ginsburg, H. (1981) 'The clinical interview in psychological research on mathematical thinking: aims, rationales, techniques', *For the Learning of Mathematics* **1**(3), 4–11.

Gormas, J. (1998) 'The centrality of a teacher's professional transformation in the development of mathematics power: a case study of one high school mathematics teacher'. Unpublished Ph.D. thesis, East Lansing, MI: Michigan State University.

Goulding, M. (1995) 'GCSE coursework in mathematics: teachers' perspectives and the performance of girls', *Evaluation and Research in Education* **9**(3), 111–119.

Goulding, M. (1997) *Learning to Teach Mathematics*, London: David Fulton.

Graham, A. (1987) *Statistical Investigations in the Secondary School*, Cambridge: Cambridge University Press in association with the Open University.

Graham, A. (1996) 'Open calculator challenge', *Micromath* **12**(3), 14–15.

Graham, A. and Galpin, B. (1998) *Calculator Maths* series, Corby: A and B Books.

Gray, E. and Tall, D. (1994) 'Duality, ambiguity, and flexibility: a "proceptual" view of simple arithmetic', *Journal for Research in Mathematics Education* **25**(2), 116–140.

Grayson, R. (1995). 'Using Geometer's Sketchpad to explore combined transformations', *Micromath* **11**(2), 6–13.

Green, D., Armstrong, P. and Bridges, R. (1993) *Spreadsheets: Exploring their Potential in Secondary Mathematics*, Leicester: The Mathematical Association.

Griffiths, H. B. and Howson, A. G. (1974) *Mathematics, Society and Curricula*, Cambridge: Cambridge University Press.

Hanna, G. (1989) 'Mathematics achievement of girls and boys in grade eight: results from twenty countries', *Educational Studies in Mathematics* **20**(2), 225–232.

Hardy, G. H. (1940) *A Mathematician's Apology*, Cambridge: Cambridge University Press.

Harnasz, C. (1993) 'Do you need to know how it works?', in Selinger, M. (ed.), *Teaching Mathematics*, London: Routledge, pp. 137–144.

Harris, J. (1995) *Presentation Skills for Teachers*, London: Kogan Page.

Hart, K. (ed.) (1981) *Children's Understanding of Mathematics: 11–16*, London: John Murray.

Hatch, G. and Shiu, C. (1997) 'Teachers research through their own mathematics learning', in Zack, V., Mousley, J. and Breen, C. (eds), *Developing Practice: Teachers' Inquiry and Educational Change*, Deakin, Australia: Centre for Studies in Mathematics, Science and Environmental Education, Deakin University, pp. 159–168.

Haylock, D. (1982) 'The mathematics of a dud calculator', *Mathematics Teaching* **101**, 15–16.

Haylock, D. (1991) *Teaching Mathematics to Low Attainers 8–12*, London: Paul Chapman.

Healy, L. and Sutherland, R. (1991) *Exploring Mathematics with Spreadsheets*, Oxford: Basil Blackwell.

Healy, L., Hoelzl, R., Hoyles, C. and Noss, R. (1994) 'Messing up', *Micromath* **10**(1), 14–16.

Henderson, A. (1992) 'Difficulties at the secondary stage', in Miles, T. R. and Miles, E. (eds), *Dyslexia and Mathematics*, London: Routledge, pp. 70–82.

Hoare, C. (1990) 'The invisible Japanese calculator', *Mathematics Teaching* **131**, 12–14.

Holt, J. (1964) *How Children Fail*, Harmondsworth, Middlesex: Pelican.

Holt, J. (1970) *How Children Learn*, Harmondsworth, Middlesex: Pelican.

Howson, G. (1991) *National Curricula in Mathematics*, Leicester: The Mathematical Association.

Hoyles, C. (1982) 'The pupils' view of mathematics learning', *Educational Studies in Mathematics* **13**(4), 349–372.

Hudson, B. (1994) 'Environmental issues in the mathematics classroom', in M. Selinger (ed.), *Teaching Mathematics*, London: Routledge, pp. 113–125.

Hunt, N. (1996) 'Spreadsheet dice games', *Micromath* **12**(1), 6–8.

Hyde, R. (1996) 'Internet Olympics', *Micromath* **12**(3), 8–11.

Inglese, J. (1997) 'Teaching mathematics to pupils with autistic spectrum disorders: exploring possibilities', *Equals* **3**(2), 18–19.

Isaacson, Z. (1992) 'Is there more than one math?', in Nickson, M. and Lerman, S. (eds), *The Social Context of Mathematics Education: Theory and Practice*, London: South Bank Press.

James, N. and Mason, J. (1982) 'Towards recording', *Visible Language* **16**(3), 249–258.

Jaworski, B. (1985) 'A poster lesson', *Mathematics Teaching* **113**, 4–5.

Jaworski, B. (1992) 'Mathematics teaching: what is it?', *For the Learning of Mathematics* **12**(1), 8–14.

Jaworski, B. and Watson, A. (eds) (1994) *Mentoring in Mathematics Teaching*, Brighton: Falmer Press.

John, P. D. (1991) 'A qualitative study of British student teachers' lesson planning perspectives', *Journal of Education for Teaching* **17**(3), 301–320.

John, P. D. (1993) *Lesson Planning for Teachers*, London: Cassell.

John, P. D. (1994) 'The integration of research-validated knowledge with practice: lesson planning and the student history teacher', *Cambridge Journal of Education* **24**(1), 33–47.

Johnson, D. *et al.* (1989) *Children's Mathematical Frameworks 8–13,* Windsor, Berkshire: NFER–Nelson.

Johnson, D. and Millett, A. (eds) (1996) *Implementing the Mathematics National Curriculum*, London: Paul Chapman.

Jones, K. (1997) 'Some lessons in mathematics: a comparison of mathematics teaching in Japan and America', *Mathematics Teaching* **159**, 6–9.

Jones, K. and Smith, K. (1997) *Student Teachers Learning to Plan Mathematics Lessons*, Occasional paper, University of Southampton Centre for Research in Mathematics Education.

Jones, L. (ed.) (1991) *Teaching Mathematics and Art*, Cheltenham: Stanley Thornes.

Jordan, R. and Powell, S. (1995) *Understanding and Teaching Children with Autism*, Chichester: John Wiley.

Joseph, G. G. (1994) *The Crest of the Peacock: Non-European Roots of Mathematics*, Harmondsworth, Middlesex: Penguin.

Katz, V. J. (1992) *A History of Mathematics*, New York, NY: HarperCollins.

Kerslake, D. (1981) 'Graphs', in Hart, K. M. (ed.), *Children's Understanding of Mathematics: 11–16*, London: John Murray, pp. 120–136.

Kerslake, D. (1986) *Fractions: Children's Strategies and Errors*, Windsor, Berkshire: NFER.

Keys, W., Harris, S. and Fernandes, C. (1996) *Third International Mathematics and Science Study: First National Report*, Windsor, Berkshire: NFER.

Kitchen, A. (1996) 'A-level maths isn't what it used to be, or is it?', *Mathematics Today* **32**(5 and 6), 87–90.

Kitchen, A. (1998) 'Using calculators in schools', *Micromath* **14**(2), 25–29.

Kitchen, A. and Lord, K. (1996) 'The interface between mathematics post-16 and higher education', in Haines, C. and Dunthorne, S. (eds), *Mathematics Learning and Assessment: Sharing Innovative Practices*, London: Edward Arnold, pp. 1.12–1.26.

Krutetskii, V. A. (1976) *The Psychology of Mathematical Abilities in Schoolchildren*, Chicago, IL: University of Chicago Press.

LAMP (Low Attainers in Mathematics Project) (1994) 'Schemes', in Selinger, M. (ed.), *Teaching Mathematics*, London: Routledge, pp. 29–37.

Larcombe, T. (1985) *Mathematical Learning Difficulties in the Secondary School: Pupil Needs and Teacher Roles*, Buckingham: Open University Press.

Lave, J. (1988) *Cognition in Practice*, Cambridge: Cambridge University Press.

Lawson, C. and Lee, C. (1995) 'Numeracy through literacy', *Proceedings of the Joint Conference of the British Society for Research into Learning Mathematics and the Association of Mathematics Education Tutors*, Loughborough: BSRLM/AMET.

Lorenz, J. H. (1982) 'On some psychological aspects of mathematics achievement assessment and classroom interaction', *Educational Studies in Mathematics* **13**(1), 1–19.

Love, E. and Mason, J. (1992) *Teaching Mathematics: Action and Awareness*, Milton Keynes: The Open University.

MacNamara, A. and Roper, T. (1992) 'Unrecorded, unobserved and suppressed attainment: can our pupils do more than we know?', *Mathematics in School* **21**(5), 12–13.

MA (1987) *Maths Talk*, Cheltenham: Stanley Thornes.

MA (1992) *Mental Methods in Mathematics: A First Resort*, Leicester: The Mathematical Association.

MA (1995a) *Why, What, How? Some Basic Questions for Mathematics Teaching*, Leicester: The Mathematical Association.

MA (1995b) *Starting as a Secondary Mathematics Teacher*, Leicester: The Mathematical Association.

Mason, J. (1994) 'Assessing what sense pupils make of mathematics', in Selinger, M. (ed.), *Teaching Mathematics*, London: Routledge.

Mason, J. (1995) 'What, why and how in mathematics', *Micromath* **11**(1), 10–14.

Mason, J. (1999) *Learning and Doing Mathematics*, York: QED.

Miles, T. R. and Miles, E. (eds) (1992) *Dyslexia and Mathematics*, London: Routledge.

Miller, L. D. (1992) 'Teacher benefits from using impromptu writing prompts in algebra classes', *Journal for Research in Mathematics Education* **23**(4), 329–340.

Morgan, C. (1988) 'Writing to learn in mathematics', unpublished M.Sc. Option Report, Institute of Education, University of London.

Morgan Jones, J. P. and McLeay, H. (1996) 'Zooming spreadsheets: putting functions under the microscope', *Micromath* **12**(1), 35–38.

Morris, G. (1986) 'The Bristol Maths Trail', *Mathematics Teaching* **114**, 2–3.

Morris, G. (1995) 'Developing the spiritual in mathematics', *Mathematics Teaching* **153**, 36–37.

Morrison, T. (1998) 'Using spreadsheets to teach differentiation', *Micromath* **14**(1), 30–33.

NCC (1989) *Mathematics National Curriculum Non-Statutory Guidance*, York: National Curriculum Council.

NCC (1990) *The Whole Curriculum*, York: National Curriculum Council.

NCC (1992) *Mathematics Programmes of Study – INSET for Key Stages 3 and 4*, York: National Curriculum Council.

NCET (1995) *Mathematics and IT: a pupil's entitlement*, Coventry: NCET.

NCET (1996) *Dynamic Geometry*, Coventry: NCET.

NCTM (1991) *Professional Standards for Teaching Mathematics*, Reston, VA: National Council of Teachers of Mathematics.

Neill, H. (ed.) (1994a) *Nuffield Advanced Mathematics, Book 1*, Essex: Longman.

Neill, H. (ed.) (1994b) *Nuffield Advanced Mathematics, History of Mathematics*, Essex: Longman.

Neill, S. and Caswell, C. (1993) *Body Language for Competent Teachers*, London: Routledge.

NICCEA (1994) *Comparing Examination Boards and Syllabuses at A Level: students' grades, attitudes and perceptions of classroom processes*, Executive Summary of a Report Commissioned by the GCE Examining Boards, Belfast: Northern Ireland Council for the Curriculum, Examinations and Assessment.

Nolder, R. (1991) 'Mixing metaphor and mathematics in the secondary classroom', in Durkin, K. and Shire, B. (eds), *Language in Mathematical Education: Research and Practice*, Buckingham: Open University Press, pp. 105–113.

Noss, R. (1992) 'The National Curriculum and mathematics: political perspectives and implication', in Nickson, M. and Lerman, S. (eds), *The Social Context of Mathematics Education: Theory and Practice*, London: South Bank Press, pp. 62–64.

Nunes, T. and Moreno, C. (1997) 'Solving word problems with different ways of representing the task: how do deaf children perform?' *Equals* **3**(2), 15–17.

O'Hara, S. (1993) *Easy Excel*, Carmel, IN: Que Corporation.

Oldknow, A. (1998) 'Real data in the mathematics classroom', *Micromath* **14**(2), 14–20.

Ollerton, M. (1991) 'Teaching versus assessment', *Mathematics Teaching* **135**, 4–6.

Open University (1989a) *Preparing to Teach*, Milton Keynes: Open University.

Open University (1989b) *Developing Own Mathematics*, Milton Keynes: Open University.

Open University (1993) *Open Calculator Challenge*, Milton Keynes: Open University, Centre for Mathematics Education.

Orton, A. (1987) *Learning Mathematics: Issues, Theory and Classroom Practice*, London: Cassell Educational.

Orton, C. (1995) 'A parent's search for a question', *Equals* **1**(3), 7–10.

Papert, S. (1980) *Mindstorms – Children, Computers and Powerful Ideas*, Brighton, Sussex: Harvester Press.

Pask, G. (1976) *The Cybernetics of Human Learning and Performance*, London: Hutchinson.

Perks, P. and Prestage, S. (1994) 'Planning for learning', in Jaworski, B. and Watson, A. (eds), *Mentoring in Mathematics Teaching*, Brighton, Sussex: Falmer Press, pp. 65–82.

Pimm, D. (1987) *Speaking Mathematically: Communication in Mathematics Classrooms*, London: Routledge and Kegan Paul.
Pimm, D. (ed.) (1988) *Mathematics, Teachers and Children*, London: Hodder and Stoughton.
Pimm, D. (1995) *Symbols and Meanings in School Mathematics*, London: Routledge.
Pimm, D. and Love, E. (eds) (1991) *Teaching and Learning School Mathematics*, London: Hodder and Stoughton.
Pinel, A. (1986) *Mathematical Activity Tiles Handbook: An ATM Discussion Book*, Derby: Association of Teachers of Mathematics.
Plato (trans. Lee, H., 1987) *The Republic*, Harmondsworth, Middlesex: Penguin.
Portwood, M. (1997) 'Step by step', *Special Children* **104**, 18–20.
QCA (1998) *Standards at Key Stage 3 Mathematics: Report on the 1997 National Curriculum Assessments for 14-Year-Olds*, London: School Curriculum and Assessment Authority.
Reynolds, D. (1996), 'The truth, the whole-class truth', *The Times Educational Supplement* **1471**, June 7th, p. 21.
Reys, R. E., Suydam, M. N. and Lindquist, M. M. (1995, 4th edn) *Helping Children Learn Mathematics*, Boston, MA: Allyn and Bacon.
Rich, B. (1993), 'The effect of the use of graphing calculators on classroom presentation', in *Proceedings of the International Conference on Technology in Mathematics Teaching* (TMT 93), Birmingham: University of Birmingham, p. 556.
Richards, P. (1982) 'Difficulties in learning mathematics', in Cornelius, M. (ed.), *Teaching Mathematics*, New York, NY: Nichols Publishing, pp. 59–80.
Rouncefield, M. and Holmes, P. (1989) *Practical Statistics*, London: Macmillan.
Ruthven, K. (1987) 'Ability stereotyping in mathematics', *Educational Studies in Mathematics* **18**(3), 243–253.
Ruthven, K. (1990) *Personal Technology in the Classroom – the NCET Graphic Calculators in Mathematics Project*, University of Cambridge: Department of Education/NCET.
Ruthven, K. (1992), *Graphic Calculators in Advanced Mathematics*, Coventry: NCET.
Savage, M. D. and Williams, J. S. (1990) *Mechanics in Action*, Cambridge: Cambridge University Press.
SCAA (1995a) *Consistency in Teacher Assessment, Exemplification of Standards, Mathematics: Key Stage 3, Levels 1 to 3*, London: HMSO.
SCAA (1995b) *Consistency in Teacher Assessment, Exemplification of Standards, Mathematics: Key Stage 3, Levels 4 to 8*, London: HMSO.
SCAA (1995c) *GCSE Regulations and Criteria, March 1995*, London: School Curriculum and Assessment Authority.
SCAA (1996a) *Standards in Public Examinations: 1975 to 1995*, London: School Curriculum and Assessment Authority.
SCAA (1996b) *Promoting Continuity between Key Stage 2 and 3*, London: School Curriculum and Assessment Authority.
SCAA (1997a) *Standards at Key Stage 3 Mathematics: Report on the 1996 National Curriculum Assessments for 14-Year-Olds*, London: School Curriculum and Assessment Authority.
SCAA (1997b) *The Use of Calculators at Key Stages 1–3*, Discussion Paper No. 9, London: School Curriculum and Assessment Authority.
SCAA (1997c) *Making Effective Use of Key Stage 2 Assessments: A Guide to Good Practice*, London: School Curriculum and Assessment Authority.
SCAA (1997d) *The Proposed A-Level Mathematics Core*, London: School Curriculum and Assessment Authority.
Schumann, H. and Green, D. (1995) *Discovering Geometry with a Computer – Using Cabri Géomètre*, Bromley: Chartwell-Bratt.
Scott-Hodgetts, R. (1986) 'Girls and mathematics: the negative implications of success', in

Burton, L. (ed.), *Girls into Maths Can Go*, London: Holt, Rinehart and Winston, pp. 61–76.

Selinger, M. (ed.) (1994) *Teaching Mathematics*, London: Routledge.

Selinger, M. and Baker, L. (1991) *The What, Why, How and When of Mathematics Trails*, Derby: Association of Teachers of Mathematics.

Selkirk, K. (1983a) 'Simulation exercises for the classroom – 4: The Potato beetle', *Mathematics in School* **12**(4), 10–13.

Selkirk, K. (1983b) 'Simulation exercises for the classroom – 5: Looking for a home', *Mathematics in School* **12**(5), 26–28.

Shan, S. and Bailey, P. (1991) *Multiple Factors: Classroom Mathematics for Equality and Justice*, Stoke: Trentham.

Shuard, H. and Rothery, A. (eds) (1984) *Children Reading Mathematics*, London: John Murray.

Simon, M. A. (1994) 'Learning mathematics and learning to teach mathematics: learning cycles in mathematics teacher education', *Educational Studies in Mathematics* **26**(1), 71–94.

Sjörstrand, D. (1993) *Mathematics with Excel*, Bromley: Chartwell-Bratt.

Skemp, R. (1976) 'Relational understanding and instrumental understanding', *Mathematics Teaching* **77**, 20–26.

SMILE (1993), *Spreadsheets from SMILE*, London: SMILE.

SMP (1992) *Calculus Methods*, Cambridge: Cambridge University Press.

SOED (1991) *Curriculum and Assessment in Scotland, National Guidelines – Mathematics, 5–14*, Edinburgh: Scottish Office.

Stigler, J. W. and Hiebert, J. (1997) 'Understanding and improving classroom mathematics instruction: an overview of the TIMSS video study', *Phi Delta Kappan* **79**(1), 14–21.

Stigler, J. *et al.* (1996) 'Traditions of school mathematics in Japanese and American elementary schools', in Steffe, L. P. (ed.), *Theories of Mathematical Learning*, Mahwah, NJ: Lawrence Erlbaum Associates, pp. 149–175.

Stradling, R. *et al.* (1991) *Differentiation in Action: A Whole-School Approach to Raising Standards*, London: HMSO.

Stubbs, M. (1983, 2nd edn) *Language, Schools and Classrooms*, London: Methuen.

Sutherland, R. and Pozzi, S. (1995) *The Changing Background of Undergraduate Engineers*, London: The Engineering Council.

Sutherland, R., Howell, D. and Wolf, A. (1996) *A Spreadsheet Approach to Maths for GNVQ Engineering*, London: Edward Arnold.

Tahta, D. G. (ed.) (1980, 2nd edn) *A Boolean Anthology: Selected Writings of Mary Boole*, Derby: Association of Teachers of Mathematics.

Tall, D. (1987) *Readings in Mathematics Education: Understanding the Calculus*, Derby: Association of Teachers of Mathematics.

TTA (1997) *Career Entry Profile Pack*, London: Teacher Training Agency.

Tyler, R. W. (1949) *Basic Principles of Curriculum and Instruction*, Chicago, IL: University of Chicago Press.

Wake, G. D. (1997) 'Improving mathematics provision for post-16 students', *Teaching Mathematics and its Applications* **16**(4), 200–206.

Watson, A. (1994) 'What I do in my classroom', in Selinger, M. (ed.), *Teaching Mathematics*, London: Routledge, pp. 52–62.

Watson, A. (1996) 'Teachers' notions of mathematical ability in their pupils', *Mathematics Education Review* **8**(March), 27–35.

Webb, N. L. (ed.) (1993) *Assessment in the Mathematics Classroom; 1993 Yearbook of the National Council of Teachers of Mathematics*, Reston, VA: NCTM.

Wells, D. (1991) *The Penguin Dictionary of Curious and Interesting Geometry*, Harmondsworth, Middlesex: Penguin.

Wells, D. (1992/4) *Can You Solve These?,* Series 1/2, Diss, Norfolk: Tarquin Publications.

Williams, D. and Stephens, M. (1992) 'Activity 1: Five Steps to Zero', in Fey, J. T. and Hirsch, C. R. (eds), *Calculators in Mathematics Education*; *1992 Yearbook* of the NCTM, Reston, VA: National Council for Teachers of Mathematics, pp. 233–234.

Williams, J. S. and Kitchen, A. (1989) *Modelling with Functions and Graphs*, Manchester: Mechanics in Action Project, University of Manchester.

Wood, D. (1988) (2nd edn) *How Children Think and Learn*, Oxford: Basil Blackwell.

Woodrow, D. (1989) 'Multicultural and anti-racist mathematics teaching', in Ernest, P. (ed.) *Mathematics Teaching – The State of the Art*, Lewes: Falmer Press.

Wragg, E. C. (1995, 2nd edn) 'Lesson structure', in Anderson, L. W. (ed.), *International Encyclopaedia of Teaching and Teacher Education*, Oxford: Pergamon Press, pp. 207–211.

WWF (1990) *Mathematics and Environmental Education*, Godalming, Sussex: World Wildlife Fund.

Name and Author Index

Subject Index